Adventure Guide to

Milan
& the
Italian Lakes

Catherine Richards

HUNTER

HUNTER PUBLISHING, INC.
130 Campus Drive, Edison, NJ 08818-7816
☎ 732-225-1900 / 800-255-0343 / fax 732-417-1744
www.hunterpublishing.com; e-mail comments@hunterpublishing.com

IN CANADA:
Ulysses Travel Publications
4176 Saint-Denis, Montréal, Québec, Canada H2W 2M5
☎ 514-843-9882 ext. 2232 / fax 514-843-9448

IN THE UNITED KINGDOM:
Windsor Books International
The Boundary, Wheatley Road, Garsington
Oxford, OX44 9EJ England; ☎ 01865-361122 / fax 01865-361133

ISBN 10: 1-58843-592-X
ISBN 13: 978-1-58843-592-7

© 2007 Hunter Publishing, Inc.

The Star System

If a star ★ appears next to the title of a hotel, restaurant, museum, ruin, or attraction of any kind, that means it is very significant and definitely worth a look. The stars are based on location, scenery, unusual value, or any other factor that makes a place really stand out.

★ If you have the opportunity you should experience this.

★★ This is reason enough to change your plans.

★★★ Don't miss it.

Cover photo: Villa Le Fontanelle on Lake Como
(© Jon Ferro Sims/Alamy)

Maps © 2007 Hunter Publishing, Inc.
Index by Inge Wiesen

4   3   2   1

Contents

Maps

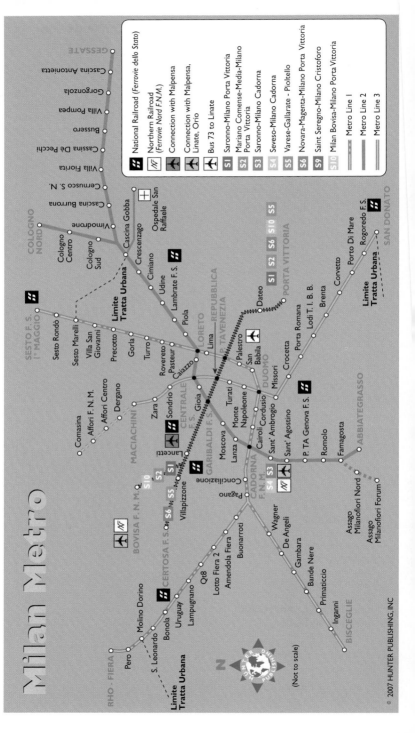

Milan Metro

Legend:

- National Railroad (Ferrovie dello Stato)
- Northern Railroad (Ferrovie Nord F.N.M.)
- Connection with Malpensa
- Connection with Malpensa, Linate, Orio
- Bus 73 to Linate
- **S1** Saronno-Milano Porta Vittoria
- **S2** Mariano Comense-Media-Milano Porta Vittoria
- **S3** Saronno-Milano Cadorna
- **S4** Seveso-Milano Cadorna
- **S5** Varese-Gallarate - Pioltello
- **S6** Novara-Magenta-Milano Porta Vittoria
- **S9** Saint Seregno-Milano Cristoforo
- **S10** Milan Bovisa-Milano Porta Vittoria
- Metro Line 1
- Metro Line 2
- Metro Line 3

(Not to scale)

© 2007 HUNTER PUBLISHING, INC

Milan

■ Introduction

For those in the know, Milan has always been a choice destination. What Milan has always offered is chic, and so discretely that many casual visitors have initially failed to spot its charms. For those who do want to discover Milan's secrets and who are prepared to venture behind the city's somewhat austere façades, the city offers a fine experience.

Milan is culturally rich. The city is home to the world famous La Scala opera house. There are enough museums and art galleries to keep any art lover happy – indeed the Pinacoteca Ambrosiana is one of the greatest European art collections. Though Milan lost buildings during World War II, it has many fine architectural examples from the Roman period through to the 20th century: basilicas, churches, chapels, castles, palaces – even the monumental Stazione Centrale is of historical and architectural significance. In fact, there has never been a better time to visit Milan, as the city is about to embark on a period of major regeneration.

For shoppers, the city's Sunday antique markets and the bohemian villages in the south of the city present another Milan – quieter, more relaxed. The neighborhood stores – the pasticcerie, the salumerie – are a delight. At the 32other end of the scale Milan is home to the world's greatest fashion houses: Versace, Fendi, Armani, Dolce e Gabbana. A great

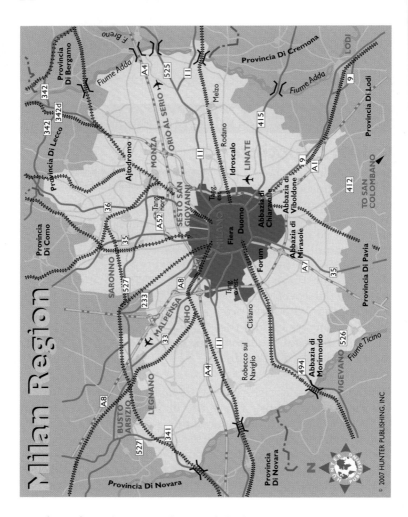

number of tourists come here solely for the fashion, to buy, to see and to be seen. At certain times of the year the fashion shows are the attraction, at other times the sales, where the promise of a Versace or Armani item at a fraction of the original cost entices shoppers from all over Europe.

Those visitors who spend only a day in Milan miss out on another virtue: its food. The Milanese take their food very seriously. Within Italy, Milanese cuisine is synonymous with luxury and sophistication, which seems appropriate in a city with the highest standard of living in the country. The history of the city can be seen in its food. Many of the dishes are heavily influenced by the foreign cultures that have occupied Lombardy over the last two thousand years: the Austrians and the Spanish, for example. Butter, cream, rice and cheese feature heavily in the cuisine, as it does throughout Lombardy, but also meat and, perhaps surprisingly, fish. The largest fish market in Italy is, in fact, located in Milan. Leaving Milan without sampling some of its cuisine would be like leaving London without setting foot inside a pub or leaving New York without riding the subway.

Milan is not an easy city to live in, nor is it easy to visit. This is a serious, working city, which at first glance can look grey, dirty and ugly. The traffic is an ever-present problem, the pollution can be a nightmare in the summer, as can the humidity and the mosquitos. It is also an expensive city, where the cost of hotels and meals can be 40% more than in places less than an hour away.

With some careful planning however, a visit to Milan can be a thoroughly enjoyable experience. With art collections to rival those in any other European city and with some stunning Romanesque and Renaissance architecture, Milan will satisfy tourists in search of culture. At the other end of the scale, it is a fun city, with superb restaurants, a lively bar and nightlife scene and excellent shopping. With a bit of planning and inside information, it's even possible to experience Milan – one of the most expensive cities in Italy – on a budget.

The second-largest city in Italy, Milan covers an area of 112 sq. miles, and has a population of 1:4 million. Located in the plains of Lombardy, Italy's most populated and industrialized region, the area known as La Grande Milano (Greater Milan) covers an area of nearly 1,200 sq. miles, with a population of four million. In common with many Italian cities, it has seen a 10% fall in the number of residents over the last 15 years. The name Milan probably comes from the Celtic "mid-lan," which meant "in the middle of the plain," The Romans, who conquered "Midlan" in 222 BC, named it "Mediolanum." Some 85% of the residents of Milan are Italian, while 5% come from other European countries, and the remaining 10% are immigrants, primarily from Asia and North Africa.

Climate

Milan does not have the most comfortable of climates: the summers can be very humid and muggy (the ever-present pollution problem doing little to improve the situation) and the winters can be cold, with fog and snowfall between January and March fairly common. Spring and early autumn are the ideal times.

The average temperature in January is 35°F; in July it's around 72°. Average yearly rainfall is 38.3 inches. All of which makes Milan's weather pretty similar to that of Baltimore.

Try to avoid spending time here in August. Not only does most of the city leave for the coast, the lakes or the mountains (including most restaurant, shop and hotel staff), but the humidity and the mosquitos can make for a pretty uncomfortable experience!

Economy

Major Industries: Fashion and textile manufacturing, banking and finance, chemical manufacturing, food manufacturing, tourism.

Currency

Italy adopted the euro (€) on January 1st 2002. The euro is divided into 100 cents. Notes come in denominations of €500, €200, €100, €50, €20, €10 and €5. Coins come in denominations of €2 and €1, and 50, 20, 10, 5, 2 and 1 cents.

What to read: Duca and the Milan Murders *by Giorgio Scerbanenco. Duca Lamberti, Scerbanenco's doctor-turned-crime solver. Not so easy to find, but check out www. alibris.com for used copies.*

Public Holidays

Jan 1st – New Year's Day
Jan 6th – Epiphany
April – Good Friday

April – Easter Monday

April 25th – Anniversary of the Liberation

May 1st – Labour Day

June 2nd – National Day

August 15th – Assumption

November 1st – All Saints Day

December 7th – Saint Ambrose's Day (Sant' Ambrogio, patron saint of Milan)

December 8th – Feast of the Immaculate Conception

December 25th – Christmas Day

December 26th – St Stephen's Day

Practicalities

Telephone

Country code: 39

Milan code: 02

You need to dial the city code even if you are calling from Milan (the same is true for all district codes in Italy) and you need the initial 0. If a city code begins with an 8, the number is toll free.

Useful Toll-Free Telephone Numbers

Carabinieri (police), ☎ 112

Emergency public assistance, ☎ 113

Ambulance, ☎ 118

Breakdown assistance (ACI), ☎ 116

Fire brigade, ☎ 115

Emergencies

Hospitals

San Raffaele, Via Olgettina 60, Milan 20132, ☎ 39 02 264 31.

Fatebenefratelli (24-hour), Corso di Porta Nuova 23, Milan 20121, ☎ 39 02 636 31.

24-Hour Pharmacies

Farmacia della Stazione, Stazione Centrale (Galleria delle Partenza), Milan 20124, ☎ 39 02 669 0735. Open 24 hours, 365 days a year.

Farmacia Ferrarini, Piazza 5 Giornate 6, Milan 20129, ☎ 39 02 551-94867. Open day and night, except daily closure from 12:30-3:30 pm, Sun 8:30 am-8 pm and Mon morning.

Getting Here

Airport Information

Malpensa

 ☎ 39 02 7485 2200, www.sea-aeroportimilano.it.

Milan's international airport lies around 30 miles north of the city. To get into the city you have a couple of options.

Train: The Malpensa Express is the fastest and most comfortable. The trains leave from Terminal 1 every 30 minutes and take around 40 minutes. You arrive at Cadorna, which is just north of the historic center. Cost is around €9. Tickets can be bought on board though they are 25% more expensive.

From Piazza Cadorna: first train 5:50 am; last train 9:20 pm.

From Malpensa Terminal 1: 6:45 am; last train 10:15 pm.

Bus: The Malpensa Shuttle operates regular bus services between Malpensa and the city center (Stazione Centrale) and Milan's other airport, Linate. Though affordable – around €5 one-way from Malpensa to the city center – the trip can take anywhere between the advertised 50 minutes and 90 minutes, depending on traffic. Tickets can be purchased on board as well as in advance from various points. For timetables and other details check out www.malpensashuttle.it.

Taxi: A taxi from Malpensa to the city center can cost around €70.

Car rental: All the major companies have a presence at both Malpensa and Linate: Avis; Hertz; Europcar; eSixT.

 Author's tip: Malpensa's Terminal 1 generally handles most European flights and all transcontinental flights, while Terminal 2 handles mostly charter flights. Make sure you know which terminal you need. Buses run between the terminals so a lot of stress is guaranteed if you get it wrong and are running late!

Linate

☎ 39 02 7485 2200, www.sea-aeroportimilano.it

Linate, which serves mainly domestic flights and European routes, is located 15 minutes east of the center. There is currently no train service into the city center, though there are plans to build a connecting subway line.

Taxi: About €25-30 into the center, less if traffic is very light. If you want to spend a little more on a private car, or you need a mini-bus, have a look at www.limos.com. They have details of companies all over the globe offering such services.

Bus: The local bus service stops right outside the main arrivals terminal. No 73 runs to Piazza San Babila. You cannot buy tickets on the bus, but there are machines located at the bus stops or in the airport. Runs from 5:35 until 12:35 pm. About €1.

A pullman service operated by STAM (☎ 39 02 717106) runs every 20-30 minutes or so from the airport to Piazza Luigi di Savoia, alongside Stazione Centrale. Around €2.50.

 Warning: Though there are ATM machines at Linate airport, there are not enough and they don't always work. Don't rely on them if you can help it. If you're arriving too late to exchange your money at the banks in the airport, then change some before you leave home. Post offices in Italy also have exchange facilites.

Consulates

American Consulate, Via Principe Amedeo 2/10, Milan 20121, ☎ 39 02 290351, ☎/fax 39 02 29035273, http://milan.usconsulate.gov.

British Consulate General, Via San Paolo 7, Milan 20121, ☎ 39 02 723 001, fax 39 02 8646 5081, www.britain.it.

Canadian Consulate General, Via Vittor Pisani 19, Milan 20124, ☎ 39 02 6758 3420 or 02 6758 3422, fax 39 02 6758 3912, www.canada.it.

Getting Around

Public Transport

 For information on routes, timetables and tickets, have a look at the website of the **Azienda Trasporti Milanesi** (ATM): www.atm-mi.it. The website is also in English.

The Metro

Entraces to the Milan subway, "the metropolitana," are designated by a red letter M. There are currently three lines, (M1 in red; M2 in green; M3 in yellow), though a further three are either in the construction or planning stage. The network runs for around 50 miles. Make sure you validate your ticket in the machines in the metro hall, and hold on to your ticket until you leave the metro. Random inspections are common. In comparison to other European cities, Milan's metro is relatively modern. The first line opened in 1964, though a subway system had first been proposed back in 1848!

TICKETS FOR PUBLIC TRANSPORT

Tickets are sold at metro stations, many tobacconists, recognizable by the T sign outside (look for the ATM logo on the window), and at virtually every newsstand (called an edicola).

Single tickets cost €1, a day pass costs €3, and a two-day pass is €5.50. If you think you'll need it, buy a "carnet," a booklet of 10 tickets. (2006 prices)

Tickets are valid for up to 75 minutes on trams, buses and the metro.

Trams

Milan has one of the most extensive tram/streetcar networks in the world, with more than 286 km of track – that's around 177 miles. Unless you have a particular reason to use the subway, I would recommend sticking with the streetcars when moving around Milan.

There are currently five different kind of trams whizzing around the city, the majority a distinctive orange color, with the oldest dating from 1928.

Buy your ticket before you board, and remember to validate it!

Taxis

Milan's taxis are all white, and are reasonably priced. You generally cannot hail a cab in the street but must look for a taxi-rank in one of the city's piazzas, or order a cab at one of the following numbers: ☎ 02 8585, 02 6969, 02 4040. Tipping is optional: aim for around 5-10% or round up the fare to the nearest euro.

> **Author's tip:** Milan's Trade Fairs are among the biggest and most important in the world. If there's a trade fair on when you're visiting the city, taxis will be much harder to find. Book well in advance if that taxi trip is essential.

Tipping

The cover charge ("il coperto") that the majority of Italian restaurants impose (for bread and service, dependent on the number of people eating) means that tipping is optional even when dining out. 10% is usually more than enough if you feel you want to reward good service. Should you make use of a porter, €1 a bag is standard.

Tourist Information

 The **APT Milano Information Office** (☎ 39 02 7252 4301), on the corner of via Marconi and Piazza del Duomo, has maps, guidebooks and a free monthly magazine, full of listings and events, called *Milano Mese*. Also available as a PDF document from their website, www. milanoinfotourist.com.

Available here as well is the **The Welcome Card**, which comes complete with a map, public-transport information, a 24-hour travel pass, and discount vouchers for attractions and concerts. Around €10. Open Mon-Fri 8:30 am-8 pm (7 pm Oct-April), Sat 9 am-1 pm, 2-7 pm (6 pm Oct-April), Sun 9 am-1 pm, 2-5 pm.

Tours

The **APT Milano Information Office** organizes a three-hour walking tour of the city on Mondays, which includes entry to La Scala. Via Marconi 1, ☎ 39 02 7252.

Private guided tours of Milan and its sights and museums are also offered by the **Centro Guide Turistiche Milano**, with offices at the same location. Contact them at info@centro-guidemilano.net.

Check out **http://discountmilan.com** for walking tours of the city. Not economical if there is just one of you, but good for a group.

For limousine tours of Milan and Lakes Como and Maggiore (full-day excursions) with English-speaking drivers, check out **Ideal Limousines**. They also offer a day-trip to a designer outlet just over the Swiss border at Mendrisio. One to three people in a Mercedes sedan will cost around €400. www.idealimousines.com. Another option is **Girasole**. They arrange walking tours of Lake Maggiore, Lake Lugano and Lake Como over a six-day period. Tours start and finish in Milan. www.girasole.com.

 Unique experience: Why not consider a tour of the city in an historic streetcar – Line 20 which starts from Piazza Castello. Headsets provided for tourist info. Cost is around €20 per person. Between April 1 and October 31, the tours run every day at 11 am, 1 pm and 3 pm, except May 1 and the second and third week of August. In winter, only on Saturdays and some holidays at 11 and 1 pm. Contact Autostradale Srl, ☎ 39 02 33910794, or ask at the APT office. www.milanoinfotourist.com.

Trade Fairs

Milan wouldn't be Milan without its trade fairs. If you want to know what's on and when, have a look at the Milan Tourist Board site, www.milanoinfotourist.com, which lists upcoming shows, the addresses of fashion and design shops and other related information. Look under "Business."

■ The History of Milan

Prehistoric & Roman Milan

Before the Etruscans arrived in the fifth century BC, northern Lombardy had been inhabited by Indo-European populations, and by the Ligurians in the third century. The mighty Romans arrived in 222 BC, conquering the Po River valley and all of its cities. "Mediolanum," as the Romans called Milan, became an autonomous province, and, thanks to its geographical position, which gave it both a trading and military importance, the city quickly grew in size and prosperity. Such was its importance that in AD 286 it became the capital of the Western Roman Empire, a title it held until AD 402. The second-most important city in the Empire after Rome itself, Milan became a center for Christianity and, with the Edict of Milan granted by Constantine the Great in AD 313, Christians throughout the Western Roman Empire were free from religious persecution.

SANT'AMBROGIO

One of Milan's greatest historical figures and the patron saint of the city was Sant'Ambrogio, who was made Bishop of Milan in AD 374. He built four basilicas in the city: San Simpliciano; Sant'Ambrogio; San Lorenzo and San Nazaro. December 7th is the saint's feast day, when the area around the Basilica of Sant'Ambrogio is given over to a market, with antiques, Christmas gifts, food and the delicious "vin brûlé" or mulled wine.

The Early Middle Ages

Losing the status of Imperial capital in AD 402, Milan in the fifth and sixth centuries entered a period of decline, culminating in virtual destruction during the sixth century as the Goths and Byzantines battled it out, conquering and reconquering the city. At the end of the sixth century, the Byzantines lost control of the city to the invading Lombards, who themselves were defeated by the Franks in 774. The Franks were Christian, with an empire by the eighth century that included France (except Brittany, which they never managed to conquer), northern Spain, most of modern Germany, northern Italy, and today's Austria. A period of growth and prosperity followed, as the bishops regained power, trade flourished and the artisan and the merchant class grew.

With formidable power, wealth and confidence, the people of Milan rose up against the Emperor in the 11th century, declared themselves independent and the Free Commune of Milan was founded. It was at this time that a new city wall was built, complete with six gates – almost entirely destroyed in 1162 when the great Frederick Barbarossa laid siege to the city. By allying themselves with other communes from the north and forming the Lega Lombarda, Milan rose again and wrenched control of the city from Frederick in 1176.

The impressive canal network of Milan, the Navigli, was begun in the 12th century, at one time connecting Milan with the Canton of Ticino, now part of Switzerland.

13th-16th Centuries

The Viscontis

Thanks to infighting and nepotism among the rulers of Milan, power passed to the first of the Visconti signorie, Oddone, Archbishop of Milan, in 1277. The greatest artists and architects of the age were commissioned to build, re-build and decorate the city, and it was in this period that the Castello and the Duomo were commissioned. At first lords of Milan, the Viscontis became dukes at

Milan's walls, 1477

the end of the 14th century when the greatest and most infamous of the Viscontis, Gian Galeazzo Visconti, bought the title from the Holy Roman Emperor for 100,000 Florins.

GIAN GALEAZZO VISCONTI

Gian Galeazzo Visconti, who had secured the title of Lord of Milan by overthrowing his uncle, Bernabo, had great expansionist ambitions, and rarely let anything get in his way. Infamous for devising a 40-day torture for anyone who might need it, the so-called Lenten Treatment, Galeazzo set about seizing the cities of Verona, Vicenza and Pavia, and soon had control of much of the Po Valley. Taking Bologna and then turning his attention to Florence was his next move. His dream of a united Italy came to an end unexpectedly in 1402, when he died of a fever. His entire empire soon crumbled as his successors squabbled among themselves.

The great Italian film director, Luchino Visconti, Duke of Modrone, was the last of the Visconti line. He died in Rome in 1976.

The Sforzas

From 1447 when the Visconti dynasty died out, Milan enjoyed three years of autonomy, under the Ambrosian Republic. Having stormed the Visconti Castle on the death of the last Visconti Duke, Filippo Maria Visconti, the citizens of Milan declared a Republic, and then ordered the castle to be demolished. The heady days were shortlived: in 1450 **Francesco Sforza** entered the city, taking advantage of a coup engineered by the

Francesco Sforza

powerful families of Milan. The city surrendered, Sforza declared himself "capitano del popolo" (leader) and through his wife – Filippo Visconti's daughter – the new Duke of Milan.

Francesco Sforza had none of the expansionist ideas of his predecessors, and Milan now entered a period of great prosperity and relative peace. The badly damaged castle was rebuilt and renamed **Castello Sfozesco**. It swiftly became one of the most important Renaissance courts in Europe. Today it's among the must-see sights of Milan. Other architectural additions to the city were the **Ospedale Maggiore** (or Ca Grande) – an incredibly modern design concept, with separate facilities for men and women, intended to unite the city's 30 hospitals. It is now part of the city's university.

Lodovico Sforza, second son of Francesco Sforza, is credited with bringing the great **Leonardo da Vinci** to Milan, along with countless other architects and artists. In 1492 the architect Bramante remodelled **Santa Maria delle Grazie**, which houses Leonardo's famous work *The Last Supper* (1498).

France & Spain

"O Franza o Spagna purché se magna"
(Either France or Spain, as long as we eat)

Carlo Borromeo

From the first half of the 16th century Milan endured endless wars between France, Spain and the Austrians. In1559 the Spanish wrestled control from the French, holding onto Milan until the Spanish War of Succession in the early 18th century.

The Spanish built new city walls in the mid-16th century. All that remains of them is the **Porta Romana** – though not in its original location. **San Carlo Borromeo** (1538-84), Cardinal and Archbishop of Milan, is one of the greatest Milanese figures of this period. (See *Lake Maggiore* for more information.)

I Promessi Sposi (The Betrothed) *by Alessandro Manzoni is considered one of the greatest works in Italian literature, and is the most widely read novel in the Italian language, possibly because generations of school kids have to read it! Written when Milan was under Austrian rule, the story is in fact set in the late 17th century, when the city was ruled by the Spanish. It contains superb descriptions of the so-called Great Plague of Milan, which carried off more than 280,000 people. Also recommended for the descriptions of Lake Como. Penguin Classics publishes an English translation.*

The Austro-Hungarian Empire

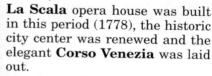

The Treaty of Baden in 1714 ceded Milan to the Austro-Hungarian Empire, where it remained for nearly a century and a half, aside from a brief period of Napoleonic rule and the Cinque Giorni Revolt of 1848 (Five Day Revolt). The early days of Austrian rule were good for Milan. Economically, culturally and intellectually the city thrived – largely thanks to **Maria Theresa** of Austria, the first and only female head of the Hapsburg dynasty.

Maria Theresa

La Scala opera house was built in this period (1778), the historic city center was renewed and the elegant **Corso Venezia** was laid out.

Napolean as King of Italy

Napoleonic forces entered Milan in 1796, and eight years later **Napoleon** was crowned Emperor in the cathedral. When he was driven out a few years later, the Hapsburgs regained control of the city, though the Hapsburg rulers had none of the charm of Maria Theresa, and the majority of Milan's population – intellectuals, traders, working men and women – wanted the Austrians out. Milan became a center for the movement known as Romanticism, and of the struggle for Italian independence and unity, which reached a peak in 1848 with the "Cinque Giornate Revolt" (The Five Day Revolt). Though it lasted less than a week and ended with much bloodshed, the Milanese drove the Austrians out of the city – albeit temporarily.

 Milan features in two of Shakespeare's plays: *Two Gentlemen of Verona* and *The Tempest*, though there is no evidence that he ever set foot on the Continent, let alone Milan.

The Unification of Italy

Gallerie Vittorio Emanuele I

The unification of Italy was a long process that began in 1815 with the Congress of Vienna, and reached its culmination in 1879 with the Franco-Prussian war. After much fighting and bloodshed, in 1861, Victor Emmanuel was proclaimed King of Italy which by then included most of modern-day Italy.

Throughout the 19th century Milan continued to grow in size and would continue to grow. In 1861 it had a population of 240,000; in the years after World War I it had tripled in size and was fast approaching 850,000. The world's earliest shopping center – Gallerie Vittorio Emanuele I – was built in 1866; the Pirelli tire company was founded in 1872 and the famous newspaper *Corriere della Sera* was established in 1876. Such rapid population growth was the cause of much social tension and dissatisfaction, which helped fuel the formation of trade unions and the rise of socialism. Strikes and demonstrations were commonplace and, as Europe greeted the 20th century, the artistic and intellectual movement known as Futurism was born in Milan.

FUTURISM

Founded by Filippo Tommaso Marinetti, along with the artists Umberto Boccioni, Giacomo Balla, Carlo Carrà and Gino Severini, Futurism glorified technology, speed and machines, and extolled the virtues of war. Marinetti was acutely aware that Italy was a comparatively backward country, with great poverty and half of its population illiterate. Its 19th century attitudes, complete with a powerful church and monarch, in a 20th century world was, for Marinetti, a huge hurdle to be overcome. There was clearly a close relationship between Futurism and Fascism, and this relationship has tainted the reputation of Futurism ever since. For a great collection of 20th-century Italian art, head to the **Civico Museo d'Arte Contemporanea** (CIMAC) in the Palazzo Reale. Open Tues-Sun 9 am-5:30 pm. Admission free. At the time of writing closed for restoration.

Post-War Milan

By 1946, Milan's population had grown to 1,800,000, Mussolini was dead – his body and that of his mistress left hanging upside down in Piazzale Loreto – and the city of Milan was starting to rebuild after the terrible destruction of the Allied bombing: a quarter of the city was in ruins. The new La Scala opera house, having been bombed to bits in 1943, was reopened in 1946, with Alberto Toscanini conducting. The Torre Velasca – Velasca Tower – was erected in 1956-8, looking very much like a modern take on a medieval tower, and in 1955 work began on the famous Pirelli building – not impressive in terms of size these days, but for the Milanese the tower was, and is, an important symbol. The famous San Siro sports stadium was also rebuilt in the 1950s (it was originally built in 1926).

The city busied itself with regeneration for the following 20 years, and then in 1969 a terrorist bomb in the Banca Nazionale dell'Agricoltura in Piazza Fontana exploded, killing 16 and injuring 84 people. It marked the beginning of "The Years of Lead" – 20 years of political violence, bombings, kidnappings and assassinations throughout the country.

In 2001, an Italian court finally sentenced three men for the bombing in Piazza Fontana in 1969. The investigation had lasted more than 30 years. Seven trials had collapsed as fresh allegations emerged or for lack of evidence. One defendant turned witness for the state. He was, according to the news agency Reuters, a CIA informer at the time of the bombing. In spite of the fanfare surrounding the convictions, accusations of a political cover-up still continue.

Contemporary Milan

Fashion, business, and more fashion. It is hard to imagine Milan without fashion, though we don't have to go too far back to the days when Rome and Florence were the fashion capitals of Italy. In the 1960s, as fashion itself changed and ready-to-wear became the thing, Milan began to lead the way and today is not only the fashion capital of Italy but of the world. In the heart of Milan is the Quadilatero della Moda, the fashion district, made up of via Monte Napoleone (probably the most famous fashion street in the world), via della Spiga, via Manzoni; via Bagutta, via Sant'Andrea and via Santo Spirito. This is designer heaven – and certainly not for those traveling on a budget.

 Author's tip: Milan is generally packed with media, models and wannabes in the spring and fall for the fashion shows. Bear this in mind. Hotels get booked up, taxis are hard to get, but it's certainly a fun time to be in the city.

Teatro alla Scala interior

As Milan entered the 21st century, it continued to build and rebuild. La Scala was reopened in December 2004 after a three-year renovation project led by the Swiss architect Mario Botta. It cost $67 million and has the largest stage in

Europe. The city will see more skyscrapers too. A team of architects, led by Daniel Libeskind and backed by three of the country's largest insurance companies, has won the right to build three skyscrapers on a site formerly occupied by the fiera – Milan's trade fair. The plans include more green space (sorely needed in the city) and a few thousand apartments. Plans are also underway to build a new urban park in the center of Milan, which will sit between the two main railway stations, Central and Porto Garibaldi.

■ What to See

Milan's Top Sights

 ★★★**Pinacoteca Brera:** One of the most important collections in Italy, with masterpieces from the 13th to the 20th century. Particularly strong on Renaissance art. Not to be missed.

★★★**Pinacoteca Ambrosiana:** A stunning collection of paintings from the 15th century.

★★★**Castello Sforzesco:** Dating from the 14th century and one of the most important courts in Renaissance Italy under Francesco Sforza and his son. See Michelangelo's unfinished Rondanini *Pietà*, the Trivulzio Tapestries and the splendid Sala del Asse.

★★★**Duomo:** The symbol of Milan and the third-largest church in the world. To get a feel of it before you go, check out http://milan.arounder.com for a virtual tour. For an unforgettable view, head to the roof.

★★★**Sant'Ambrogio:** With fourth-century origins, the basilica is a must-see. Don't miss the fourth-century Sarcophagus of Stilicho and the ninth-century Golden Altar.

★★★**The Last Supper:** Leonardo's masterpiece in Santa Maria della Grazie. Queues, timed tickets, booking in advance – but worth it.

★★★**La Scala:** One of the most famous opera houses in the world. Take a guided tour of the backstage area, visit the museum, catch a classical performance or, if you're lucky enough to get a ticket, attend the opera.

★★**Cimitero Monumentale:** 300,000 square yards of peace and greenery in an otherwise frenetic city. Visually a treat, tranquil and moving – particularly the derelict Jewish plot.

★★**Galleria Vittorio Emanuele II:** If only all shopping malls looked like this. Italy's first glass and iron building, and a place to wander, get a coffee and people-watch.

★★**Stazione Centrale:** Majestic, chaotic, noisy, monumental – and one of my favorite railway stations in Europe.

★★**Quadilatero della Moda:** You don't have to buy, but an hour spent window shopping in Milan's fashion district is fun. Guaranteed to make most of us feel underdressed and unattractive.

★**The Da Vinci Passageways:** Private, group tours. Spooky and mysterious, great for bored teenagers. 1,640 ft of tunnels below Castello Sforezco – possibily designed by the great Leonardo da Vinci.

★★**Naviglio Grande:** In the southwest of the city. Bars, music, cheap eats, art galleries, and an antiques market on the last Sun of the month running along the canal towpath.

★**The Skull Chapel:** Not on everyone's must-see list but very unusual and great for those bored teenagers with no interest in fashion, food or art. 3,000 skulls and other assorted bones dating from the 17th century. In the church of San Bernardino in piazza Santo Stefano.

Roman columns facing Basilica di San Lorenzo Maggiore

★★**San Lorenzo alle Colonne:** Dating from the 4th century, this church still retains its original quatrefoil plan. Don't miss the 5th-century mosaics in the chapel of Sant'Aquilino.

★★**Ca' Grande:** Originally a hospital, now part of the city's university with the earliest parts dating from 15th century. The 15th century facade and courtyards are beautiful.

Milan

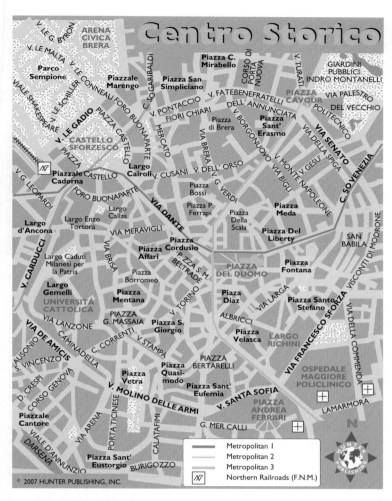

  Tip: The majority if not all of the churches and basilicas in Milan open early, but take a long lunch break: closed from around noon until 3-3:30pm. Plan your sightseeing accordingly!

Historic Center

Piazza del Duomo

A magnet for visitors to the city, this is a good place to start a tour of Milan. Opened in 1865, the piazza was designed by

Piazza del Duomo

Giuseppe Mengoni, who, at the same time and in an effort to bring harmony to the piazza, renovated all the surrounding buildings. Today thronged with people, the piazza sits on the remains of the fourth-century church of St Tecla. In the center of the piazza is Ercole Rosa's monument to King Vittorio Emanuele II.

★★★**The Duomo**. The biggest Gothic church in the world, the third-largest church regardless of style in the world, and Milan's most enduring symbol. Consecrated in 1418, the Duomo wasn't finished until the 19th century, when Napoleon ordered the construction of the façade. Originally fired bricks were chosen as the building material, but in 1387 Duke Gian Galeazzo Visconti declared that marble be used throughout. Mark Twain referred to the duomo as a poem in marble, though doubtless the workers charged with getting the marble from the Candoglia quarries near Lake Maggiore felt less poetic about the whole thing.

157 m/515 ft long, with a capacity of 40,000, the interior has five aisles separated by 52 piers (supports) – the number chosen to represent the weeks of the year – and contains more than 3,500 statues. Open daily 6:45 am-7 pm; Roof open 9 am-5:30 pm (4:30 pm in the winter).

What to See in the Duomo

■ The very impressive **stained glass windows**: some date from the 15th century, though the majority are 19th-century,

The Duomo

and depict scenes from the Bible. The apse is illuminated with three enormous windows by the Bertini brothers.

■ The **crypt** contains the body of San Carlo Borromeo, the Duomo Treasury with its fine collection of religious objects and vestments, and the Coro Jemale, a beautifully decorated 16th-century room.

■ The left transept holds the bronze **Trivulzio Candelabrum**, five m (16 ft) high and in two pieces. The base is the oldest part, attributed to Nicolas of Verdun, a 12th-century goldsmith. In the right transept is the 16th-century monument to **Gian Giacomo Medici**. Once attributed to Michelango, it is actually the work of Leone Leoni. Medici, referred to as Il Medeghino, was not related to the Florentine Medicis, but was Milanese, brother of Pope Pius IV and one-time bodyguard to Francesco II Sforza.

■ In the dome itself, right above the choir in the apse, you'll see a red light, marking the spot where a **nail from Christ's crucifixion** has been kept since 1461. One of the strangest things you're likely to see in a church takes place every year on September 14th. The Bishop of Milan is hoisted up to the niche to retrieve the nail and show it to the thousands gathered below.

■ Don't miss the **view from the roof**. From the dome you can see as far as

Switzerland on a clear day. Take the stairs or use the lift. (Open daily 9-4:45 in winter, to 5:45 pm in summer).

■ **Museo del Duomo**. The cathedral museum has a fascinating collection of art (including Tintoretto's *Christ Among the Doctors*, 1530) and religious artifacts collected since the 15th century. Particularly impressive is the early 16th-century wooden model of the cathedral.

The Palazzo Reale (Piazza del Duomo). For centuries the palace of the various rulers of Milan, this was once the site of the city's first permanent theater. Mozart performed here as a child. Though closed for restoration at the time of writing, the palazzo usually houses the excellent **CIMAC** (Civico Museo d'Arte Contemporanea) collection of 20th-century Italian art. The Futurist works are temporarily on display at the **Palazzo della Permanente**, near Piazza della Republica.

To the west of Piazza del Duomo at Via Torino 9 is the church of **Santa Maria Presso San Satiro**. Redesigned by the architect Bramante in 1478, the church contains a 13th-century fresco above the high altar, which Bramante salvaged from the façade of the original church.

A few moments walk and you reach the ★★★**Pinacoteca Ambrosiana** on Piazza Pio XI. One of Milan's finest art galleries, the

Santa Maria Presso San Satiro

Ambrosiana was founded in 1618 by Cardinal Federico Borromeo, San Carlo's cousin. The Borromeo Collection contains the most famous paintings so, if time is short, head for this gallery first. See da Vinci's *Portrait of a Musician*, Caravaggio's *Basket of Fruit*, the *Madonna del Padiglione* by Botticelli and Raphael's cartoon for the School of Athens,

Portrait of a Musician (da Vinci)

which now hangs in the Vatican. Open Tues-Sun 10 am-5:30 pm, www.ambrosiana.it.

The Biblioteca Ambrosiana was opened in 1609, one of the first public libraries in the world. The library contains over 1,000 pages of Leonardo da Vinci's *Codex Atlanticus* – which Napolean borrowed in 1796. It was not returned, in part, until 1815!

★★**Galleria Vittorio Emanuele II**. Designed to connect the Piazza del Duomo with Piazza della Scale, the Galleria is all glass, iron, shops, cafés and restaurants. Opened in 1867, it was designed by Giuseppe Mengoni, who tragically slipped and fell from the roof only days before it was completed. Spend a little time (and a little money) and have a light lunch at Biffi or coffee at Salotto. Check out the heraldic symbol on the floor under the central dome. This is the Savoy family crest: a white cross on a red background. Surrounding it are the arms of four of Italy's important cities – the bull of Turin is particularly notable, as the Milanesi believe that swirling on your heel where his testicles would be brings good luck!

Teatro alla Scala

★★★**Teatro alla Scala**. One of Milan's most famous buildings, the opera house was reopened after a costly and extensive renovation in 2004.

Originally built in 1776-78 by Giuseppe Piermarini, the building was badly damaged by Allied bombing in the Second World War, and was rebuilt a couple of years later. The lat-

Inside la Scala

est renovation has given La Scala an enormous stage, with a seating capacity of over 2,800. A visit to the interesting theater museum – Museo del Teatro – gives you the opportunity to look inside the theater itself and is recommended to theater and opera fans.

See too the mirrored foyer, designed in 1936, with a bust of Toscanini. The opera season opens on December 7th, on the feast of Sant'Ambrogio. If you want to experience a performance here, be organized. Some hotels have tickets available for guests, the tourist board sometimes have them available, or book online – be warned, however, that tickets for operas are like gold dust. www.teatroallascala.org

Palazzo Marino sits opposite the theater, and though closed to the public, take a peek through from Via Marina to the beautiful courtyard of honor.

Alessandro Manzoni

★**San Fedele**. On Piazza San Fedele. Commissioned by San Carlo Borromeo and designed by Pellegrino Tibaldi in 1569. The work continued for nearly a century, with the dome, crypt and choir added between 1633 and 1652 by Martino Bassi. A good example of Counter-Reformation architecture. In 1873, at the ripe old age of 88, the celebrated author Alessandro Manzoni suffered a fatal fall on the steps of the church. His death certificate is kept in San Fedele, and a statue was later erected to him in the square.

Casa degli Omenoni

Heading east, you come to **Casa degli Omenoni**, built by sculptor Leone Leoni in 1565. Closed to the public, but with a very striking façade – eight mythical figures act as pillars (telamones, which the Milanese call omenoni).

Around the corner at Via Morone 1, is Alessandro Manzoni's house. Now the **National Center of Manzoni Studies**, the house functions as a museum (9-12 am; 2-4 pm Tues-Fri. Closed public holidays).

Northeast of the Historic Center

★★**Museo Poldi Pezzoli**, at Via Manzoni 12, houses a superb collection of paintings, sculpture, armor, porcelain, textiles and glass. Works by Pollaiuolo's (his 15th-century *Portrait of a Girl* being one of the best-known paintings in Italy); Mantegna's *Madonna and Child* is here as well. Open Tues-Sun 10 am-6 pm.

★**Museo Bagatti Valsecchi**, Via Gesù 5. A delightful museum that offers a fascinating insight into the lives of the wealthy 19th-century collector.

Portrait of a Girl (Pollaiuolo)

Much more of a house than a museum, with tapestries,

ceramics, furniture and paintings. Open afternoons only,
Tues-Sun 1-6 pm, www.museobagattivalsecchi.org

★★Fashion District: the Quadilatero

You can't come to Milan without a stroll through the fashion
district, home to the world's top designers. Four main streets
make up the block: Via Montenapoleone, Via Manzoni, Via
Sant'Andrea and Via della Spiga. If you can't remember the
last time you went shopping with any pleasure, and frankly,
can't see what all the fuss is about, the area has some fine
aristocratic residences from the 16th, 17th and 18th centuries. See too the **Archi di Porta Nuova**, on the corner of Via
della Spiga and Via Manzoni. It is one of only two surviving
gates from the medieval city walls.

★★The Brera District

San Simpliciano

The Brera distict is a
great place to wander,
with lots of bars,
cafès, antique shops
and nightclubs. The
Greenwich Village or
the Portobello of
Milan?

Here too is the very
early church of **San
Simpliciano** (AD 402) on Piazza San Simpliciano 7, which
was one of four basilicas founded by Sant'Ambrogio. Though
the façade dates from the 19th century, San Simpliciano has
preserved much of its early Christian architecture.

 San Simpliciano is the venue for some great organ
concerts, a wonderful way to end the evening. Pick
up information at the church or ask the Tourist Office for details. You can also call ☎ 39 02 862 274.

See also the the 13th-century church of **San Marco**, on
Piazza San Marco. San Marco has a Latin cross plan and nine
patrician chapels, added between the 14th and 19th
centuries.

Also worth a look is the church of **Sant'Angelo** on Piazza San Angelo. Built in the mid-16th century by Domenico Giunti, the church is an important example of its kind.

On Via Brera, on the third Saturday of every month, there's an **antique market**.

Finding the Body of St Mark (Tintoretto)

The ★★★**Pinacoteca Brera**, Via Brera 28, is the highlight of the district. One of Italy's finest art galleries, with masterpieces from the 13th to the 20th centuries. The gallery was founded by Napoleon, who busied himself suppressing monasteries and religious orders and relieving them of their treasures. There are 31 rooms, with works displayed chronologically. Much of the original collection was made up of works taken from suppressed monasteries and churches in the 17th century. Must-sees include Mantegna's *Dead Christ*, a superb exercise in foreshortening, Raphael's *Marriage of the Virgin*, Piero della Francesco's *Montefeltro Altarpiece*, and Tintoretto's *Finding the Body of St Mark*. Open Tues-Sun 8:30 am-7:30 pm (last admission one hour before closing).

Dead Christ (Mantegna)

Author's tip: The Brera Gallery is one of the few that opens at 8:30 am. It makes a lot of sense to come here first thing, not only to avoid the crowds but to take maximum advantage of your time in the city.

Beyond the Brera District

Just beyond the Archi di Porta Nuova lie the **Giardini Publici**, the largest city park in Milan, first opened in 1786. The park is bordered by Via Manin, Via Palestro, the famous Corso Venezia and Bastioni di Porta Venezia. Closes at sunset.

 Kid-friendly: Check out Milan's **Natural History Museum** in the Giardini Publici, nearest entrance Corso Venezia. With displays of insects, reptiles, mammals, and reconstructed dinosaurs, it may will suit younger members of the family.

★★**Villa Reale & Galleria Arte Moderna**. Villa Reale is a Neo-Classical villa built in 1790, and was once the residence of Napoleon (albeit briefly) and later Marshal Radetsky. A must for admirers of European art from the 19th and 20th century: the main gallery has 19th-century works from Italy, while the Grassi and Vismara collections show European works of the 19th and 20th centuries, including pieces by the Impressionists, Matisse and Picasso.

Casa Fontana-Silvestri

★**Corso Venezia**. Stroll down one of Milan's most elegant streets (traffic notwithstanding) toward the church of **San Babila**, built originally in the 11th century and rebuilt in the 15th century. The façade is a more recent addition – 1906 – while the bell tower was rebuilt in 1820. Like most churches, it's open from around 7:30 am until 7 pm, but closed for a long lunch between 12 and 3:30 pm. Corso Venezia itself has some fine palazzi, including the Renaissance **Casa Fontana-Silvestri**. It's on the left as you approach San Babila. Unfortunately the villas are not open to the public.

Other Sights in Northeast Milan

★★**Cimitero Monumentale**. A cemetery may not be everyone's idea of a fun day out, but this one is well worth seeing. Measuring 300,000 square yards, the cemetery was first laid out in 1866, and it not only provides welcome relief from the noise and chaos of the city, but it's so full of incredible tombs and sculpture that it functions as an open-air gallery to boot. Some great examples of Art Noveau sculpture can be seen here. The derelict Jewish cemetery is particularly moving. Entrance free. Open 8:30 am-

In the Cimitero Monumentale

5:30 pm Tues-Sun. Closed Mon. Holidays open 8:30 am-1 pm.

The **Pirelli Building** is very much the symbol of Milan. Not particularly impressive in size or design these days, when it was first built (1955-60) it was actually the largest reinforced concrete skyscraper in the world. It stands on the site of Giovan Battista Pirelli's first tire factory and was built as the company's headquarters. Today it houses regional government offices. In 2002 a Swiss pilot from Locarno on Lake Maggiore crashed his light aircraft into the tower killing himself and two lawyers.

Stazione Centrale

★★**Stazione Centrale**. If a cemetery isn't your idea of a fun afternoon out, no doubt the train station won't be either, though Milan's central station in one of the largest in Europe, and certainly one of the grandest and most monumental.

Inspired by the Art Nouveau movement, the station was finally opened in 1931, after 19 years of work. It's the second-largest building in Milan after the Duomo and a brief visit here is fun.

Southeast Milan

Corso di Porta Romana

Laid out by the Romans in the second and third century AD, the Corso di Porta Romana led all the way to Rome. Today it ends at Porta Romana (1598), in Piazzale Medaglie d'Oro, and is lined with impressive villas dating from the 17th and 18th centuries. Take it a short distance to the church of San Nazaro Maggiore, in Piazza San Nazaro. On the way you'll see another symbol of post-war Milan: the **Velasca Tower**. Built in 1956-58, it houses offices and apartments.

★★**San Nazaro Maggiore** is an ancient church, originally built in 382-86 AD by Sant'Ambrogio. At first dedicated to the Apostles Andrew, John and Thomas, whose remains are buried here, it was later dedicated to San Nazaro, whose remains were found and reburied here in 396. Rebuilt in the 11th century after a fire, the church contains frescos from the period, as well as the remains of the Apostles and San Nazaro. The prolific architect Bramantino designed the hexagonal Cappella Trivulzio to house the tomb of Giangiacomo Trivulzio. A Milanese by birth, Trivulzio fought for the French, leading the attack against Lodovico Sforza and the city in 1499. He later became the French-installed governor of Milan.

Francesco Sforza

★★**Ca'Grande**, once the city's hospital, was built in 1456 on the orders of Francesco Sforza. Originally designed to unite the city's 30 hospitals, Ca Grande was remarkably modern for its time – and, incredibly, remained in use as a hospital until 1939. Since the 1950s it has housed part of Milan's university. See the 15th-century decorated façade and courtyards, and the Cortile Maggiore, designed by Francesco Maria Richini. Open 7:30 am-7:30 pm Mon-Fri; 8 am-noon Sat. Closed Sun and holidays (though open 7:30 am-3:30 pm the first three weeks of August).

Head up to Piazza Santo Stefano, for one of Milan's strangest sights. Next to the church of Santo Stefano Maggiore is the ossuary chapel of **San Bernadino alle Ossa**. Small, dark and entirely covered with skulls and bones (that's what ossa means) taken from suppressed monasteries and cemeteries in the 17th century, this will not be on everybody's must-see list but a surefire winner if there are teenage boys in your party! Open 7:30 am-noon and 1-6 pm daily.

In San Bernadino alle Ossa

For those more interested in architecture than bones, have a look at the austere **Palazzo di Giustizia** on Corsa di Porta Vittoria, which runs off Via Sforza. This houses the law courts of Milan and is a good example of architecture from the Fascist period (built 1932-40 by Marcello Piacentini).

★**Abbazia di Chiaravalle** is a lovely Cistercian abbey located slightly outside of Milan city at Chiaravalle. Dating to the 12th century, the Abbey was suppressed by Napoleon in 1798 and fell into disrepair. The 14th-century bell tower (called "ciribiciaccola" or clever contraption by the Milanese) with its 80 marble columns, was designed by Francesco Pecorari. Bramante's chapter house survives,

Abbazia di Chiaravalle

though the 15th-century cloister he designed was demolished in the 19th century to make room for the railroad. Don't miss the 17th-century wooden choir and 14th-century frescoes.

The Abbey is easily reached by Metro 3 to Corvetto. Open 9-11:30 am, 3-6 pm Tues-Sat, 3-4:30 pm Sun.

Southwest Milan

The primary sights here are the superb churches of Sant'Ambrogio and San Lorenzo alle Colonne, and the Naviglio canals: the Naviglio Grande and the Pavese.

The area was sited outside of the Roman walls, and contained early Christian burial grounds as well as Milan's Roman Arena. Sadly, there is little in the way of archeological evidence left, aside from fragments of Emperor Maximian's Circus, and a few remains hidden in the private villas and courtyards of the area.

 The third-century Roman Emperor, Maximian, built a number of structures in Milan: the Arena, the thermal baths and the Circus, used for chariot races. At 1,656 feet long, it was one of the most impressive in the entire empire. The bell tower of the church of San Maurizio on Corso Magenta was originally one of the entrances to the Circus. The only other remains to be seen are on the corner of Via Cappuccio and Via Circo.

★ ★ ★**Sant'Ambrogio.** This is the burial place of Milan's patron saint, and arguably the most beautiful of all of Milan's sights. Built by Ambrogio himself in 379-86 AD, the basilica was enlarged in the eighth century, and then again in the ninth, 11th and 12th centu-

Sant'Ambrogio (Ilva Beretta)

ries. Much of the building seen today dates from the 11th century, and is considered an excellent example of Lombard Romanesque architecture. Open 7 am-noon, 2:30-7 pm daily. Metro 2, Sant'Ambrogio.

WHAT TO SEE IN SANT'AMBROGIO

■ The **Golden Altar**, made in the ninth century by Volvinius for the remains of Saint Ambrogio. On the rear of the altar are reliefs from the life of Ambrogio, while the front is decorated with reliefs from the life of Christ.

■ The **Sarcophagus of Stilicho**, under the pulpit, made in the fourth century, and beautifully decorated with relief figures from the New and Old Testaments.

Sant'Ambrogio (Ilva Beretta)

■ The **Chapel of San Vittore in**

The Pusterla

Ciel d'Oro, fourth century, at the end of the south aisle. The funerary chapel contains stunning fifth-century mosaics, one of which is presumed to be a portrait of Sant'Ambrogio himself. There are also portraits of saints Gervasio and Protasio, whose remains are kept at Sant'Ambrogio.

■ The **Pusterla**, the gate to the basilica, houses a small museum with weapons and grisly instruments of torture.

★★★**San Lorenzo alle Colonne**. One of the oldest churches in Western Christendom, San Lorenzo was built in the fourth century using not only Roman building material but also, it seems, Roman architects and masons.

San Lorenzo alle Colonne

The visitor passes under 16 Corinthian columns from the second and third centuries – from an unidentified Roman villa – to the church's main entrance. The bronze statue in the center of the courtyard is a copy of a Roman statue of Emperor Constantine, who issued the Edict of Milan in AD 313 that granted religious freedom to Christians.

The **Capella di Sant'Aquilino** dates from the fifth century, and contains superb mosaics that once entirely covered the chapel.

The **Capella di San Sisto** contains 17th-century frescoes by Gian Cristoforo Storer, while the dome, the largest in Milan, was built in the late 16th century after the earlier dome collapsed in 1573.

Open 9 am-5:30 pm daily. The Cappella di Sant'Aquilino closes an hour later at 6:30 pm. Take the Metro 3 to Missori and walk, or take Streetcar 3.

 Piazza della Vetra, behind San Lorenzo, was, until 1840, the site of executions!

Naviglio Grande. Hard to believe, but work began on Milan's canal system as early as the 12th century, with Lodovico il Moro enlisting the help of Leonardo da Vinci to enlarge the network in the 15th century. Though some sections of the canals were filled in during the Fascist period, navigation didn't cease completely until 1979. For the next couple of decades, not a great deal happened, though the Naviglio Grande is now one of the liveliest

Naviglio Grande

and friendliest areas of the city, with cheap restaurants, jazz clubs and artists' studios. On the last Sunday of every month there's an antique market running along the canal, with as many as 400 dealers. www.navigliogrande.mi.it

Northwest Milan

The main draws here are the Castello Sforzesco, Santa Maria delle Grazie and Leonardo's *Last Supper*.

★★★**Castello Sforzesco**. One of the symbols of Milan, it's hard to believe that the castle was saved from demolition in the 19th century by architect Luca Beltrami, who was responsible for turning the castle into the museum center it is today. First built in 1368 by Visconti, it was greatly enlarged by Francesco Sforza and his son Lodovico, who enlisted the help of the great Leonardo da Vinci and the architect Bramante. At its height it was one of the greatest of the Renaissance courts. Metro 1 Cairoli-Cadorna, or Metro 2 Lanza-

Castello Sforzesco

Cadorna. Also a number of streetcars take you to the Castello: 1, 3, 4, 12, 14 and 27.

The castle today houses a number of art collections: the **Civici Musei d'Arte e Pinacoteca del Castello** (open Tues-Sun 9 am-5:30 pm), an archeological collection containing sixth-century BC bronzes and Lombardian Iron Age finds, and the **Museum of Musical Instruments**, with over 600 wind and string instruments, and a spinet that was once played by Mozart.

Star sights include the ***Rondanini Pietà***, Michelangelo's last work. The sculptor spent nine years on this, altering it at

Rondanini Pietà

least three times. Abandoned by the artist, who became convinced that he could not capture God in his work, it remained unfinished at the time of his death.

See too the **Sala delle Asse**, a pergola decorated by Leonardo da Vinci, and the stunning **Trivulzio Tapestries**, 12 16th-century Italian tapestries designed by Bramantino.

Under the Castello Sforzesco, there are 1,640 ft of tunnels, the **Da Vinci Passageways**. There are private group tours in English that are great for bored teenagers, though not suitable for those with young children or if you have a nervous disposition. Book ahead, ☎ 39 02659 6937. Cost is around €80 per group.

Via Dante leads you down from Piazza Cordusio to the Castello. If you're trying to get away from Milan's ever-present traffic, Via Dante is a good place to stop and have lunch – it's pedestrianized.

Behind the Castello stretches Milan's biggest park, **Parco Sempione**, redesigned at the end of the 19th century as an

Trivulzio Tapestries detail

English-style garden. In the 15th century the park functioned as the Sforza's hunting reserve, covering 740 acres. Today it's a third of the size, and contains the **Arena Civica**, built in 1806, used today mainly for athletic events and concerts, a number of monuments, and the Triennale di Milano, built in 1932-3 by Giovanni Muzio. The Triennale hosts art exhibitions and conferences.

Kid-friendly: The Acquario Civico, the city's aquarium, is on Via Gado, close to the Arena Civica. With 100 species of fish, it's a good place for the kids.

GREAT VIEWS

On Piazza Sempione, climb to the top of the **Arco della Pace**, for a good view of the castle and Corso Sempione. Originally designed in honor of Napoleon, the arch was finally inaugurated in 1838 to commemorate the crowning of Ferdinand I, ruler of Lombardy-Veneto.

Another of Napoleon's grand designs, Corso Sempione today is a long, busy thoroughfare. The section towards the Arco della Pace is pedestrianized. At No. 36 is **Casa Rustici**, designed by Como-based Modernist architect Giuseppe Teragni in 1931. See the section on Como for more information on his life and work.

To the west of the Castello, lies Corso Magenta and the famous church of Santa Maria delle Grazie, site of Leonardo's *Last Supper.*

★★★**Santa Maria delle Grazie**. Built originally by Guniforte Solari between 1463 and 1490, Santa Maria delle Grazie was altered in 1492 by Bramante under Lodovico il Moro. Possibly the finest Renaissance church in Lombardy, it was hit by a bomb in 1943, which destroyed the main cloister.

Before you head in, note the brick façade designed by Solari, the doorway by Bramante, and the lunette with a painting by Leonardo da Vinci of Lodovico di Moro and

Santa Maria delle Grazie

his wife Beatrice d'Este on either side of the Madonna.

You don't need to be an expert to notice the difference between Solari's Lombard-Gothic architecture, with its decorations and arches, and Bramante's Renaissance style – an alto-

gether purer form, with less decoration. Bramante designed
the apse, the choir, the small cloister and the sacristy.

 One of the painted wardrobes in the old sacristy
hides a secret doorway to an underground passageway. The passageway was designed to allow
Lodovico il Moro to travel on horseback to and from
the castle!

★★★THE LAST SUPPER

The Last Supper

If there is anything that draws visitors to Milan –
certainly not the easiest Italian city to visit for those
in search of la dolce vita – it's this painting by da
Vinci, a masterpiece of Renaissance art.

Painted in the refectory for Lodovico il Moro, the
Last Supper captures the moment when Christ de-
clares that one of his apostles will betray him.

Christ, his mouth half-closed, has just spoken, and
the apostles are dismayed, turning to one another to
express and gesture their disbelief. Judas, momentarily stunned but every inch the guilty man, stares
unrepentently at Christ.

The painting is not a fresco – where paint is applied
quickly to wet plaster (fresco meaning fresh). Leonardo chose to paint in tempera on glue and plaster.
Though it gave him the time he needed to reapply
paint, and build up the tone and depth, it also meant

the painting suffered great deterioration over the years. The great 16th-century art historian, Vasari, called Leonardo's mistake a dazzling blotch

By the early 17th century the deterioration was such that it was considered a lost work. Further damage was done in the Napoleonic era when the refectory was used as a stable. A bomb in 1943 seriously damaged the room, though, incredibly, the painting survived, protected as it was with sandbags and mattresses! Flooding later caused further damage. In 1977 restoration work that was to last 18 years was begun, dealing not only with the deterioration and damage of 500 years but also the six previous restoration attempts, some of which had done nothing but damage the work further.

 Did you know? The face of Judas, seen in profile on Christ's right, was inspired by the prior in the convent, who repeatedly asked da Vinci when the work would be finished.

TICKETS & BOOKING

These days timed tickets are sold to view the *Last Supper*, allowing 15 people in at a time, and booking these in advance is required. Tickets can be sold out weeks in advance, so if you're only in town for a couple of days don't wait too long to book or you might be disappointed, particularly in high season. Consider booking a tour via the Tourist Office, which inludes entry to the *Last Supper*, ☎ 39 199 199 100 for reservations. Open Tues-Sat 9 am-7 pm; Sun 9 am-8 pm. In the summer the closing times may well be extended on Thursday and Saturday evenings. Metro 1,2 Cadorna. Tram 24.

Civico Museo Archeologico, Corso Magenta 15, houses Roman, Greek and Etruscan exhibits. If you want to know how Milan looked in the days of the Romans, come here for a model of the city and to see the only remaining pieces of the Roman walls. Open 9 am-5:30 pm.

Walking east along Corso Magenta back towards the center, you'll find the church of **San Maurizio**, built by Gian

Giacomo Dolcebuono in 1503. Many of the frescoes are the work of Bernardino Luini, a pupil of Leonardo da Vinci.

Musical moment: San Maurizio is the venue for concerts of medieval and Baroque music. A special experience guaranteed and a great way to wind down after a day's sightseeing. Phone for details or ask at the Tourist Office, ☎ 39 02 760 05500.

More Museums & Galleries

Casa Museo Boschi-Di Stefano houses 270 modern works collected by artist Marieda di Stefano and her husband, Pirelli engineer Antonio Boschi, on display in the couple's former apartment. Crammed floor-to-ceiling with pieces by Giorgio de Chirico, Lucio Fontana, and still-life painter Giorgio Morandi, the exhibit is just the peak of the couple's mountainous

2,000-piece collection. In the Porta Venezia district. 15 Via Jan; ☎ 39 02 2024 0568. Metro 1 to Lima.

In winter 2005 textile heiresses **Gigina and Netta Necchi's** '30s house (12 Via Mozart; www.fondoambiente.it) was opened to the public. Treasures include paintings by Canaletto and Tiepolo, Chinese ceramics, and original furniture by the house's architect, Piero Portaluppi.

■ Music in Milan

Sala Verdi del Conservatorio di Milano

via Conservatorio 12, Milan 20122
☎ 39 02 76005500 (concerts Tues evenings only)
Milan's Sala Verdi is a concert hall within a traditional conservatory with a music school and its own 70-strong symphony orchestra. After La Scala, it is one of the city's most important venue for classical concerts. The hall seats 1,600 people, and is centrally located, near the Piazza 5 Giornate.

Auditorium di Milano

Largo Gustav Mahler, Milan 20136

☎ 39 02 833-89201, www.orchestrasinfonicamilano.it

Inaugurated in 1999, this 1,400-seat concert hall in the Navigli area is home to Milan's Symphony Orchestra and Choir. Musical director Riccardo Chailly has a marked preference for works of the late 19th and early 20th century, and he is known especially for his performances of Mahler and Shostakovich.

Teatro Dal Verme

via S. Giovanni sul Muro 2, Milan 20121

☎ 39 02 879-05, www.dalverme.org

After a tortuous restoration, spanning several decades, this 19th-century theater re-opened in 2001. Its concert program is primarily symphony concerts by the resident Orchestra I Pomeriggi Musicali, and tends towards the traditional.

■ Adventures

On Foot

Select Italy offers private walking tours of Milan – for culture vultures and shopaholics. They're also the people to contact regarding tickets to La Scala and other musical events in the city. www.selectitaly.com

On Water

Aquatica is a great place for the kids. Nearly 1,000 ft of water slides, including the toboga, the twister and – not one for scaredy cats – the kamikaze! There's a baby pool and a lazy river for those who just want to slow down and take it easy. The city campsite is next door (see *Camping*). Via Rivoltana 64. www.parcoaquatica.com.

The **Idropark Fila** is a huge water park (more like a lake) located close to Linate Airport. Rowing, water-skiing, swimming (in designated areas), sunbathing, cyling – all kinds of activities and events take place. Take the airport Bus 73, and then change onto Bus 183, which runs the short distance between the Idropark and the airport. infoidropark@provincia.milano.it, ☎ 39 02 7020 0902.

Milan has its huge outdoor swimming pool, the **Lido**, at Piazzale Lotto 15, which is a great place to escape the heat and humidity of the city. In addition to the outdoor pool, there are tennis courts, five-a-side soccer pitches and mini-

Idropark Fila

golf. Cheap and cheerful fun, ☎ 39 02 39 2791

Centro Solari, on Via Montevideo 20, has a 25-m/82-foot, five-laned pool. It's not far from San Abondio, Metro 2. Various opening times. Call for details or look under Impianti on the Milano Sport website, www.milanosport.it, ☎ 39 02 469 5278.

You have to travel to one of the lakes for fishing, or to a river. Try the **Adda River**, near Sondrio. Around 40 miles from Milan. The catch-and-release section of this river is in an area called the Piateda Riserve. Contact the Unione Pesca Sportiva della Provincia di Sondrio, ☎ 39 342 217257.

Tethys, based in Milan, organizes six days of whale spotting with a team of English-speaking researchers. As you might expect, the program doesn't take place in Milan but in the Ligurian sea. An unforgettable experience for those with sea legs, ☎ 39 02 720 01947, www.tethys.org.

On Wheels

Mountain bike through the **Parco del Ticino**, an area of outstanding beauty south of Milan that extends over more than 252,000 acres. **Blu River** organizes excursions at all levels of difficulty, rents bikes and cycle helmets, though you may need some Italian to understand their website, www.bluriver.it. If you prefer two wheels to four (or instead of two feet) why not rent

In the Parco del Ticino

a motorbike in Milan and hit the road? **Beach's Motocycle**

Adventures has a range of bikes for hire for a minimum of one week. www.beachs-mca.com/rental/italpric.htm.

Bianco Blu also rents out motorobikes from Milan, and scooters too. Reasonable rates. www.biancoblu.com.

Air-Stop Travel organizes a half-day bike excursion along the canals of Milan on the first Sunday of every month. info@airstop.net or www.airstop.net. Around €100 for half a day.

Speed Control is an Italian company offering advanced driving courses at the Monza race track. www.speedcontrol.it. If you'd rather watch, take yourself off to Monza race track for any number of annual events. Check their website for details, www.monzanet.it.

On the Tennis Court

 The **Harbour Club** has masses of excellent facilities, including tennis courts, swimming pool, golf driving range, a crèche facility for those with young children, and beauty center. Special membership arrangements for ex-pats in Milan. English-speaking staff, ☎ 39 02 452 861, www.harbourclub.it.

The **Associazione Sporting Club Corvetto** has 13 indoor tennis courts, a gym, bar and restaurant – and does not require membership. Via Massino 15/4, ☎ 39 02 531 436.

The **Centro Sportivo Mario Saini** has 12 courts, both covered and open. Around €12 an hour. Via Corelli 136, ☎ 39 02 756 1280.

On the Golf Course

 La Rovedine Golf Course is Milan's only public course. Around 10 minutes or four miles west of the city at a place called Noverasco di Opera, ☎ 39 02 576 06420, www.rovedine.com.

Castello di Tolcinasco is a top-quality golf and country club with a 36-hole golf course. Located at Tolcinasco, south of the city, ☎ 39 02 904 67250, www.golftolcinasco.it.

On Horseback

 Michele Maggi arranges horse-drawn tours in the Parco del Ticino. Groups of up to six people in a Break Wagonette, tours last up to two hours. A lovely way to see the countryside. You can also go out for excursions on horseback with Michele – not, as he says, at a gallop, but a relaxing excursion through the beauties of the park. Located near the village of Besate, southeast of Milan, and not too far from Vigèvano. info@carozza.it, www.carozza.it.

You can stay here too – it's an agriturismo and wellness center, **Cascina Caremma**, full of charm and great for those with kids or looking to get away from it all. www.caremma. com.

In the Kitchen

The **Scuola Leonardo da Vinci** offer cookery courses for amateurs and professionals, with one three-hour session. Courses take place on a weekly basis. Some knowledge of Italian needed. www. scuolaleonardo.com.

With Wine

The **Scuola Leonardo da Vinci** gives very short courses on Italian wines in Milan. Two three-hour sessions over a two-week period. www.scuolaleonardo. com.

Cellar Tours conducts wine tours from Milan of the Piacenza region. The private chauffered tour also includes visits to local wineries and to a medieval castle. They also have a Gourmet Day Wine Tour to the Franciacorta region near Lake Iseo, and a three-day break to the same region, complete with luxury hotel, optional spa treatment or cookery course, and meals in a Michelin-starred restaurant. www.cellartours. com.

With Language

Adventures Abroad gives Italian language lessons for business travelers in Milan. Accommodation is arranged, along with some leisure activities. www. adventuresabroad.com.

The **Scuola Leonardo da Vinci** offers accredited language courses in modern air-conditioned facilities including a WiFi zone. Located in the Navigli district, the school is recognized by a number of American universities, so you can gain credits towards a degree. www.scuolaleonardo.com.

AmeriSpan gives language courses and arranges accommodation with host families or in apartments in Milan. Airport pickup is included as well. info@amerispan.com, www. amerispan.com.

For older travelers – 50 plus – **Apple Language** conducts so-called Club 50 courses twice a year in Milan. One week, three hours of lessons a day with a full excursion program, including a day-trip to Lake Como. www.applelanguages.com.

With Art

Art Courses in Italy offers an excellent range of art, fashion and design courses in Milan throughout the year. These courses are international and generally require knowledge of Italian. http://www.art-courses-italy.com./

The **Scuola Leonardo da Vinci** has Italian art history courses, running for two weeks twice a month. A knowledge of the Italian language is required – a lower intermediate level apparently, though you should check directly with the school for details. www.scuolaleonardo.com.

With Fashion

Fashion is synonomous with Milan, so if you've always wanted to get a behind-the-scenes look at the industry, check out **Global Experiences'** six-day tour, in Milan and Florence. Included are an English guide, visits to fashion studios, outlets, and textile museums. Contact the Italy Fashion Coordinator for information, ☎ 877 432 2762 (US), www.globalexperiences.com.

Global Experiences also organizes **internships** in Milan, notably within the fashion industry. Each program includes intensive language training – two-, three-or six-month programs are currently offered. www.globalexperiences.com.

With Yoga & in the Spa

 Very well known in his field, **Lino Miele** gives Ashtanga workshops on selected dates throughout the year in Milan. Lino Miele has also produced books and teaching videos, available from his website, www.astanga.it.

The **Italian Association of Ayurveda and Yoga** is based in Milan. Workshops and courses are offered throughout the year. Contact Amadio Bianchi at ☎ 39 02 487 12863, cysurya@cysurya.milano.it, www.cysurya.milano.it.

There are a good number of well-known spas and wellness centers in Milan, at prices to suit most budgets. If the heat and chaos of the city gets to you, consider pampering yourself for an hour or more at one of the following centers.

Find sheer luxury at **Gianfranco Ferré's E'Spa**, attached to his boutique at Via Sant'Andrea 15. Try a purifying herbal linen wrap or a salt and oil scrub (25 minutes treatment at approximately €45) or go the whole hog and experience the Rejuvenate Retreat – a holistic facial using hot stone therapy, followed by the Life Saving back massage (2½ hours, around €250). Check out VR Mag for a virtual tour of the spa: www.vrway.com, ☎ 39 02 7601 7526, reservations@gianfrancoferre.com, www.gianfrancoferre.com.

At the **Moresko Hammam Café**, Via Rubens 19, you might be forgiven for thinking you were in Turkey. Separate facilities for men and women, and a whole range of treatments including the 2½-hour Moresko (hot tiles, sauna, body exfoliation, whirlpool and massage for around €70 during the week, a little more on the weekend). There's a bar and restaurant here too – for €25 you can have aperitivi and a massage – "Oriental Happy Hour with Massage." Advance booking is essential, ☎ 39 02 4046936, info@moresko.it, www.moresko.it.

If you ever wanted to know how it felt to be a Roman, then take a few hours out and head to **Aquae Calidae**, Via Santo Sofia 14. With beautiful interiors – stone, marble, pebbles, tiles and copper – it's one of the chicest places to unwind in the city. Their programs for brides and grooms-to-be are intimate and ritualized – quite something! www.aquaecalidae.it.

Habits Culti Day Spa, Via Angelo Mauri 5, is a place to spend an entire afternoon. There's a shop with great products for the home, a restaurant and the minimalist spa. Or perhaps your partner can browse through the store, then have some lunch, while you enjoy a rejuvenating massage and nail treatment?

■ Where to Stay

Milan is not the place for budget accommodation. Even basic hotels seem to cost twice as much as they would elsewhere and affordable options get booked up fast. Having said that, there are affordable hotels for those who know where to

HOTEL PRICE CHART	
Double room with tax & breakfast	
€	Under €80
€€	€80-€130
€€€	€131-€180
€€€€	€181-€250
€€€€€	Over €250

look, and for those in search of luxury, whether its in a large chain or a small boutique hotel, Milan won't disappoint.

Author's tip: If you want to know precisely where your hotel is located before you land, check out the Milan streetfinder on www. citylightsnews.com.

City Center

Park Hyatt, 1 Via Tommaso Grossi. www.milan.park. hyatt.com, ☎ 800 778 7477 or 39 02 882 11234. €€€€€. 117 rooms and word has it the largest bathrooms of any hotel in the city – sunken bathtubs, double-washbasins, capacious showers. Great restaurant and bar. Very central, very luxurious and expensive.

Park Hyatt

Straf, Via San Raffaele 3, www. straf.it, ☎ 39 02 805 081. €€€€€. Milan's most avant-garde hotel, with 64 rooms, a stunning interior, all slate, concrete, glass and metal. Cool and very hip. Gym, therapy rooms, bar and two restuarants. Very central, within spitting distance from the Duomo.

Straf

Hotel Gray, www.hotelthegray. com. €€€€€. A designer hotel, very chic and moments from the Duomo. Member of the Design Hotels Group, with 21 rooms, and a tiny restaurant/bar. Not pretensious, nor is it cheap.

Gran Duca di York

Gran Duca di York, Via Moneta 1. www.ducadiyork.com, info@ducadiyork.com, ☎ 39 02 874 863. €€€. In an 18th-century building, newly refurbished and decorated in yellows and creams, this hotel represents great value for the location, moments from the Pinacoteca Ambrosiana. Pay a little more for access to a pretty terrace. 33 rooms.

Spadari al Duomo, Via Spadari 11, www.spadarihotel.com, reservation@spadarihotel.com, ☎ 39 02 720 02371. €€€€. A small hotel in the center of the city. Not quite the value it once was but a good location. A number of artists worked on the design of this hotel in the early 1990s and, though arty, it's neither avant-garde nor hip. 36 rooms.

Spadari

Grand Hotel Duomo

Grand Hotel Duomo, www.grandhotelduomo. com, ☎ 39 02 883 3. €€€€€. Right in the heart of Milan, on Piazza del Duomo. 162 rooms and 20 suites, many of which have a view of the Duomo. Built originally in 1860, it was turned into a hotel in 1950. Three restaurants.

Starhotel Rosa, Via Pattari 5. www.starhotels.com, rosa. mi@starhotels.it, ☎ 39 02 883 1. €€€. What it lacks in atmosphere, the Rosa makes up for in value for money. Recently renovated and very central, with all the facilities that a hotel of this size should have: fitness room, restaurant, bar, coffee bar and more. 246 rooms.

Northwest of the Center

3rooms, Corso Como 10, www.3rooms-10corsocomo.com, ☎ 39 02 626 163. €€€€. Designed by American architect Kris Ruhs, this has three suites with Arne Jacobson furniture, Bisazza tiles, Joe Colombo lights. Not central but very fashionable.

Bedroom in 3rooms

Antica Locanda dei Mercanti, Via San Tomaso 6, www. locanda.it, ☎ 39 02 805 4080. €€€. Just 14 rooms, some with private terraces. Bright, simple and fresh. No TV but books and magazines provided. Very much a country feel in a big, noisy city. Breakfast, not included in the room price, is served in your room. Between the Duomo and the Castello. Book well in advance.

Antica Locanda Leonardo, Corso Magenta 78, www.anticalocandaleonardo.it, ☎ 39 02 480 14197. €€€€. A small family-run hotel with a lovely fresh interior and lots of blue and white and cherrywood furniture. Rooms

Antica Locanda Leonardo

recently refurbished. The hotel represents good value in a good location: on Corso Magenta, moments from Leonardo's *Last Supper*, but set back from the road. Rooms overlook the garden or internal courtyard. Book early.

Southwest of the Center

Hotel Zurigo, Corso Italia 11/a, http://brerahotels.com, ☎ 39 02 720 22260 €€€. Just south of the Duomo on Corso Italia. 40 rooms. Complimentary bicycle use offered. All the facilities you would expect, and modern. Good value. Part of the Brera Hotel Group.

Hotel Pierre

Hotel Pierre, Via de Amicis 32. www.hotel-pierremilano.it, ☎ 39 02 720 00581. €€€€€. Away from the tourists and the traffic, the Hotel Pierre has all the conveniences of an ultra-modern hotel with a lot of charm and comfort. 51 rooms, including some suites.

Northeast of the Center

Bulgari Hotel

Bulgari Hotel, Via Privata Fratelli Gabba 7/b, www.bulgarihotels. com, ☎ 39 02 805 805 1. €€€€€. Sumptuous hotel, and the only one in the center of Milan with its own private garden. All the quality and facilities you would expect from the name... and more. Natural materials used throughout: stone, marble, teak and oak, and beautiful furnishings. The tones are neutral and natural. Restaurant and spa.

Starhotel Ritz, Via Spallanzani 40, www.starhotels. com, ritz.mi@starhotels.com. €€€. Excellent value for money in this Italian chain hotel. A short walk from Corso Buenos Aires. 195 rooms, plus meeting rooms, bar and restaurant.

Starhotel Ritz bedroom

Antica Locanda Solferino, www.anticalocandasolferino. it, info@anticalocandasolferino.it, ☎ 39 02 657 0129. €€€. With 11 rooms, very traditional and charming – if old-world is your thing. You'll need to book well in advance to get in here. If faded 19th-century isn't your taste, the Locanda now has two apartments to rent, furnished in a late-'60s style. Located in the Brera district.

Aspromonte, Piazza Aspromonte 12/14, www.hotelaspromonte.it, info@hotelaspromonte.it. €€. Farther out of the city center, but with easy access via the Metro to all the sights. The Aspromonte is modern, basic and a very good value. Close to Stazione Centrale.

Lombardia, Viale Lombardia 74/76, www.hotellombardia. com, info@hotellombardia.com, ☎ 39 02 289 2515. €€. Reasonable prices here. Rooms are comfortable and recently refurbished. A couple of Metro stops east from Stazione Centrale. Restaurant and bar.

The Best Hotel, Via Benedetto Marcello 83, ☎ 39 02 294 04757. €. Great little budget hotel a few moments from Corso Buenos Aries. Ask for a room overlooking the garden.

Hotel Mercure Milano, Piazza Oberdan 12, www.mercure. com, booking@hotelmercuremilanocentro.it, ☎ 39 02 294 03907. €€€. A small chain hotel with 30 rooms, completely refurbished in 2005. Bar, but no restaurant. Located on Piazza Oberdan near the Giardini Publici.

Sheraton Diana Majestic bedroom

Sheraton Diana Majestic, Viale Piave 42, sheraton-dianamajestic@sheraton.com, ☎ 39 02 205 81, www.starwoodhotels.com. €€€€€. Beautiful Liberty-style hotel. Tradition and state-of-the-art technology combined in 107 rooms – some with balcony or terrace overlooking the private garden. Restaurant and chic bar. Expensive but a good value.

Principe di Savoia, Piazza della Repubblica 17, www.luxury-collection.com, ☎ 39 02 623 01. €€€€€. Luxury hotel, with 404 rooms, including the Presidential Suite, originally built in 1927. Superb restaurant and impressive guest list.

Principe di Savoia

Grand Hotel et de Milan, Via Manzoni 29, www.grandhoteletdemilan.it, ☎ 39 02 723 141. €€€€€. Luxury hotel with 95 rooms. The Grand opened in 1863 and has an impressive guest list that includes Verdi, Hemingway and contemporary supermodels.

Four Seasons, Via Gesù 8, www.fourseasons.com, ☎ 39 02 770 88. €€€€€. Luxury hotel, with 118 rooms, in a converted 15th-century monastery. Very chic, very comfortable and very expensive.

Room in the Four Seasons

Bed & Breakfasts

Female Friendly: The following four B&Bs are all run by women, and, though outside of the city center, they are a good option for those travelling alone and/or on a budget.

Dolce Vite, www.ladolcevite.net, ☎ 39 02 489 5 2808. €€. B&B in a delightful villa in the Solari district, with pretty garden, two cats and a dog. Three double rooms and private bathroom. 12-minute walk to the Metro station. Closed August.

B&B Milan, Via Vetta d'Italia 14, www.bedandread.it, ☎ 39 02 468 267. €€. Small house converted by its owner, and offering three simple double rooms with breakfast. Private bathrooms. 15 minutes walk to the Metro station (S.Agostino or Pagano).

Buon Soggiorno, Via Carlo Fornanini 1, www.buonsoggiorno.it, ☎ 39 02 717 951. €€. Located east of the city center, in the university area of Milan. Two double rooms and one single. Private bathrooms. Simple and bright.

Elefante Giallo, Via Moise Loria 50, www.elefantegiallo.it, ☎ 39 02 423 5586. €€. In the Solari district, off Via Foppa. Two double rooms with bathroom. Bright and cheerful.

Apartments

For serviced apartments in Milan have a look at **MoveandStay.com**. They have a good selection. For families or groups this could be an affordable and convenient solution if you plan to spend a few days in the city. www.moveandstay.com.

For luxury, **Select Italy** has beautiful apartments to rent at a daily rate. See www.selectitaly.com – look under Villas & Apartments.

Camping

 Milan itself has a couple of campsites. **Camping Milano** is a four-star campground, with tent pitches, bungalows, rustic cabins with outside bathrooms and large tents available for groups. Sports facilities and bike/scooter rental. West of the city, not too far from the San Siro stadium. Via Gaetana Airaghi 61. Reachable by M1 to De Angeli and then Bus 72. www.campingmilano.it. The great water park, Aquatica, is nearby, www.parcoaquatica.com.

There's also a nice-looking campsite close to Monza race course, **Camp Monza**. It covers more than 90,000 square ft, with room for 220 tents, and asphalt roads. Check the Monza website for details www.monzanet.it (look under Services), or campmonza@libero.it for more information.

South of Milan near Pavia, close to the Ticino National Park, is **Camping Ticino**, www.camping.it/lombardia/campingticino, and **Camping Ticina**, near Vigevano, Loc. Ponte Ticino, ☎ 39 0381 347348.

■ Food & Wine

 There is no excuse not to eat well in Milan. It would be a crying shame not to eat well here, and there are a huge number of restaurants to suit all tastes and pockets. If you're travelling on a budget, the best areas for cheaper eats are in the Navigli, Brera and Ticinese districts.

Milan's cuisine reflects its history: there are dishes that have their origins in Spain, or France, or farther afield in Austria, and there are dishes that are a testimony to the number of workers who flooded into Milan from other regions of Italy after World War II.

The influence of the French is evident in the amount of butter that is used in Milan and Lombardy – and cream, which is quite unusual if not unheard of farther south. The costoletta alla Milanese, a veal chop in breadcrumbs, is more than a little similar to the Austrian/German specialty Wiener schnitzel.

Milanese Specialties

DID YOU KNOW?

If you think pasta is the number one staple all over Italy, think again. In Lombardy, it's rice. Italy produces more rice than any other country in Europe, with the majority of the production in Lombardy and neighboring Piedmont.

Though Milan doesn't really have a specialty, there are a number of dishes that are considered local.

Minestrone (la minestra) is thought to have originated here, though the Ligurians say otherwise, and of course the famous **risotto alla Milanese**, with its distinctive yellow color cortesy of saffron. **Cassouela** is a classic Milanese dish, a hearty pork casserole cooked with cabbage and other vegetables. If your meat generally comes packaged in plastic from a supermarket, be warned that cassouela contains some interesting parts of the pig... trotters, ribs and ears! Veal is a very popular meat – try **ossobucco**, braised veal on the bone, complete with marrow.

Milan has the largest fish market in Italy, and though traditional cuisine rarely uses any fish aside from freshwater varieties, you'll find many fish dishes and fish restaurants in the city.

The Milanese love their cheese – sweet **Mascerpone**, **Grano Padano**, from the Po Valley, and the famous **Gorgonzola** all originate in the province.

Milan does not produce much notable wine. Wines from Franciacorta, the area to the east of Milan, around Brescia and Lake Iseo, are very interesting – particularly the whites. Red wine is producted in much smaller quantities here.

Where to Eat

 Warning! If you have to be in Milan in August, plan your meals ahead. Most restaurants are closed, with the staff on summer vacation. Finding any restaurant that's open is a bonus. Likewise, not all restaurants open on Sunday, or Saturday lunchtime and very few on public holidays. Plan and reserve ahead.

City Center

DID YOU KNOW?

At the very beginning of the 19th century, each box in La Scala had an area where food could be prepared. Curtains were drawn to give the occupants some privacy as they tucked into dinner. It soon became clear however that theater goers were more interested in the music – and so the post-theater dinner was born. The famous restaurants Biffi and Savini have their origins in this period.

Bistro Duomo, Via San Raffaele, bistroduomo@ gmristoriazio, ☎ 39 02 877120. €€€. On the top floor of Rinascente, the chic department store. Probably the best view in town. Not an extensive menu but great quality. Closed Sun, Mon lunchtime.

Cracco-Peck, Via Hugo 4, ☎ 39 02 876 774. €€€€. Blow your budget and your taste buds at this Michelin-starred restaurant under the supervision of acclaimed chef Carlo Cracco. Closed Sat lunch and Sun.

Biffi Scala & Toulà, Piazza la Scala 2, ☎ 39 02 866 651. €€€€. Famous eaterie popular with opera goers. A lovely dining room. Milanese cuisine. Closed Sat lunch and Sun.

DINING PRICE CHART	
For three courses, excluding wine	
€	Under €20
€€	€20-€40
€€€	€41-€70
€€€€	Over €70

Boeucc, Piazza Belgioso 2, ☎ 39 02 760 20224. €€€€. Milanese cuisine in a delightful 18th-century palace. Very elegant.

Don Lisander, Via Manzoni 12/a, ☎ 39 02 760 20130. €€€. For a romantic dinner or relaxing lunch head to Don Lisander. When the weather permits you eat in the pretty courtyard. Milanese, national and international cuisine. Closed Sun.

Savini

Savini, ☎ 39 02 720 03433. €€€€. One of Milan's most famous historic restaurants, in the Galleria Vittorio Emmanuele. All crystal, mirrors and history. Classic Milanese cuisine.

Hostaria Borromei, Via Borromei 4, ☎ 39 02 864 53760. €€€. Unpretentious and pretty courtyard restaurant in Milan's Business district. Eat outside in the summer. Closed Sat lunch and Sun.

Trattoria Milanese, Via Santa Marta 11, ☎ 39 02 864 51991 €€€. Again, tucked away in a small street in the financial district, and well worth the effort it takes to find.Two small rooms and typical Milanese cuisine at a good price.

Taverna Visconti, Via Cerva 18, ☎ 39 02 795 821. €€€. An osteria in a quite street, a wine bar and bistro upstairs, with a restaurant downstairs. As you might expect, a great choice of wine. National cuisine.

Agnello, ☎ 39 02 864 61656. €€. Good pizzeria, moments from the center. Closed Tues.

Artidoro, Via Camperio 15, ☎ 39 02 805 7386. €€€. Innovative restaurant with huge wine list and a great selection of grilled meat. A short walk from Piazza Cordusio. Closed Sun.

Alla Vecchia Latteria di Via Unione, Via Unione 4-6, ☎ 39 02 874401. One of the last remaining latterie, this one serves only vegetarian food from a small menu. Open only for lunch. Family-run for nearly 50 years. Hogging tables when you've long since eaten not encouraged!

Northeast of the Center

Santini

Santini, Via San Marco 3, ☎ 39 02 655 5587, www.ristorantesantini.it. €€€€. In the heart of the Brera district, this elegant restaurant serves modern, refined food – though always has some traditional dishes on the menu. Offers a business lunch with two courses – which makes the whole experience a little more affordable.

Stendhal, Via Ancona, on the corner of Via San Marco, ☎ 39 02 657 2059. €€€. Relaxed café/osteria with a decidedly Parisian feel. Popular with journalists and a chic, creative crowd. Lovely garden space too. Eat brunch here, or come for a drink in the early evening. Closed Mon.

Frienno e Magnanno, Via Benedetto Martcello 93, ☎ 39 02 29403654. €€. Good cheap pizzeria. Closed Mon.

Anema e Cozze, Via Palermo 15, ☎ 539 02 864 61646 (also at Corso Sempione & Via Regina Margherita). €€. An Italian pizza chain, with four restaurants in Milan and two in Naples. Bright, modern interiors, with seafood and pizza the specialties. Perhaps the best pizza outside of Naples.

La Bitta, Via del Carmine 3, ☎ 39 02 720 03185. €€. Popular Tuscan trattoria in the Brera district with a menu that's very strong on fish. Good value for money.

Piero e Pia, Piazza Aspari, 2, ☎ 39 02 718 541. €€. Located farther east of the center, this restaurant offers specialities from Piacenza. Lots of meat dishes and very popular. Closed Sun.

Il Doge di Amalfi, Via Sangallo 41, ☎ 39 02 730 286. €€. If it's pizza you're after, head here. Also good for fish. Highly rated. Closed Mon.

Vecchia Napoli, Via Chavez 4, ☎ 39 02 261 9056. €€. The best known pizzeria in Milan – and winner of the Best Pizza in Europe prize for their Pizza Flesh. Big place (seats 200), very popular, and deserving of praise. Closed Sun lunch.

Da Abele, Via Temperanza 5, ☎ 39 02 261 3855. €€. A trattoria in the traditional sense, with a choice of risottos, meat and fish dishes. Relaxed atmosphere and well priced. Closed Mon.

Joia, Via Panfilo Castaldi 18, ☎ 39 02 295 22124, www.joia.it. €€€€. One of the best restaurants in Milan. Vegetarian and fish cuisine by Swiss chef Pietro Leeman. Lovely atmosphere. Closed Sat lunchtime and Sun.

Joia

Antica Osteria di Via Gluck, Via Gluck 10 (Via Sammartini 43), ☎ 39 02 669 82898. €€€. Simple trattoria with a predominantly fish menu – though meat eaters certainly won't be disappointed. Closed Sat lunch and Sun.

Osteria del Treno, Via San Gregorio 46, ☎ 39 02 670 0479. €€€. Very popular restaurant, with traditional and not-so-traditional cuisine. Call to check opening times as they could be closed at lunchtime and on Sat – though not according to some guidebooks!

Sukrity, Via P. Castaldi 22, ☎ 39 02 201 315. €€. The first Indian restaurant to have opened in Milan, and consistently good. Well priced food too, so it's good for those watching their wallets! This may be an option if you find yourself in Milan in August – but phone and check.

Arturosa La Latteria, Via San Marco 24. €€. Only nine tables here. No reservations taken and, thanks to its proximity to the offices of one of Italy's biggest newspapers (Corriere della Sera), it's pretty difficult to get a table. Great food and relaxed atmosphere Try going early. Closed Sat and Sun.

East & Southeast of the Center

Pane e Farina, Via Pantano 6, ☎ 39 02 869 3274. €€. Pizzeria/restaurant. Relaxed, young crowd and always busy. Order at the counter. Closed Sat and Sun lunch.

Masuelli San Marco, Viale Umbria 80, ☎ 39 02 551 841 38. €€€. Traditional Milanese and Piemontese cuisine in this friendly trattoria – owned by the same family since 1921. Closed Sun and Mon lunchtime.

Dongiò, Via Corio 3, ☎ 39 02 551 1372. €€. Very simple, friendly, with great pasta and lovely desserts! Very fairly priced too – the kind of place you rarely see in Milan any more. Closed Sat lunch and Sun.

LifeGate Cafè, Via della Commenda 43. ☎ 02 545 0765. €€. Organic food, meat, fish and organic pizza. Nice atmosphere here. Closed Tues and Sat lunch.

Trattoria del Nuovo Macello, Via Lombroso 20, ☎ 39 02 599 02122. €€. Lovely, minimalist interior, mouthwatering menu. Closed Sat and Sun. No credit cards taken here, but this inconvenience is balanced out by the very reasonable prices and the fact that service and cover charge is included in the price.

South & Southwest of the Center

Da Theresa, Via Pavia 3, ☎ 02 581 11126. €€. Good Puglian food in this trattoria – and a very popular restaurant so book ahead! Outdoor eating in the summer. Very nice prices to boot.

Sarla, Via G. Stampa 4, ☎ 39 02 890 95538. €€. Iindian restaurant, good prices and nice atmosphere. Set menu at lunchtime which won't break the bank.

Trattoria Tradizionale, Via Bergognone 16, ☎ 39 02 422 92026. €€. In a reconstructed brick-walled factory, with plenty of space and atmosphere. Lots of fish on the menu and also pizza (made with organic flour if you ask nicely!) Closed Sat lunch.

Premiata Pizzeria, Alzaia Naviglio Grande 2, ☎ 39 02 894 00648. €€. Good pizza in the Navgli district. Closed Tues

Super Pizza, Viale Sabotino 4, ☎ 39 02 583 20410. €€. Again, good, well-priced pizza. Closed Mon.

L'Ape Piera, Via Lodovico il Moro 11, ☎ 39 02 891 26060. €€€. Elegant, very pleasant atmosphere with fine food and a well-priced, simple lunch menu. Closed Sun.

Lungolanotte, Via Lodovico al Moro 133, ☎ 39 02 891 20361. €€. In the Naviglio Grande area. Short menu but good and well-priced. You can get wine by the glass here – which is not always possible in Milanese restaurants. Closed Sat lunchtime and Sun.

L'Ape Piera

Al Pont de Ferr, Ripa di Porta Ticinese 55, ☎ 39 02 8940 6277. €€€. Well-known trattoria in the Navigli district. Friendly, homey food. There is usually a vegetarian option here too. Good for a lazy lunch – and open when other restaurants may be closed!

Ponte Rosso, Ripa di Porta Ticinese 23, ☎ 39 02 837 3132. Relaxed, informal atmosphere, regional Italian cuisine – sometimes with a twist. Closed Mon lunch and Sun.

Northwest of the Center

Insalatiera delle Langhe, Corso Como 6. €€. If you're after a light lunch come here. It's next to the very famous 10 Corso Como Café (see below).

Porta Ticinese

10 Corso Como Café, ☎ 39 02 290 13581. €€€. Modern, fashionable and a good place for brunch – it's open from 11 am – or an aperitivo. Food is international. See *Shopping* for more information about 10 Corso Como. Closed Mon lunchtime.

Al Baitone, ☎ 39 02 392 16589, Viale Teodorico 26. €€. Great pasta and pizza in a large, high-ceilinged, wood-beamed room. Closed Tues.

Emilia e Carlo, Via Giuseppe Sacchi 8, ☎ 39 02 875 948. €€€. Close to the castle, this is one of best restaurants in the area. Great menu that changes frequently and an extensive wine list. Closed Sat lunchtime and Sun.

Tagiura, Via Tagiura 5, ☎ 39 02 489 506 13. €€. Predominantly for lunch, though Thurs and Fri evening it's open for dinner. Fixed-price menu and reservation obligatory. Great salami, pasta, and other traditional dishes. Friendly, relaxed atmosphere.

Osteria La Tagliata, Via Ariberto 1, ☎ 39 02 8940 2461. €€. Great Sardinian cuisine, predominantly meat-based and hearty.

Al Garibaldi, Via Monte Grappa 7, ☎ 39 02 659 8006. This place serves until late – 1 am – which is very unusual in Milan. Closed Fri, though open in August. Best to reserve in advance.

Happy Hour – Milan & Aperitivi

 Milan does aperitivo time very well indeed. Forget a quick beer and a bag of nuts after work. Aperitivo time in Milan is something else. Kicking off from around 6 pm until 9 pm, you get to drink, eat the complimentary nibbles, which can be substantial indeed, and people-watch until it's time to think about dinner. Or not. Many places continue to serve traditional finger-food, though the bigger, chicer and more contemporary bars offer what amounts to supper for a very small charge, between €5 and €10.

The chicest of places have stunning interiors and beautiful people – and you can blow your budget if you get carried away. For a more relaxed crowd, the Navigli district is good, as is the Brera district, just north of the Duomo. The idea is that you move from one place to another – not like an English pub where you settle into your fireside seat and remain there all night. Remember too that all hotel bars will be serving aperitivi. If you can't afford to stay there (or eat there), drink there instead!

 Insider tip: If budget is your concern, or you just don't enjoy eating dinner after 8 pm, why not make lunch your main meal, and spend a leisurely hour or three sipping aperitivi – making the complimentary canapès your supper? In some places you'll be offered an array of dishes, or a buffet; in others, finger-food, which can be substantial enough.

Diana Garden, Viale Piave 42, ☎ 39 02 20581. Well-known bar at the Sheraton Diana Majestic. Beautiful garden and indoor bar/lounge. A fashionable/arty crowd.

10 Corso Como, ☎ 39 02 290 13581. One of the chicest places in town and full of beautiful people. Even the doormen are beautiful.

Living, Piazza Sempione 2, ☎ 39 02 331 00824. Overlooking the Arco della Pace, a very popular (and mostly always packed) bar. Outside space for warmer weather, great interior – unless you hate orange furniture. Have a look at their website: www. livingmilano.com.

Bar Basso, Via Plinio 39, ☎ 39 02 294 00580. Relatively unchanged since it opened in 1947, Bar Basso is dark, comforting and reassuringly not cutting-edge – though the crowd is, as always, elegant. The signature cocktail here is the Negroni Sbagliato (sbagliato means mistaken or wrong). The drink, the result of a mistake by a stressed barman, uses spumante in place of gin. Try it! Closed Tues.

Bar Martini Dolce & Gabbana, Corso Venezia 15, ☎ 39 02 760 11154. Now this really is chic... no sign indicates it even exists, but walk through the shop to reach the bar in a courtyard at the back. Black, red and glass. Bar closes at 9:30 pm.

Bar Martini Dolce & Gabbana

Four Seasons, Via Gesù 6/8, ☎ 39 02 770 88. In one of Milan's loveliest hotels, subdued elegance complete with log fire in the winter months.

Bar Brera & Art Cafè, Via Brera 21 & 23. Really close to the Brera Art Gallery. Both of these are relaxed and popular with the student crowd. Buffet served at both bars from 6 pm.

Light, Via Maroncelli 8, on the corner of Tito Speri, ☎ 39 02 626 90631, www.lightlounge.it. Big place in a converted 17th-century building. Two bars, a restaurant, and often hosting events and launches. Great interior and resident DJ. Closed Mon.

ATM, Bastioni di Porta Volta 15, ☎ 39 02 655 2365. Housed in an old bus station, ATM has a young crownd and a good cross-section of people here. Avoids the painfully pretentious vibe of some Milanese bars. Open until 2 am. Closed Sun.

Roialto, Via Piero della Francesca 55, ☎ 39 02 349 36616. Former industrial warehouse; cool but unpretentious crowd. 50s-style furniture. Closed Mon.

Sayonara, Via Ippolito Nievo 1, ☎ 39 02 436 635. If you care little for la moda and are in search of service and style that has all but disappeared, head to this piano bar, pay a little extra and... relax.

Trattoria Toscana, Corsa di Porta Ticinesi 58, ☎ 39 02 8940 6292. A restaurant but also a popular place for aperitivi. Closed Sun.

Trussardi Alla Scala Café, Piazza della Scala 5, ☎ 39 02 806 8821. Ground-floor bar for an aperitivo or lunch with a very elegant crowd. Closes at 10 pm. Upstairs restaurant newly renovated in 2006 – good views of La Scala from here.

Pacino Café, Piazzale Baccone 9, ☎ 39 02 890 74195. Relaxed and chic crowd northeast of the city center.

Bhangrabar, Corsa Sempione 1, ☎ 39 02 349 34469, www. bhangrabar-milano.com. Every Thursday night, international residents of Milan come here for so-called Meltin Pot night. Close to the Arco della

Bhangrabar

Pace, Bhangrabar is Indian-inspired, very comfortable and fun. Buffet served here with the aperitivo – a good selection of

selection of international dishes. Until 10 on most days; until midnight on Wednesdays. Come here for brunch on Sun too.

∎ Nightlife & Clubs

Venues come and go here, so check the listings in publications such as Wednesday's edition of *Corriere della Sera*, Thursday's *La Repubblica*, or pick up a copy of *Spettacoli Milano* or *Mese Milano* at the Tourist Office. On weekends the crowds will be from the suburbs or out of the city – the Milanese go clubbing midweek.

Blue Note, Via Borsieri 37, ☎ 39 02 690 16888. Good mix of European and American musicians here – inspired by the famous American club. You can eat here too. See who's playing and book online at www.bluenotemilano.com

Scimmie, via Ascanio Sforza 49, ☎ 39 02 894-02874. Jazz, blues and world music here, in the heart of Navigli district. Adjoining restaurant.

Blues House, ☎ 39 02 270 03621, Via S.Uguzzone 26. Also in the Navigli district. Blues, rock cover bands and the like. Look at their very blue website for listings, www.blueshouse.it. Music starts quite late here – around 11 pm.

Rolling Stone, Corso XXII Marzo 42, www.rollingstone.it. Rock, disco and hip-hop. Open Fri-Sun from 10 pm until 3 or 4 am. Live music and disco.

Rocket Club, Via Pezzotti 52. Closed Sun. Open until 2 am. No trend, no wannabes. Indie, electronic, et al. www.therocket.it.

Ragoo, Viale Monza 140, www.ragoo.it. Calls itself a discobar... very relaxed, informal and alternative crowd. Admission free!

Cafe Atlantique, Viale Umbria 42, ☎ 39 02 199 111 111, www.cafeatlantique.com. Great for aperitivi, for a Sun brunch (from 12:30) or for the music and dancing, which continues until 4 am. Huge place – over 1,000 square yards and always very popular.

■ Excursions

★★★Pavia

A short train ride (from Milan Central Station, around 30 minutes) south of Milan, Pavia is a beautiful university town. It's one of the oldest universities in Europe and one of the most prestigious in Italy. With a long history. The Goths established their capital here, as did the Lombards in the sixth century. With masses of walkable sights along pedestrianized or bicycle-filled streets, Pavia refreshes the senses that Milan can assault.

See the **Duomo**, with its ugly, unfinished exterior, begun in 1488, and fiddled with for more than 400 years. Giovanni Antonio Amadeo, Leonardo da Vinci and Bramante were all involved in its design, along with many others, though

The Duomo and Broletto

the dome itself wasn't added until 1855. Next to the Duomo you'll see the remains of the 11th century **Torre Civico**, which collapsed in the 1980s. Right behind the Duomo, in the Piazza del Duomo, is the **Broletto**, with eighth-century origins. The loggia dates from the 15th century, while its north wing has 12th-century origins.

The **university** itself was founded in 1361 by Galeazzo Visconti, though Pavia had long since been an important center of learning. There is little left to see of the 15th-century structures, but the elegant, yellow-hued buildings are a delight – the work of Maria Theresa of Austria and architect Giuseppe Piermarini. In Piazza Leonardo da Vinci, there are three medieval towers, and the remains of a 12th-century crypt.

Pavia was once called Civitas Centum Turrium – the city of the hundred towers. Many were built in the 10th, 11th and 12th centuries – though they didn't last. A map from 1525 shows only 50 were still standing.

The Castello Visconteo (Giorgio Gonnella)

Pavia's castle, the **Castello Visconteo**, is a wonderful sight. A quadrangle with two of the original towers still standing, the castle was first built in 1360 by Gian Galeazzo II, though it suffered heavy damage in the Battle of Pavia, 1525, when Emperor Charles V captured Francis I of France. Its arcaded courtyard is stunning. Today the castle houses the Civic Museum.

See also the churches of **San Pietro in Cielo d'Oro**, close to the castle, **Chiesa di Santa Maria del Carmine** and **Chiesa di San Michele**. If you want to get away from stone and bricks, try the botanical gardens here – the **Orto Botanico di Pavia**. It has 2,000 species of plants; the rose garden alone has 400 varieties. Off Viale Gorizia.

★★★Certosa di Pavia

This is one of the most remarkable religious buildings in Italy, located about two miles outside of Pavia. You'll need to take a taxi or the Pavia-Milan bus if you're without a car. The bus stop is about a mile from the Certosa. You could even rent a bicycle.....

Begun in 1396 by Gian Galeazzo Visconti, the Certosa took more than 200 years to complete, and involved a great many architects and craftsmen. The primary architect, however, was Giovanni

Certosa di Pavia

Antonio Amadeo, who worked on the place with his successor Bergognone for 30 years. The church itself has a splendid ornate marble façade. On a summer's day when the sky is a deep blue and the grass of the courtyard a lush green, the contrast is stunning and will have you reaching for your camera.

The church itself contains the tombs of Lodovico il Moro and his young wife Beatrice d'Este and the tomb of Gian Galeazzo Visconti. The plan is Gothic, though the decorations are primarily Renaissance with Baroque additions. Leaving the church, you enter the Little Cloister. What you see here will have you gasping in surprise and reaching for the camera again – rich terracotta, stone spires and upwards to the cupola of the church. The tour continues into the **Great Cloister**, one of the best surviving examples of a Renaissance cloister, with its arcades, 24 cells around a large grassed square. Take a look inside one of the cells, and out into the tiny garden that each monk would have tended. See too the **Refectory**, where monks would meet to eat on Suns, listening to a sermon conducted from the pulpit.

Open Tues-Sun, Oct-Mar 9-11:30 am, 2:30-4:30 pm, April closes at 5:30 pm, May-Sept closes at 6 pm. If you want to stay in Pavia, try the central **Hotel Ariston**, www.aristonpavia.it, or, five minutes outside of Pavia, the **agriturismo Maiocchi** at Borgarello – it also happens to be a stud farm. www.laramaiocchi.it. Also try **Hotel De La Valle**, which is around four miles from Pavia in a nice

Certosa di Pavia Cloister

location and with lots of facilities: www.hotel-delavalle.com. If you're on a budget, try **Locanda Alla Stazione**, with clean, cheap rooms in a private home. Don't expect someone to be here all the time though. Call ahead: Viale Vittorio Emanuele II, 14, ☎ 39 0382 29231.

 Author's tip: If the idea of staying in Milan doesn't appeal, why not stay a couple of nights in Pavia, and make a day-trip or two to Milan?

★★★Vigevano

About 25 miles from Milan, Vigevano is beautiful and well worth a visit – though many guidebooks inexplicably ignore it. With one of the largest fortifications in Europe, and with one of the most beautiful Renaissance piazzas, Vigevano is better known today as a center for shoe manufacturing, but 500 years ago was an important Lombardian city. Begun in the late 15th century by Luchino Visconti, its heyday came

Piazza Ducale and Duomo, Vigevano

under Lodovico il Moro, who extended the **castle** with the help of architect Bramante. The castle complex extends over an area of more than 23,000 square ft, with a courtyard of over 12,000 square ft, making it the largest fortified complex in Europe. See the stunning **Piazza Ducale**, with its three porticoed sides, and the **Bramante Tower**, built in 1492. There's a great panoramic view from here.

The **Duomo**, dedicated to Sant'Ambrogio, was built in 1532 by order of Francesco Sforza, and contains paintings by Bernardino Ferrari and Macrino d'Alba. The **Keep (Il Maschio)** is the oldest, much modified part of the castle. From an entrance on its left you enter the so-called covered street, in fact a fortified bridge, 164 m/ 538 ft long and seven m/23 ft wide.

Castle tower

The castle is open 8 am-6 pm (6:30 on holidays), and the Bramante Tower is open Tues-Fri 11-12 , 3-6 pm, Sat and holidays 10-12:30, 2:30-6 pm.

For those with a liking for shoes, there's a fascinating **shoe museum** in Vigevano, at Corso Cavour 82. Open Mon-Fri 10:30-12 , 3-6 pm, weekends and holidays 10-12:30, 2:30-6:30 pm. If you want to stay in the area, try the agriturismo **Cascina Caremma**, a few miles away. www.caremma.com.

Buses run between Milan, Pavia and Vigevano, if you don't have a car. Contact www.vigevano.org for more tourist information, maps and events.

★★Monza

Famous today for its racetrack, Monza has had a long and illustrious past. With Celtic origins, it assumed great political and commercial importance under the Lombards in the sixth and seventh centuries, thanks primarily to the religious conversion of regent Theolinda. It became an independent or free commune in the 11th century. In 1334 it was conquered and suppressed by Milan – and from then on in its history was that of Milan.

Duomo di Monza

See the **Duomo**, on Via Napoleone, built in the 13th century on the remains of a sixth-century temple. The Duomo, dedicated to St John the Baptist, has a striped marble façade, and an excellent collection of religious artefacts. The **Chapel of Theolinda** contains frescoes by Zavattari. The Iron Crown, emblem of regents in Italy, is here, as is a nail from the cross of Christ, so the story goes.

Villa Reale

Villa Reale is an 18th-century palace with fine gardens and an enormous park. The villa itself houses an art gallery with northern Italian art from the 15th, 18th and 19th centuries and can be visited by appointment through the Tourist Office. Group tours only. www.monza.net. The chapel behind the villa commemorates Umberto, King of Italy, who was assassinated here in 1900 by Italo-American anarchist Gaetano Breschi.

The parkland – 2,200 acres in total – is big enough to contain the Monza Grand Prix track (built in 1922), a horse-racing track and the 27-hole Golf Club Milano.

Take the train from Porto Garibaldi (journey time 15 minutes) or the bus from the same place. Trains also run, albeit less frequently, from Stazione Centrale. If you want to stay in Monza, (or eat lunch), try the **Hotel de la Ville** if your budget allows. It has a beautiful interior, overlooking the park and with an excellent restaurant. The restaurant is closed for Sat and Sun lunch. www.hoteldelaville.com. €€€€

 Something to buy: Head to the **Pasticceria Vecchia Monza** near the Duomo for chocolates made in the strangest shapes you've every seen: pliers, keys and bolts – all celebrating the local metallurgical industry!

■ Shopping in Milan

 You can't come to Milan without being tempted to open your wallet – it's one of the best cities in Europe for shops! After fashion, Milan is famous for design – lighting, homeware, furniture – and is full of small stores selling handmade products. Don't think you have to spend a fortune either. The Italians themselves are clever shoppers and head to the outlets or stockhouses for last season's clothes or slight seconds at huge reductions. If fashion isn't your thing and you don't want to carry anything home, Milan's food stores, particularly the salumerie, will have your taste buds working overtime.

F. Pettinaroli cards

F. Pettinaroli, 2 Piazza San Fedele, has been selling exquisite handmade stationery and writing accessories since 1881. This is the place to go if you're looking for something a little special to take home with you. It's moments from the Duomo. www.pettinaroli.ch.

More handmade paper and stationery can be found at **Fabriano**, in business since 1872 and perfect for gifts or a souvenir to take home. Via Pietro Verri 3. Open Tues-Sat 10 am-7 pm. Mon 3-7 pm.

La Rinascente, Via Santa Radegonda 3, is the only true department store and conveniently located right in the center of the city near the Duomo. Spend the morning shopping and then have lunch in their excellent rooftop restaurant. Neither the store nor the restaurant are cheap.

Alessi Iconic is design famous the world over for inexpensive and fun gifts for the home, as well as pricier and larger objects. Corso Matteotti 9.

Basement, Via Sentato 15, is one of Milan's best known designer outlets. It carries a lot of labels, including Gucci, D&G, Prada, Moschino and Jimmy Choo. For opening times or information call ☎ 39 02 76317913.

Salvagente, Via Bronzetti 16, is similar – a designer outlet with a good range of clothing, including a small men's section. Clothing and accessories from European and American designers, as well as labels you may never have heard of. 50-70% discounts. Check out their website at www.salvagente.it for information on how to get there and opening hours (in

English). They also have a children's stockhouse, **Salvagente Bimbi**, at Via Giuseppe Balzaretti 28.

 Cash or American Express. No Visa or MasterCard accepted at Salvagente!

Dmail

Utterly inelegant but as practical and fun as it gets, **Dmail** sells all sorts of things for the house that you never thought you needed, such as a stick-on thermometer for the window or a table-top Madonna in a grotto. If you're seeking something for a few dollars that will have your neighbors guessing, this is the place to go! Via San Paolo 15, below the British Consulate. www.dmail.it.

Cioccolatopuro sells an incredible range of chocolate-covered fruits and fillings, from chestnut (maron glacé) to figs, lavander, cherries, orange and lime. Beautiful shop for chocaholics. Even the packaging is delectable. Piazza del Carmine 1.

10 Corso Como is well-known among those who like to shop. Calling it a general store hardly does it justice. It's a 13,000-square-foot complex with an art gallery that features mainly

photographc work, a bookstore (art and design predominantly), a boutique for men and women and luxury or must-have items for the home. There's a bar and restaurant here too.

The Lakes

Perennially popular, a visit to one of Northern Italy's lakes never fails to delight. With views that inspired Roman poets and Renaissance painters, a host of 18th-century writers and 19th-century composers, the Italian and Swiss-Italian lakes are not to be rushed. Forget about doing the lakes in a week. These are places to savor, to discover and, above all, places to unwind. A week on one lake alone would never be sufficient, and it's no surprise that visitors return year after year to discover just a little more. If the beauty of the lakes were not enough, with their glass-like surfaces and the brightly-painted fishing villages huddled close to the shore, there's the backdrop of snowed-capped mountain peaks to inspire.

Then there's the climate – each lake is blessed with a micro-climate that allows palms, figs, olive trees, lemons and pomegranates to flourish. Lake Maggiore is known worldwide for its spring display of camellias, Lake Iseo for its olives and for the Franciacorta and its wines, while Lake Garda is famous for its lemons and olive oil. The gardens and parks on every lake delight garden-lovers and horticulturists the world over. The gardening heyday was undoubtedly the 18th and 19th centuries, as European aristocrats, royalty, composers, writers and a fair share of simply the very wealthy, escaped to the lakes for health or pleasure.

■ History

The Italian lakes lie across the ancient trade routes through the Alps, their geographic importance making them strategically vital for thousands of years.

After the Romans came the Franks, then the Hungarians. In the 10th century much of Lombardy fell to the great Otto I, King of the Saxons. The Middle Ages saw battle after battle, as Milan, Como and Venice fought it out. The 12th to 15th centuries was the era of the city states: Milan, under the Viscontis and the Sforzas, Verona, under the Scaligeri, and

Venice. They slugged it out continually. After the feuds and intrigues of the early Renaissance, much of Lombardy fell to the Spanish under King Charles V in the early 16th century. In 1713, after the Spanish War of Succession, the Austrians took control of Milan and most of Lombardy. For the next 80 years or so, under the cultured Maria Theresa and her son Joseph II, Lombardy underwent great economic and cultural reform. Theaters, streets, parks and villas were built, the majority of which survive today. Then it was Napoleon's turn to dominate the region, a brief period at the turn of the 19th century, followed by the Austrians again, though this time with none of Maria Theresa's culture.

In the middle of the 19th century, the unification of Italy began, and the areas around the lakes saw bloody battles with tremendous loss of life. It wasn't until the latter half of the 19th century, and the early 20th century, that tourism took off. The lakes and the valleys beyond were discovered by the traveling British, and the Austrians and Germans, who flocked there for rest cures. Grand hotels were built and the railway came, villas were remodeled, gardens laid out, and golf arrived – one of the earliest courses was at Menaggio, developed by a Britain who had retired to Lake Como.

■ What to See

Which lake to visit is the question. All, is the answer, though which you do first depends on what you are looking for. Each lake has its own character, from the sophistication and glamor of **Lake Como**, with its elegant 18th-century villas and luxury hotels, to the tranquility of tiny **Lake Orta**, with the most beautiful lake island in the whole of Italy, as yet undiscovered by most travelers. **Lake Maggiore** is an altogether quieter, more natural affair, aside from the fantastical Isole Borromei at its southern tip, but one with splendid vistas and the opportunity to head into Switzerland for yet more stunning landscapes and great walking.

Lake Lugano, most of which sits in Switzerland, is sophisticated and moneyed, though it also has tiny lakeside villages that are inaccessible by car. And then there are the Eastern lakes: little **Lake Iseo**, with a backdrop that inspired Leonardo's *Mona Lisa* and the Franciacorta wine-growing area to its south, or **Lake Garda**, the biggest, the warmest and busiest of the lot, with its sunshine, olive and lemon trees and fabulous views.

■ What to Do

 You can happily spend a vacation at any lake doing very little. Swim in the lake, as the locals do, lie on the lake beaches, stroll through pretty medieval villages, and watch the sun go down with a glass of local wine amid the scent of jasmine and bougainvillea.

All around the lakes, particularly Garda, Maggiore, Lugano and Como, are mountains with trails and treks to be enjoyed. Those looking for easy routes will not be disappointed, while experienced walkers will be able to climb to more than 6,000 ft and enjoy stunning views. The tourist boards are increasingly aware of the demand for this type of vacation, and many have brochures describing recommended trails.

Mountain biking is also popular. Renting a bike is easy, and the tourist boards have information on routes all around the lakes.

Hiking Ticino (Catherine Richards)

There are companies that organize guided cycling trips or who provide transport to take you to the start/end point of a trail.

As for water sports, the lakes will not disappoint. The best for windsurfing is Lake Garda, though the north of Como is also good. Learn to sail here, dive, water-ski, or simply rent a boat and strike out. Many boats do not require a pilot's license.

Some lakes prohibit fishing to protect local stocks, though in others, buying a day's license is easy – just contact the tourist board. If you can't fish in the lake, there are no end of rivers where you can enjoy the sport.

Given the mountains that surround the lakes, it is little wonder that paragliding is a popular sport. If you've never done it, consider a tandem flight – after some basic safety instruction, up you go to do nothing but enjoy the view. Rock-climbing, potholing and abseiling are also popular. The Ticinesi valleys (near Locarno on Maggiore) are well-established destinations

Paragliding Lago
Maggiore (Catherine Richards)

for climbers, though these activities are easily available around all the lakes.

The golf courses by the lakes are enough to inspire most people to take up the sport. They range from simple local courses to very well-designed, internationally famous courses, many with superb views over the lake. Prices vary, but Swiss green fees are almost invariably more than Italian.

Families are also well catered for on the Lakes. Italians and their northern neighbors have been vacationing here for generations. Though you might occasionally wish that certain lakes weren't quite so popular – Lake Garda and Lake Como in particular – it is relatively easy to avoid the crowds by getting off the beaten track. If you rent a car to explore the hills and the countryside beyond the lake shores, not only will you get a better feel for the people and the region but you will leave the day-trippers behind.

If you're on a budget or with a family, consider camping or trying the very Italian agriturismo, a kind of farm-stay vacation, where you often help with some of the farm tasks. Your experience will be more authentic, often of excellent quality and at half the price you would pay in a hotel. Camping, on the other hand, is a fun, budget option that should prove a hit with the kids. Many campsites are right on the lake shore, with the best views in town. Many offer chalet-type accommodation as well or caravans to rent.

■ Where to Go

Almost inevitably, there are areas on most lakes that seem over-popular, over-hyped or just over-priced. **Bellagio** on Lake Como, **Stresa** on Lake Maggiore, **Sirmione** on Lake Garda can be heaving with visitors in the summer season. You can do two things: stay elsewhere and enjoy them as day-trips, or pay the prices, stay there and enjoy the relative peace that descends when the day-trippers go.

The Lakes

Lago Maggiore (DTLS/Andrea Lazzarini)

On **Lake Garda**, the south and the east of the lake seem much busier – more sun, more package tours, and Gardaland. The north of **Lake Como** is quieter, most visitors not having the inclination or the time to venture farther than Bellagio. The southern tip of **Maggiore** is busier, the resorts of Stresa, Arona, and Baveno attracting hordes, particularly day-trippers from Milan, or tourists doing the lakes. **Lake Iseo** is pretty quiet whenever you go, even in August, as is the delightful **Lake Orta**.

■ When to Go

 And, finally, a note on when to go. August is holiday time for the Italians. The cities are all but empty, including Milan, and the resorts fill up. Anyone who has taken a beach holiday in August in Italy knows what this means. Booking ahead is vital, not only for accommodations but also for a table at dinner. Finding a quiet spot on a beach can be virtually impossible. Fabulous vibe if you love people-watching and enjoy crowds. Frustrating if you don't. That said, **Lake Iseo** seems to suffer less from crowds than the major lakes. If you are anywhere at the end of August, the last few days in particular, avoid driving. Thousands of Italians head back home after the holidays and heavy traffic on the freeways is inevitable. May through September are probably ideal months to visit the lakes.

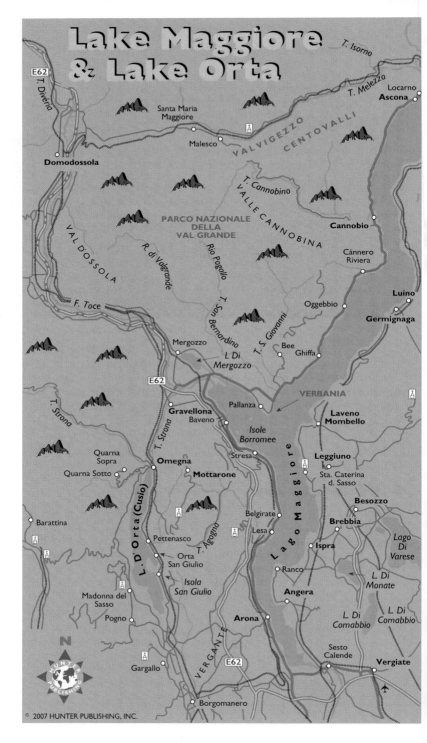

Lake Maggiore & Lake Orta

E62
T. Divèria

T. Isorno

T. Melezzo

Locarno
Ascona

Santa Maria
Maggiore

VALVIGEZZO

CENTOVALLI

Malesco

Domodossola

T. Cannobino

VALLE CANNOBINA

Cannobio

PARCO NAZIONALE
DELLA
VAL GRANDE

VAL DOSSOLA

R. di Valgrande

Rio pogallo

Cànnero
Riviera

F. Toce

T. San Bernardino

T. S. Giovanni

Oggebbio

Luino

Germignaga

Mergozzo

L Di
Mergozzo

Bee
Ghiffa

E62

T. Strona

VERBANIA

Gravellona
Baveno

Pallanza

Laveno
Mombello

Isole
Borromee

T. Strona

Stresa

Leggiuno

Quarna
Sopra

Omegna

Sta. Caterina
d. Sasso

Quarna Sotto

Mottarone

Besozzo

Lago Maggiore

Belgirate

Brebbia

Lago
Di
Varese

Barattina

Lesa

Ispra

L. D'Orta (Cusio)

T. Agogna

Pettenasco

Orta
San Giulio

Ranco

L. Di
Monate

Madonna del
Sasso

Isola
San Giulio

Angera

L. Di
Comabbio

L. Di
Comabbio

Pogno

VERGANTE

Arona

N

Gargallo

E62

Sesto
Calende

Vergiate

HUNTER
PUBLISHING

Borgomanero

Lago Maggiore

Lake Maggiore is Italy's second-biggest lake. The westernmost of the lakes, it extends over two regions – Lombardy and Piedmont. And, like Lake Lugano, it can also claim to be in two countries at once, since its northern tip stretches into Switzerland. Its main towns are Locarno (Switzerland), Arona, Pallanza, Intra, Stresa and Luino.

All of the Italian lakes have huge charm, but Maggiore – also called Verbano – is quieter than most. Less star-studded and glitzy than Como, less crowded than Garda, Maggiore is a more natural experience. That only applies until you reach Stresa, however, where the fantastical and the grandiose rule.

Lago Maggiore

FAMOUS RESIDENTS

"When a man has a heart and a shirt he should sell the shirt in order to see Lake Maggiore." (Stendhal)
All manner of writers, artists and musicians have loved Lake Maggiore, with writer Stendhal being particularly effusive. *"Nothing in the world can compare to the fascination of these ardent days of summer spent on the lakes... in the chestnut woods, so green they seem to have immersed their boughs in the water...."* he wrote.

Other admirers have included Charles Dickens, Winston Churchill, who honeymooned here, Queen Victoria, and Ernest Hemingway, who was invalided here during World War I, and then returned in the 1948 to write part of *A Farewell to Arms*.

Brissago Islands (Catherine Richards)

Unlike Como, Maggiore has a number of islands, with the most famous the three Borromean Islands in the south. There are also the Swiss Isole di Brissago, with their botanical garden and the Castles of Cannero, once a stronghold of infamous lake pirates but now romantically (or spookily) ruined. On Maggiore you get to nod off on a ferry boat and wake up in another country, great fun if you remember your passport; less amusing if you haven't.

Location/Geography

Lake Maggiore lies about 35 miles from Milan's Malpensa airport. The lake itself is some 33 miles long, has a maximum depth of 1,220 ft and is up to 7½ miles wide. With three tributary rivers, the Ticino, the Maggia and the Toce, the lake has only one outlet – the Ticino, itself a tributary of the Po. Its eastern shore sits in the province of Varese, Lombardy, while its western shore is in the province of Novara, Piedmont. Its northern tip stretches eight miles into Switzerland.

Surrounded by the Pre-Alps, the Alpine backdrop is one of the lake's attractions. From the eastern shore on a clear day you get to see Monte Rosa (4,633 m/15,196 ft), which is not a single mountain but a glacier-covered massif with 10 summits. Four of these peaks are among the highest in the Alps.

Economy

Tourism, agriculture and mining are the principal industries on and around Maggiore. The area of Varese is well-known for electromechanical engineering, and the cotton and silk industry. The opening of the Simplon Pass, which Napolean had built as a protected route into northern Italy, and the introduction of ferries onto the lake did much to open the area up to trade and tourism.

The Climate

As with all the Italian lakes, the micro-climate means endless sunshine and palm trees, though it's a good few degrees cooler than on Garda and Como. The climate means that a number of famous gardens have been established here, many open to the public. The spring display of camellias (for which the Maggiore area is well known) and azaleas is particularly impressive.

December and January are the coldest months, though February and March can be pretty chilly too, with the heaviest rainfall typically in October. Summer temperatures rarely go beyond 30°C/86°F. The Easter period, and from late June through to September, are the busiest times, when reservations are essential.

ST. CHARLES BORROMEO

Born in the Castle of Arona in 1538, son of Count Gilberto Borromeo and Margherita de Medici, his uncle was Pius IV, who became Pope in 1559. Charles Borromeo became Bishop of Milan in 1563, and earned a reputation for humility and self-discipline. Known as a reformer who found the excesses of the Catholic Church disturbing, he survived an assassination attempt by three priors from the oorder of the Humilitati (the Brothers of Humility).

He was a man of the people, often walking miles into inhospitable Alpine country to reach peasants in northern parts of his diocese who were virtually abandoned by his clergy. He died at the age of 48, and was made a saint in 1610. Quite against his wishes, a statue of him was erected in Milan Cathedral, where he was buried. It is anyone's guess what he would have thought of the giant copper statue of him in Arona – more than 30 m/98 ft high. If you visit the statue, see what you think about his ears.

Tours

Guided tours are given around the **Nature Park Lagoni of Mercurago** (Arona) and the **Nature Reserve of Fondotoce** (Verbania) in the summer months, ☎ 39 338 4742759, www.parchilagomaggiore.it.

Take one of a variety of hiking tours in the **Parco Nazionale Val Grande** – known as the wildest area in Italy. From April through to October. All levels of difficulty, ☎ 39 0323 557960, www.parcovalgrande.it/visitare/eescursioni.html.

For those based in Milan for whom budget is not an issue, take a private tour to Lake Maggiore with **Geo Passage Tours**. Chauffeur-driven from Milan to Stresa, a guided tour of the Borromean Islands and a boat trip up the lake are included. Geo Passage Tours are also available from Milan to Lake Como. www.geopassage.com/economist/daytours. asp?city_id=4&site_ID=2.

There are guided tours available of the **Borromeo Islands**. Book online at www.isoleborromee.it.

Lake Tours offersa variety of tours of Lake Maggiore, for individuals or groups. Contact them at www.laketours.it/ excursions or e-mail info@laketours.it for more information regarding prices and schedules.

Claudia Ruschena is a multilingual guide who offers extensive tours of Maggiore, Lake Orta and the surrounding provinces. Particularly interesting for those travelling in groups. E-mail her at claudia@lagomaggiore-tour.it or consult www. lagomaggiore-tour.it.

If you're looking for help deciding what to see, where to go and where to stay, a local company, **Ticino Tours**, organizes vacations and tours on Lake Maggiore and in Canton Ticino. Run by a British-Swiss, who can help with walks, treks, watersports, as well as cultural and gastronomic tours. info@ ticinotours.com, www.ticinotours.com.

When to Go & What to Pack

The best time for experiencing the lake is between April and October. Outside of these months not only are many hotels and sights closed, but the winters can be surprisingly cold and snow is common from November. Bring a sweater year-round for the evenings, as the lakeside can feel cool at night. June, July and August can be hot and sunny, and impressive thunderstorms are common in August. Early spring can be cool, but the displays of spring flowers make an April visit memorable.

Public Holidays

January 6 . . . . Epiphany
April 8th/9th (2007) . . . . Easter
April 25 . . . . Liberation Day
May 1 . . . . Labor Day
June 2 . . . . Birth of the Italian Republic
August 1 . . . . Swiss National Holiday
. . . . (fireworks in the Swiss part of Lake Maggiore)
August 15 . . . . Assumption
November 1 . . . . All Saints Day
December 7 . . . . St Ambrose Day (Milan)
December 8 . . . . Immaculate Conception
December 25 . . . . Christmas Day
December 26 . . . . Santo Stefano Day

 The Distretto Turistico dei Laghi has a website in English that gives a lot of information about events throughout the lake area. www. distrettolaghi.it/en/index.html. On the Italian version of the site there is a PDF document with an excellent listing of events throughout the year. (*Brochure Manifestazioni* under *Eventi*). The Swiss tourist authority has an excellent site covering the Swiss part of the lake and the area around it. www.maggiore.ch.

Getting Here

Milan's **Malpensa Airport** is the nearest to the Italian part of the lake – 34 miles away. Milan's **Linate** is also relatively near, though you could consider flying to Switzerland and taking the train to Locarno if you want to include Switzerland in your trip.

Lago Maggiore

There is an hourly service from Milan's central station with **Trenitalia** to Stresa, the best known resort on the lake. www.trenitalia.it, ☎ 039 89 20 21.

These days Milan's majestic Stazione Centrale boasts plenty of automatic ticket machines, so standing in the wrong line for 45 minutes is something you need do only if you're killing time between trains. Currently, the machines do not sell tickets from Italy into Switzerland however. If that is what you are after, make sure you're in the right line! Only a couple of counters seem to handle foreign tickets.

Trenitalia's Swiss cousin, **SBB CFF FFS**, is a lot easier to navigate if you want to book tickets to Locarno.

Holiday Taxis offers transfers to various points on Lake Maggiore from Milan Malpensa via car or minibus for up to eight passengers. One-way transfer by car costs about €125. www.holidaytaxis.com.

Driving from Milan is quick – around 45 minutes – unless it's a Friday evening or public holiday, when the roads everywhere in Italy are much busier. Take the A8 freeway, which connects with the A26 in the direction of Gravellona Toce. Exit at Capugnino-Stresa.

If you're coming from Turin (two hours), take the A4 freeway and then join the A26 toward Gravellona Toce.

Driving from Zurich takes three hours, though in summer the traffic jams at the Gotthard Tunnel can add an hour or more.

With a car, you get to see all the little villages above the lake, though the roads around the lake get VERY busy in the peak season. Hertz, Avis and SIXT all have a presence at Malpensa Airport.

Remember that car rental in Italy is particularly expensive – as is gas! (Italians drive over the border to Switzerland to refuel).

Practicalities

Tourist Offices

Arona
Piazzale Duca d'Aosta
28041 Arona-NO
☎ 39 0322 243601, ☎/fax 39 0322 243601
arona@distrettolaghi.it.

Baveno
Piazza Dante Alighieri, 14
28831 Baveno-VB
☎ 39 0323 924632, ☎/fax 39 0323 924632
baveno@distrettolaghi.it.

Cannero Riviera
Via Roma, 37
28821 Cannero Riviera-VB
☎ 39 0323 788943, ☎/fax 39 0323 788943
cannero@distrettolaghi.it.

Cannobio
Viale Vittorio Veneto, 4
28822 Cannobio-VB
☎ 39 0323 71212, ☎/fax 39 0323 71212
cannobio@distrettolaghi.it.

Stresa
Piazza Marconi, 16
28838 Stresa-VB
☎ 39 0323 30150, ☎/fax 39 0323 31308/32561
stresa@distrettolaghi.it.

Verbania
Corso Zanitello, 6/8
28922 Verbania-VB
☎ 39 0323 503249, ☎/fax 39 0323 507722
verbania@distrettolaghi.it.

Verbania
Via delle Magnolie, 1
28922 Verbania-VB
☎. 39 0323 557676, ☎/fax 39 0323 557676
prolocoverbania@distrettolaghi

Internet Cafés

Stresa

The **Idrovolante Café**, near the Monte Mottarone cable car station also functions as an Internet café.

Locarno

Check out the **cyber chiosk**, close to the ferry terminal. There can't be too many other Internet cafés in the open air!

Lago Maggiore

Getting Around

 On Lake Maggiore this is best done by boat. For updated boat services on the lake check out navigazionelaghi.it or pick up a timetable at your hotel. ☎ 39 (0) 800-55 18 01 or ☎ 39 031 57 92 11.

The funicolare, a common sight around Lago Maggiore
(Catherine Richards)

The fastest service from Locarno in the north to Arona on the southern tip of the lake takes around 1 hour 45 minutes. If you really want a fly/drive experience, **Magic Camper** in Verbania rents campers/motorhomes (though these are decidely smaller than US versions), www.magicamper.com. If you would like to rent a car with driver, have a look at www.gilardetti.net, info@gilardetti.net, fax/☎ 0322 844744, ☎ 335 474599 (cell) or try www.stresa.net/cars-drivers (ferrara.t@libero.it, ☎ 0323 31000, ☎ 335 6445319 (cell).

There is an extensive bus service in the area, though their website (www.vcoinbus.it/unico/uno.htm) is currently only available in Italian. The interactive route map is helpful, and the local tourist office can give more information on tickets, bus stands, etc.

The Swiss Maggiore website (www.maggiore.ch) has a lot of information on traveling around in Ticino, available in English. Look under *Getting Around*.

For wonderful views, take the **Stresa-Alpino-Mottarone cable car**. There are hiking trails that begin here too (more on this under *Hiking*). The cable car station is located in Piazzale Lido, Stresa. In 20 minutes you reach a height of nearly 1,500 m/4,920 ft. On a good day you can see all seven lakes from here (Lake Maggiore, Lake Orta, Lake Mergozzo, Lake Varese, Lake Camabbio, Lake Monate, Lake Biandronno) and even, apparently, Milan's cathedral!

Want to rent a **bike** but don't want to expend too much energy? Have no fear – electric bikes are for hire in Locarno and Ascona at selected hotels and campsites. For more information contact www.maggiore.ch, buongiorno@maggiore.ch, ☎ 41 (0) 91 791 00 91.

Boats can be rented on the lake too, either bare if you have a license, or crewed. Remember that anything over 40 HP requires a license. In Ronco, near Brissago in Switzerland, **Linneo Poroli** has small motor cruisers, 6.4 m/20 ft long, to rent for around $250 a day. They can carry up to five people. www.poroli.ch, info@poroli.ch, ☎ 44 (0) 91 791 7428, or ☎ 44 (0) 91795 2004.

Cantiere del Verbano near Stresa has a selection of boats for hire, qualified personnel to help or advise and a clubhouse complete with private beach and swimming facilities. www. cantieredelverbano.com.

General Markets

Arona: . . . . Tuesday
Ascona (CH): . . . . Tuesday
Baveno: . . . . Monday
Cannero: . . . . Friday
Cannobio: . . . . Sunday
Laveno: . . . . Tuesday
Locarno (CH): . . . . Thursday
Luino: . . . . Wednesday
Stresa: . . . . Friday
Verbania: . . . . Saturday

What to See & Do

Stresa

Known as the Pearl of Verbano, Stresa is one of the most beautiful of Maggiore's towns. A popular holiday resort since the 19th century – Winston Churchill honeymooned here – and host to conferences and international

Stresa

congresses, Stresa gets very busy on spring weekends and in the summer season.

★★★ **The Isole Borromeo**. These are Isola Bella, Isola Pescatori and Isola Madre (www.borromeoturismo.it). **Isola Bella** is indeed beautiful, and very theatrical. An Italian Baroque palace with terraced gardens was built here by Count Carlo III at the end of the 17th century for his wife, Isabella. It's been described as an enormous tiered wedding cake, and French composer Gabriel Fauré wasn't

Isola Bella (G. Gnemmi)

overly impressed: "on Isola Bella... nature has been tortured into artificiality," he wrote, though Dickens was a fan and reasoned (that) "...however fanciful and fantastic the Isola Bella may be, and is, it still is beautiful." Love it or hate it, but see it you must.

Isola Madre (G. Gnemmi)

There's a fine art collection here, 16th-century Flemish tapestries, and the room in which Napolean slept in 1747. It was here that Italian, British and French leaders met in 1935 for the Stresa Conference. **Isola Madre** is the largest of the islands and perhaps the most composed. The Borromeo family home was open to the public in 1978, and comes complete with peacocks, parrots and pheasants, plus a garden that is particularly beautiful from early spring. The Borromeo family still holds all fishing rights to the lake and spends a couple of weeks in the summer here. A flag will be hoisted when the family is in residence. **Isola Pescatori** is an island of working fishermen and their families. It's hopelessly picturesque, and packed in high-season. Consider staying a night here, but book well in advance.

Insider tip: Get up early and take the 9:15 am launch across to avoid the crowds, or go outside peak season. Beware the hordes of boatmen at Stresa encouraging you to take a boat to the islands – they are private taxi boats and will cost you an arm and a leg, though you can certainly try to haggle. Buy tickets from the Navigazione Lago Maggiore office, and ask for a day pass if you want to visit all three islands or others towns along the lake.

Hemingway was an invalid here in 1918 when it served as a hospital in the First World War. He came back in 1948 and set some of *A Farewell to Arms* here. If that doesn't appeal, pick up a copy of *Good Blood* (2004) by Aaron Elkins – a mystery, set in Stresa and on the fictitious Isola de Grazia.

Lago Maggiore

★★**Villa Pallavicino**, ☎ 39 0323 32407, www.parcozoopallavicino.it. A 19th-century villa and gardens on the lake shore that was developed into a zoological park in 1954 by its owner, the Marquise Pallavicino. The gardens are lovely and, with 40 different species of animals and birds, miniature train, restaurant and play area, it's a good place for the kids. Open from the end of February through to early November.

 Excursion: Consider taking a day-trip to Varallo, in Piedmont. Around 32 km/19 miles from Stresa, Varallo's Sacro Monte, is a UNESCO World Heritage Site, and is the oldest and most evocative religious site in northwestern Italy. Founded in the 15th century by

Bernardo Caini, a friar from Milan, the Sacro Monte was intended to evoke the atmosphere of the Holy Land and to bring to life the story of Jesus. Set in a landscape of natural beauty, there are more than 40 chapels complete with lifesize terracotta models behind iron gates – a tableau vivant. There are nine Sacri Monti in Piemonte and Lombardy. Virtually all are beautifully intergrated into the environment and are still considered centers of religious pilgrimage.

Angera

★★**Rocca di Angera**, ☎ 39 0331 931 300. Around five miles from Stresa at Angera, the Rocca di Angera is a superb castle, with 11th-century origins. Originally owned by the Visconti family and purchased by the Borromeo family in the 15th century for the princely sum of 18,500 lire. See the *Sala di Giustizia*, the Justice Room, for superb astrological frescoes from the early 14th century. The castle is often a venue for pseudo-medieval

Rocca di Angera interior

events – Gandolf get-togethers – and is also the location of Italy's best known doll museum (the biggest of its kind in Europe) with over 1,000 exhibits. Open from the end of March until end October.

Santuario della Madonna della Riva. A 17th-century church built following a local woman's claim to have seen the Virgin Mary crying tears of blood. Work began in 1662, though the bell tower is 18th-century and the façade is from 1943. There are 15th-century frescoes and work by Baroque painter Morazzone.

Baveno

Baveno is a smaller, quieter resort than Stresa, with a number of business hotels and conference facilities.

★★The parish church of **SS. Gervasio and Protasio** is well worth a look. Built from local granite, it dates from the 11th century, and retains its original plain façade, complete with Roman tombstones uncovered when the church was being built. The tiny, octagonal baptistery alongside dates from the fifth century and contains some beautiful frescoes.

SS. Gervasio and Protasio

Villa Fedora, in Baveno, is a 19th-century villa once owned by composer Umberto Giordano. It was here that he wrote his opera *Fedora*. The gardens are open to the public in the summer. In the early 1940s Villa Fedora was the hideout of a Jewish refugee, E.Serman, and his family. One night in 1943 the Germans arrived, and E. Serman was murdered. What happened to the rest of his family is not recorded.

Lago Maggiore

TAKE A HIKE

Near Villa Fedora take the road up to Monte Camoscio (890 m/2,919 ft) for superb views. The walk takes two hours if you are fit. If you have a car you can drive as far as the camping site La Tranquila and walk from there, which will take 1½ hours. Much of the pink granite that Baveno is famous for is extracted here. The trail is well-signposted with the standard red and white signs of the CAI (Club Alpino Italiani) There is a mountain rifugio, or refuge, which is sometimes open. Ask in advance at the Tourist Office to be sure.

Laveno

Laveno is a pretty town, with an ancient history and was once known for its ceramic industry. There's a **Museum of Ceramics** at **Palazzo Perabo** (☎ 0332 666 530) – the building itself is a late Renaissance structure. In the center of Laveno is **Villa de Angeli Frua**, a mid-18th-century villa with its gardens open (free) to the public.

 Great Views: the mountain of ★★**Sasso del Ferro** (1,060 m/3,477 ft) can be walked in its entirety (four hours or so) from the village of Cittiglio, just outside Laveno. Or take the cablecar from Laveno. Fabulous views of the lake.

Leggiuno, near Laveno

★★★**Santa Caterina del Sasso**. Three churches unified in the 16th century, Santa Caterina del Sasso is well worth a visit not only because of its location – clinging to the sheer cliffs of Sasso Ballaro – but because of its history. In the 12th

century a wealthy merchant and money lender named Alberto Besozzi was sailing on the lake when, in a storm, his boat capsized. He prayed to St. Catherine of Alessandria to save him, which she seemingly did. An enormous wave swept Alberto up, depositing him on a rocky ledge. By way of thanks he dedicated the next 40 years of his life to St Catherine, spending every day of those 40 years in a cave as a

Santa Caterina del Sasso **(Markus Bernet)**

hermit. Locals lowered food and water to him in a basket, while he developed quite a reputation for his piety. The convent, deserted since 1770 when the Austrians suppressed it, dates from the 13th century. An incredible feat of engineering and of religious devotion. Open every day between Mar and Oct. Closed for lunch between 12 and 2 pm. From November to end February, open on Saturdays and holidays.

Luino

Luino is the most important Lombardian town on Maggiore, and is pleasant enough, though without the charm or draw of other lakeside towns. There's a small **archeological museum** here and an **art gallery** in the restored **Palazzo Verbania**. Free entry. ☎ 39 0322 532 057.

Luino is believed to be the birthplace of painter Bernadino Luini, who was Leonardo da Vinci's chief follower. The church of Santi Pietro e Paolo contains a fresco attributed to Luini.

Check out the market here on Wednesdays.

 Luino is the birthplace of Italian writers Piero Chiaro and Vittorio Serreni, and of Dario Fo, who won the Nobel Prize for Literature in 1997. And it was in Luino that Garibaldi – though sick with malaria – successfully defended the city against a surprise Austrian attack in 1848.

Verbania: Pallanza & Intra

It was Mussolini who in 1939 decided that Pallanza and neighboring Intra should be merged to form Verbania. Pallanza is the prettier of the two, with less traffic, while Intra is the more industrial.

★★★**Villa Taranto**. Located between Pallanza and Intra, these gardens, laid out by Scotsman Neil McEacharn in 1931, are world-famous. More than 20,000 varieties, including superb examples of wisteria, giant Amazon lilies, conifers and Japanese maples. The spring displays of camelias and rhododendrons are well worth seeing. Captain McEacharn was laid to rest in the specially-built chapel at the center of the park in 1964.

Villa Taranto (DTLS/Andrea Lazzarini)

The villa is named after an ancestor of the Captain, one Field Marshall MacDonald who was given the title of the Duke of Taranto by Napolean. Open 1 April-30 Oct from 8:30 am until 7:30 pm. Note: the villa itself is not open to the public.

★★**Villa San Remigio**. Inspired by Romantic ideals of the 19th century, the Irish painter Sophia Brown and her poet/ musician husband the Marquis Silvio della Valle di Casanova rebuilt the original structure and laid out the gardens, with Italianate terraces, an English garden, an enclosed garden in the style of the Renaissance and a natural wooded area. The property was donated to the region of Piemonte in 1977. The gardens are only open to guided tours, which must be pre-booked. Individuals have access on designated days – again, by guided tour only. ☎ 39 0323 503249.

Terrace, Villa San Remigio

★★**Oratory of San Rimigio**. Adjacent to Villa San Remigio, the oratory dates from the 11th century and has two symmetrical naves and apses. Declared a national monument in 1908, the oratory contains frescoes from the 11th century. Guided tours of the villa sometimes include the oratory, or you can phone the Parish of San Leonardo to arrange a visit, ☎ 39 0323 503526.

Museo del Paesaggio. Houses a nice collection of paintings, sculpture and archaeology in the **Viani-Dugani Mansion**, with 5,000 examples of painted votive offerings (offerings or gifts to a god) in the nearby **Biumi-Innocenti Mansion**. Via Ruga, 44. Open April-Oct. Closed Mon and for lunch 12-3:30 pm. ☎ 39 0323 556667.

There are some interesting churches in Verbania, including **Madonna di Campagna**, Viale Azzari, 113, open 9-12 pm and 4-6 pm), a Renaissance church designed by Swiss architect Giovanni Beretta.

Also worth seeing is the **Parish Church of San Leonardo**, Via San Leonardo 6, and the **Parish Church of Santo Stefano**, Piazza Rosario, 9, dating from the 12th century. On view is a Roman votive tablet from the first century AD, found during excavations.

Cannero Riviera

Cannero is a very attractive village, sunny, small and generally quiet. If you like lying in the sun, the lakeside beach here is pleasant and comfortably spacious.

From here you can see the **Castles of Cannero**. The two tiny islands were once the stronghold of pirates who terrorized the lake (in fact, it was a group of brothers called Mazzarditi). They

Cannero (DTLS / Andrea Lazzarini)

were defeated by Filippo Maria Visconti in 1441. The ruined castles you see today were built by Ludovico Borromeo in 1521.

 Of the four beaches on the Italian part of Lake Maggiore awarded a Blue Flag (an international indicator for clean and safe bathing areas), three are in Cannobio, and the other is on Cannero Riviera.

Cannobio (Catherine Richards)

Cannobio

Cannobio, a small town with a population of 6,000, lies only a couple of miles from the Swiss border. It has medieval origins, a very attractive historic center and lakeside promenade, with one of the most popular Sunday morning markets in the area (open 8 am-1 pm).

The **Palazzo della Ragione** (the Town Hall) was built at the end of the 13th century, and remodelled in the 17th century. The tower has 12th-century origins. Though not generally open to the public, it can be visited on request – ask at the Tourist Office.

Also worth a look is the 16th-century **Santuario della Pieta** – built initially at the beginning of the 16th century and remodelled by Charles Borromeo in 1583. The church houses a 16th-century altarpiece, *Ascent to Calvary* by Gaudenzio Ferrari. Ferrari was best known for his series of paintings at the Sacro Monte in Varallo.

View from Canobbio (Catherine Richards)

The Ossola Valleys

To the west of Lake Maggiore lie seven unspoiled valleys – Anzasca, Antrona, Bognanco, Divedro, Antigorio, Formazza and Vigezzo – and not one, but three national parks, including Italy's wildest, the **Val Grande National Park**.

Fifty years ago, logging was a principal activity in the center of the Val Grande, which was scattered with hamlets and villages. Today there is nothing left of those villages but ruins, and the center of the park is so inhospitable in places that trails can only be attempted with guides. Many of them are difficult, dangerous and unsignposted, former mule tracks, shepherds' paths and smugglers' routes. The park's website has detailed information on the treks. Check out www.parcovalgrande.it for detailed, downloadable route maps. For less experienced trekkers, there are many Sentieri Naturi (nature trails) around the park that don't require guides and are suitable for everybody.

Residents of the Val Grande include golden eagles, peregrine falcons, blackcocks, hazel grouse, eagle owls, chamois, roe deer, and smaller mammals like badgers, foxes, martens and weasels. Even wolves have been sighted here again after a long absence. Let's hope a return of other former residents, such as wild cats, lynxes, otters and bears, is on the way.

Val Vigezzo

If you see one valley at Lake Maggiore, then the Val Vigezzo is probably your best choice. It is lush, peaceful and easily accessible (the Centovalli train line between Domodossola and Locarno runs through the valley, with plenty of hopping-off points). Val Vigezzo is known locally as the "Valley of the Painters," not only for its inspirational colors and landscapes, but also for the number of home-grown artists it has produced over the centuries.

 The Val Vigezzo was the birthplace of Gian Paolo Feminis, a barber, who emigrated to Cologne. In 1709 he created a perfumed water, which he named Aqua Admirabilis, scented with bergamot, lavender, neroli and rosemary. It was so popular that he employed his nephew, Giovanni, to market the stuff, which became known as Eau de Cologne!

This is also the place that turned out chimney sweeps by the dozen, and where you can see a museum dedicated to the trade at the **Museo della Spazzocamino** in the grounds of Villa Antonia in Santa Maria Maggiore. In the neighboring village of Malesco there is a statue dedicated to Faustino Cappini, one of the many child sweeps from the area, who died at the age of 14, having been electrocuted by high-tension cables on the roof of a Milanese house whose chimney he had just swept (ask at the Tourist Office for opening hours).

Visit the parish church at **Santa Maria Maggiore**, which has its origins in the 10th century (remodelled in the 18th century) and has work by the artist Borgnis. Have a look at the art gallery here, **Scuola di Belle Arti** in Via Rossetti Valentini.

In the village of Re, also on the Centovalli line, there is the collosal **Sanctuary of the Madonna del Sangue**, a complex of buildings that includes a 17th-century church and a modern sanctuary constructed in the early 1920s.

Madonna del Sangue

Tip: If you want to do a round-trip between Stresa and Locarno, including a rail trip on the Centovalli railway, stay overnight in the Val Vigezzo at a place like Santa Maria Maggiore, and continue your trip by rail the next day. Try **Albergo Miramonti** in Switzerland, a small chalet-like place with a good restaurant and only 11 rooms (Piazzale Diaz 3, 28857 Santa Maria Maggiore (VB), info@almiramonti.com, ☎ 39 0324 95013, ☎/fax 39 0324 94283.

Ascona

In the early 20th century Ascona was a well-known artist's community, its Bohemian atmosphere, stunning setting and favorable climate attracting the likes of Paul Klee, Ben Nicholson, Marianne Von Werefkin, Karl Jung, Hermann Hesse and Carl Gustav. With its cobbled streets, pastel-painted houses, chic boutiques and art galleries, it is no wonder that it is one of the most popular tourist destinations in Switzerland. Bohemia has long since departed, however, to be replaced by the bourgeois (expect

Ascona (Catherine Richards)

to pay more here for your beer than you would elsewhere on Maggiore). The promenade along the lake is one of the few spots that is undisturbed by traffic, the road having been diverted through a tunnel some years back.

★**Monte Verità** – which means Hill of Truth – is located above Ascona, walkable (uphill) in around 20 minutes. At the turn of the 20th century, Monte Verità had a reputation as a center or colony for European intellectuals, philosophers, spiritualists, artists, dancers, and even the occasional anar-

Lago Maggiore

Ascona wall painting

chist. Now a conference center with a restaurant, it can be a very peaceful place for lunch on the terrace, or a walk around the gardens and woods. Great views over the lake.

The small **Museum of Modern Art** in Ascona (the Museo Comunale d'Arte Moderna, Via Borgo 34, closed Mon) is well worth a look. It houses a good collection of work by Marianne Von Werefkin, associated with the German Expressionist movement Das Blau Reiter.

Take a boat from Ascona to **Brissago Island**, Isola di Brissago (Mar-Oct, 9 am-6 pm). There's a botanical garden, with more than 1,500 species of plants, a restaurant and art exhibitions, but its best feature is a superb location slap bang in the middle of the lake, with water all around and an Alpine background. A good place for lunch, either at the restaurant, which can get very busy in high season, or take a sandwich (be discrete) and a good book.

Ascona at night

 Kid-friendly: Ascona Lido is as close to a beach as you can find on a lake. With safe swimming in the lake, a swimming pool, café, toilets and plenty of grass and trees in addition to the sand, this is a great spot for families.

FESTIVAL

Jazz Ascona is the biggest New Orleans jazz festival in Europe. An annual event, it runs for 10 days at the end of June. A great atmosphere, very affordable tickets, stunning locations – stages and tents set up along the lake promenade – and some very big names in modern and traditional jazz. With more than 80,000 visitors over the 10 days, the hotels get booked up early. Book ahead if you're interested! Checkout the festival website www.jazzascona.ch.

Locarno

A small town with a population of around 20,000, Locarno is best known as the setting for the signing of the Locarno Treaties of 1925, and more recently, the host of one of Europe's biggest film festivals. It's a clean and picturesque town with a good lido and beach, an historic center, and the jumping-off point for exploring the stunning valleys of Ticino.

★★★THE LAKE MAGGIORE EXPRESS

Take a round-trip between Stresa and Locarno via Domodossola. You take the tiny Centovalli railway, which twists, climbs and creaks its way between Switzerland and Italy through the Centovalli (Hundred Valleys) and the Valle Vergozza. From Domodossola to Stresa you take a regular Trenitalia train. Lake travel is by boat. The scenery is quite something. Craggy rocks with the bluest of lakes way below you (gulp), waterfalls, chestnut woods, tiny rustici (stone built houses) just feet away from the train window. Getting the train early in the morning is recommended. Catch the first train from Locarno and you might have it all to yourself. Late afternoon in the summer guarantees a less tranquil experience. www.centovalli.ch.

Did You Know? Locarno is one of Switzerland's sunniest spots, with more than 2,300 hours of sunshine a year. It is also one of Switzerland's lowest points, only 637 ft above sea level.

Sanctuary of Madonna del Sasso

★★★The **Sanctuary of Madonna del Sasso** is one of Locarno's must-see sights. Consecrated in the 15th century, this enormous Capuchin monastery is built on a rocky crag above the city. If you don't have the energy to walk up here, there's a little funicolare railway that runs every 15 minutes from Locarno town. The museum has a nice collection of sacred art. Open all year round.

A few stops from the Sanctuary is the impressive ★★★**Cardada-Cimatta cable car** that swings you up to 1,700 m/ 5,577 ft for stunning views of the Alps and Lake Maggiore as it twists and turns into Italy. Designed by Swiss architect Mario Botta, the cable car is pricey, but the experience

Cardada-Cimatta cable car
(Catherine Richards)

is well worth the expense. Great for picnics, or try one of the restaurants up here for a simple lunch or a coffee. There are plenty of well-signed walking trails and a play area for the kids. The cable car is closed between November and mid-December for annual maintenance.

TAKE A HIKE

Take the cable car to Cardada, then follow the path to Alpe Cardada and the panoramic point at 1,496 m/4,908 ft. If you're feeling energetic continue up to Cimetta. Descend from Alpe Cardada toward Monti di Lego through Val Resa. In Monti di Lego you can either go toward Mergoscia or continue the descent to Brione S. Minusio. Return to Locarno or Orselina by public transport or on foot. Level of difficulty: Easy. Suitable for kids and adults. A map of the route is available at www.maggiore.ch/escursioni.

★**Locarno Castle/Castello Visconteo** (April-Oct, Wed-Fri, 10-12 and 2-5 pm, Sat and Sun 10-5 pm) houses the city's archaeological museum, with a fine collection of Roman glass. The seat of the Dukes of

Castello Visconteo

Milan, the Viscontis, from 1513 to 1798, the castle was attacked and damaged extensively by the invading Swiss army. In 2004, the Italian historian Marino Vigano speculated that part of the castle may have been the work of the great Leonardo da Vinci.

★**Gamborogno Botanical Garden** is at the very end of the lake, between Piazzogno and Vairano. Famous for its collection of camelias – more than 950 varieties – as well as 350 varieties of magnolia, azalea, peonies and rhododendron. Open all year round, though spring is the best time to visit the garden, in March, April and May. Take the boat from Locarno to Gambarogno, then Bus 59. info@gambarognoturismo.ch, www.parcobotanico.ch

Lago Maggiore

FESTIVALS

 ★★★The **Locarno Film Festival** is Europe's fourth-largest film festival and the highlight of the year for the city. Every year for the last 59 years, for 10 days at the beginning of August, the city plays host to thousands of film lovers, hundred of movies from all over the world – both new and old – and is visited by well-known actors, actresses and directors. In 2005 John Malcovich and Susan Sarandon popped in to receive awards and host an acting masterclass! In addition to screening all day at various venues around the town, every night, in Locarno's Piazza Grande, films are shown on Europe's biggest outdoor movie screen. You can buy tickets on the day, though be warned that the screenings in the piazza are very, very popular. Take a sandwich, a book and arrive 90 minutes before the performance. See http://jahia.pardo.ch/ and a review of the 2005 festival at www.kamera.co.uk.

★★Bellinzona

Bellinzona (Ticino Tourism / A. Zirpoli)

Bellinzona is the canton's capital, easily reached by half-hourly train service from Locarno. Though it doesn't have a lake, it doesn't have the crowds either, and makes for a pleasant afternoon's excursion. Since the days of the Romans, Bellinzona has been a fortress town, and it boasts three castles, the earliest dating from the mid-13th century. In 2001 the castles of Bellinzona were made a UNESCO World Heritage Site. The largest of the castles, **Castello**

Grande, is superb. You can walk on the ramparts, visit the permanent art collection or eat lunch here, either at the restaurant or take a sandwich and doze on the grass. Open year-round except Dec 25 and 26, 10-6 pm in the summer, 10-5 pm in the winter, ☎ 41 (0) 91 825 8145.

Piazza Collegiata (also called Piazza Grande) is very attractive, and seems much more Lombardian than Swiss. With elegant 17th-century frescoed houses, it's here that the Saturday morning market is held (8 am-1 pm). In nearby Piazza Teatro, there is a beautiful example of a 19th-century theater, small and beautifully proportioned. It was recently reopened after an extensive refurbishing program.

★★★The Ticinesi Valleys

In the Ticino Mountains
(Catherine Richards)

There are a number of valleys in Ticino that are a haven for walkers, or for those who really are looking for peace and tranquility. Unlike many other places in Switzerland with crowds and tour groups all vying for some rest and relaxation, Ticino is not well known outside of the country, and you can walk for miles and miles without seeing another soul. Those in the know say that the best walking to be had in Ticino is here. **Vallemaggia**, the **Val Verzasca** and the **Val Onsernone** can all be reached easily from Locarno. Waterfalls, pools of the deepest greens and blues imagineable, flora, fauna – and silence.

 Insider Tip: If you want somewhere to stay in Valle Maggia, try **Ca Serafina**, a small pensione in the village of Lodano, around 10 miles from Locarno. A restored 19th-century house, with lovely rooms, modern comforts and lots of atmosphere. The friendly owner is English-speaking, and is on hand to help with wine tours or other excursions. Dinner by arrangement. If you are without a car, you can get here by taking the No10 bus from Locarno, ☎ 41 (0) 91 756 5060, www. caserafina.com. Around €130 a night, double room and breakfast.

Lago Maggiore

The tourist board has plenty of information and maps of suggested walks and cycle routes in the area. The Valleymaggia Tourist Office also has an extensive selection of hikes in the area, complete with public transpost connections. Check out www.maggiore.ch/escursioni.

 Pick up a copy of *Walking in Ticino* by Kev Reynolds, published by Cicerone Guides 1992. ISBN 1-85284-098-6. More than 75 of the best walks in Ticino's valleys.

Adventures

In the Air

 The flying school in Locarno, **Aero Locarno** offer a huge range of tourist flights, from a quick 12-minute flight over Ascona, Locarno and Brissago Island, (two people pay around $40 per person, one person $60), a 35-minute flight over the whole of Lake Maggiore for $100 each for two people, to a 90-minute flight over three of Switzerland's most impressive mountains: the Eiger, Monch and Jungfrau. Two people pay about $250 per person for that one. The website is not currently in English, but ask at the Tourist Office for help if you can't read Italian – www.aerolocarno.ch/italian/panoramici.htm

On Foot

 In addition to running Alpine skiing courses in the season, the **Guide Alpine Ticino** (CH) organization offers a variety of rock-climbing activities (for experienced climbers), Alpine climbs, hiking, and canyoning, including basic courses for those with no experience, in the valleys of Ticino. All of the activities are guided by experienced instructors. info@guidealpine.ch, ☎ 41 (0) 91 968 1119, www.guidealpine.ch.

Verbano Viaggi runs guided treks with qualified and experienced personnel in the valleys around the lake: the Val Strona, Val Formazza, Val Grande and Valle Cannobina. info@verbanoviaggi.com, ☎ 39 0323 923 196, www.verbanoviaggi.com.

On Water

 There are a number of diving schools on Lake Maggiore. One is **Centro Sub Abysso International** at via Perossi 8, Verbania, info@sub-abysso. com, ☎ 39 0323 407400.

Also try **Associazione Sub del Lago** in Verbania at via Gugglielmazzi 84/A, ☎ 39 0323 502316.

 Note: These two organizations may not speak English, so if your Italian isn't good ask for help at the Tourist Office! If you want to rent a boat, remember that anything over 40 HP requires a licence (the ICC, International Certificate of Competence). The following companies have boats to hire out, both over and under 40 HP.

■ **Baveno**: **Cantiere del Verbano**, SS Sempione 10, 28835 Ferriolo di Baveno (VB). Family-owned company. info@ cantieredelverbano.com, ☎ 39 0323 28280, www. cantieredelverbano.com.

■ **Porto Ronco** (CH): **Linneo Poroli** has small motor cruisers, 6.40 m/21 ft long, to rent for around $250 a day. An hour for around $75. They can carry up to five people. www.poroli. ch, info@poroli.ch, ☎ 41 (0) 91 791 7428 or 41 (0) 91 795 2004.

■ **Tenero** (CH), at the northern tip of the lake, is a great place to try out some watersports. Marc Spiller runs his outfit **Watersports** from here, with affordable water-skiing and wakeboard lessons. Kajaks for hire and fun stuff for older kids, like the banana boat, ☎ 41 (0) 79 685 5817, www.watersports.ch.

■ Near **Bellinzona** (CH): Check out **Swissraft** for fun rafting on the river. Suitable for kids over the age of six years. info@ swissraft.ch, ☎ 41 (0) 91 921 00 71, www.swissraft.ch. In Balmuccia, one hour's drive east of Stresa is the **Monrosa Canoe and Rafting Center**, info@monrosarafting.it, www. monrosarafting.it. ☎/fax 39 0163 75298 in spring and summer, ☎ 39 0291 02155 in fall and winter. Rafting, kayaking, canoing, tubing hydrospeed and canyoning. A day's course costs about €50.

■ At at a place called **Pino Lago Maggiore** you can windsurf or kitesurf on the lake with **La Darsena school of windsurfing**. It's on the eastern shore of Maggiore, close to the Swiss border. Lessons or equipment for rent. Lessons for kids above age six as well. Book in advance if you want lessons – English is spoken well by most instructors. Open between May and Sept. info@ladarsinawindsurf.com, ☎ 39 0332 566492, www.ladarsenawindsurf.com.

Fishing on Lake Maggiore is regulated by a complex system of licence rules regarding where and when you can fish. Ask at the Tourist Office for further information. In Ticino, fly fishing is possible throughout the canton under one permit, available at the Tourist Office for about $40 for two days. The **IFFT** (International Fly Fishing Club Ticino) can organize guided trips and provide equipment. info@ifft.ch, ☎ 41 (0) 91 972 5082, www.ifft.ch. In Italy, the **Advanced Fly-Catching School** runs courses for all levels throughout the country, including Piedmont and Lombardy. info@afcs-flyfishing.com, www.afcs-flyfishing.com.

Bungy Jumps

Golden Eye Bungy Jump

A few miles from Locarno, in Valle Verzasca, is the famous **Golden Eye Bungy Jump**, named after that James Bond movie that was filmed here. This is the highest bungy jump in the world: 220 m/770 ft, and a 7½-second drop. Terrifying, exhilarating, and pricey – but something you'll never forget. Between April and Oct. **Swissraft** organizes jumps here. info@swissraft.ch, www.swissraft.ch or ask at the Locarno Tourist Office. If 770 ft is a few feet too many, consider doing a bungy jump over the River Isorno in Centovalli. It's 230 ft and half the price.

On Wheels

Bicico is located at the Mottarone cablecar station in Stresa. Here you can rent mountain bikes, which you can take up in the cable car if you wish. Bicico also arranges a host of other activities in the area, from trekking to canyoning, rafting, tennis, sailing and golf excursions. ☎/fax 39 0331 324300, info@bicico.it, www.bicico.it. If it's been a while since you exerted yourself on wheels, rent an electric bike in Locarno or Ascona. Ask for details at the Tourist Office, **Ente Turistica Maggiore**, ☎ 41 (0) 91 791 0091, www.maggiore.ch, buongiorno@maggiore.ch.

In Nature

There are summer tours of the various nature reserves around the lake, including a motorboat tour of the last reed thicket left on the lake (the **Fondotoce**) and the **Canneti Nature Reserve** at Dormelletto. Contact info@parchilagomaggiore, www. parchilagomaggiore.it. In the summer, many of the reserves allow children and bird-watchers to participate in the activities of the study center, which involve recording of the many winged visitors who use the reserves as pitstops.

Volunteers are sometimes needed in the Fondotoce Reserve for a week at a time. Check with the Lago Maggiore Park at info@parchilagomaggiore.

On Snow & Ice

Bicico – located up at Mottarone in the winter – rents out skiing equipment, snow boards and snowshoes. They also arrange courses and provide daycare if you're traveling with young children. www.bicico.it info@bicico.it, ☎/fax 39 0331 324300.

Mottarone has a 360° view over the seven lakes, the Ligurian Apenines, the Po Valley, the Swiss Alps and the Monte Rosa Massif.

Pian di Sole, at 1,065 m/3,493 ft, is great for families, with 1. 8 miles of easy to medium slops. Views of the lake. Ask at the tourist board in Stresa for up-to-date snow reports and information on skiing lessons. www.distrettolaghi.it.

VAL VIGEZZO

There are lots of winter sports in the Val Vigezzo: downhill and cross-country skiing, off-piste skiing, ice-skating. All levels of ability and from 800 to more than 2,000 m (2,600-6600 ft). The **Centro del Fondo** in Santa Maria Maggiore rents out equipment and provides skiing lessons, ☎ 39 0324 94289, www.valvigezzo.com/centrodelfondo, scvigezzo@tin.it.

 Kid-Friendly: There are usually outdoor ice-skating rinks in the center of Locarno and Stresa from early December until the end of Feb. Also deep in the heart of Val Vigezzo at the village of Malesco. Check with tourist boards for details.

On the Golf Course

There are many golf course in the Lake Maggiore area, some of them world-class (and expensive), while others are smaller and cheaper. For a list, have a look at the British golfing website, www.golftoday.co.uk and do a search or ask at the Tourist Office. It is always advisable to book ahead and to confirm fees before setting off.

Some of the best known courses are:

■ **Castelconturbia**, between Malpensa airport and the lake. Country club/hotel. 27 holes, ☎ 39 0322 832093.

■ **Des Iles Borromées**, near Stresa. 18 holes, ☎ 39 0323 929 190, golfilesdesborromees@ntt.it.

■ **Circolo Golf Pian di Sole**, near Verbania. Nine holes, ☎ 39 0323 587 135.

■ **Golf Club Patriziale** in Ascona has a superb setting and is one of the best courses in Switzerland. 18 holes. Lessons available, ☎ 41 (0) 91 791 2132, www.golfascona.ch.

On Horseback

 Club Ippico Ticino is located in Castelletto Ticino, near Sesto Calende at the southern tip of the lake. They are a riding school and also offer pony treks. ☎ 39 0331 920 187.

Between Locarno and Bellinzona at Giubiasco there are the **Al Piano Stables**. ☎ 41 (0) 91 8571512, or ask at the Locarno tourist board.

In the Kitchen

 The International Kitchen offers luxury cooking vacations on Lake Maggiore, with chef Pierangelo Bertinotti. Included are wonderful accommodations, guided tours and wine tasting. ☎ 800 945 8606 (toll-free US number), www.theinternationalkitchen.com, info@theinternationalkitchen.com.

Cooking Vacations take place in a villa on the lake, where you stay six nights. Three cooking lessons with top chefs are offered, and art lessons also available. They have a tennis court, swimming pool, and direct access to the lake.

Cheeses in the Canobbio market (Catherine Richards)

☎ 617 247 4112 (US), www.cooking-vacations.com, info@cooking-vacations.com.

With Wine

 Matasci Vini in Tenero is just a short bus ride or one stop on the train from Locarno. It offers wine tasting and a visit to the wine cellars (by appointment). There's even a small modern art gallery here. info@mataschi-vini.ch, ☎ 41 (0) 91 735 601, www.matasci-vini.ch.

 Though it may come as a surprise to learn that wine is produced in Switzerland – less than 42,000 acres of land are given over to wine production – it has a very long history of viniculture, with more than 40 varieties of indigenous grapes. Here in Ticino, almost 90% of the wine produced is Merlot, both red and white. But, although there are undoubtedly many excellent Ticinese wines, they come at a price. The high cost of production, and the enormous restaurant mark-up, means that the equivalent of $20 in a restaurant buys nothing you would care to drink. A good Ticinesi Merlot is very good indeed, however, and it's worth spending a bit more for the experience.

The tourist board can help you with the addresses of other cantinas (vineyards) in the area, or check the Ticino Tourist Board site, www.ticino-tourism.ch. Look under Gastronony, then Wines and Cellars. If you want to buy a bottle or two of Ticinesi Merlot and don't have time for a wine tour, head to a tiny shop off Piazza Grande, in Locarno: **In Vino Veritas**. The owner is helpful, friendly and a great enthusiast. Piazza Grande 20a, ☎ 41 (0) 91 751 6122.

With Language

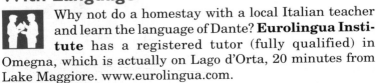 Why not do a homestay with a local Italian teacher and learn the language of Dante? **Eurolingua Institute** has a registered tutor (fully qualified) in Omegna, which is actually on Lago d'Orta, 20 minutes from Lake Maggiore. www.eurolingua.com.

With Art

Lean the art of watercolor painting on Lake Maggiore with **Webster's World** and American artists Janet and Steve Rogers. A 10-day course. ☎ 386 441 4930 (US), www.webstersworld.net, rogersart@worldnet. att.net.

As a Volunteer

There are often volunteer projects running in the area, from footpath maintenance and structural restoration to general weeding. Some are suitable for all levels of fitness and experience, while others demand a certain toughness. A two-week commitment is often required. Have a look at the excellent **Cadip** (Canadian Alliance for Development Initiatives & Projects) website: www.cadip.org. It details many volunteer opportunities in Italy and around the world, and how to get involved.

With the Spirit

In the heart of the countryside, overlooking Lake Maggiore and close to Verbania is the **Albagnano Healing Meditation Center**, opened by Lama Gangchen Rinpoche. A range of daily, weekly and evening courses are on offer, from art therapy and meditation to Tantric self-healing. infoalba.lgpt.net, www.lgpt.net.

Where to Stay

There is a good range of accommodation on Lake Maggiore, from luxury down to simple campsites. Camping, in fact, accounts for a huge proportion of overnight visitors. It's extremely popular with Europeans and the lake has some excellent

HOTEL PRICE CHART	
Double room with tax & breakfast	
€	Under €80
€€	€80-€130
€€€	€131-€180
€€€€	€181-€250
€€€€€	Over €250

campsites, especially in the Swiss part.

Prices in Switzerland for accommodation are higher than in Italy. Nearly everything you might want to buy is more expensive in Switzerland, with the notable exception of gas, chocolate and cigarettes. Make of that what you will.

Some hotels, particularly those on the lake, are closed in the winter (between November and Feb/Mar). For hotels on the lake, always specify if you want a room with a view to avoid disappointment. In high season always book ahead – resorts like Stresa are very popular.

Italian Lake Maggiore
Stresa

Grand Hotel des Iles Borromées. Beautiful 19th-century hotel, associated with Hemingway and European royalty. As with many hotels of its ilk, the décor may not be to everyone's taste, though the sense of history is a great attraction. Lungolago Umberto I, 67. ☎ 39 0323 93 89 38, www.borromees. it. €€€€€

Grand Hotel des Iles Borromées

Hotel Verbano, Isola dei Pescatori. For a unique experience, this hotel is on one of the most picturesque islands on any lake in northern Italy. Only 12 rooms, so book early. hotelverbano@it, ☎ 39 0323 304 08, www.hotelverbano.it. €€€

Villa Aminta

Villa Aminta. An award-winning luxury hotel set in its own park outside the town of Stresa. Splendid views over the lake and the Borromean islands, with excellent facilities and a restaurant. Via Sempione Nord 123, villa-aminta@villa-aminta.it, ☎ 39 0323 933 818, www.villa-aminta.it. €€€€€

Hotel Ristorante Fiorentino. Run by father and son, this budget hotel is well-located in the center of Stresa. Restaurant. Via A. M. Bolongaro, 9, ☎ 39 0323:30254, info@hotelfiorentino.com. €

Hotel Cà Mea. A good budget option – simple rooms but some with lake view. Restaurant. Via Sempione Sud 46/a. hotelcamea@libero.it, ☎ 39 0323-31162, www.hotelcamea.com. €

Baveno

Albergo Rigoli. Small, family-run hotel set right on the lake. Make sure to ask for a lake view! As with many such places, the friendliness is the attraction, not the décor. Offers very good value, considering the location. The **Residence Ortensia** next door is under the same ownership and offers year-round accommodation with kitchen. Via Piave 48, 28831, bavenohotel@hotelrigoli.com, ☎ 39 0323 924756, www.hotelrigoli.com. €€

Lido Palace Hotel. A traditional hotel with superb views of the lake, family-owned and dating back to the mid-19th century. Lots of atmosphere. Swimming pool, gym, tennis, gardens and private access to the beach. Winston Churchill passed through on his honeymoon in 1908, Wagner and Anthony Eden were guests, though the grandest visitor must surely be Queen Victoria, who was here in 1879. Strada del Sempione 30, info@lidopalace.com, ☎ 39 0320 924444, www.lidopalace.com. €€€

Lido Palace Hotel

Belgirate

Villa dal Pozzo d'Annone

Villa dal Pozzo d'Annone. This privately owned villa has six suites, beautifully furnished, and a further 12 bedrooms in the recently-opened 18th-century **Borgo**, a complex set on the grounds of the villa with a bistro/wine bar. Given as a wedding gift in 1827 to Princess Luisa Dal Pozzo della Cisterna by her husband, Ferdinando Arborio, Duke of Sartirana and Marquis of Bremè, the villa today is still owned by the Dal Pozzo family. The villa is open between Easter and October; the 18th-century Borgo is open all year round. Strada del Sempione 5, info@villadalpozzodannone.com, ☎ 39 0322 7255, www.villadalpozzo.com. €€€€€

Pallanza

Grand Hotel Majestic. Built in 1870, with a guest list that included Toscanini and Debussy, the 90-room Grand Hotel sits in landscaped gardens on a promontory that juts out into

Lago Maggiore

Lake Maggiore. Superb lake views from some rooms, excellent facilities and elegant furnishings. Via Vittorio Veneto 32, info@grandhotel-majestic.it, ☎ 39 0323 504305, www.grand-hotelmajestic.it. €€€€€

Grand Hotel Majestic

Intra

Il Chiostro

Il Chiostro. A converted 17th-century nunnery – chiostro means cloister – and certainly one of the more unusual hotels available. In the center of Intra, a short walk to the lake but without a lake view. Open all year round. Facilities include two restaurants and meeting rooms. Unusual and good value. Via Fratelli Cervi, 14, ☎ 39 0323 404077, www.chiostrovb.it. €€

Ghiffa

Hotel Ghiffa. A three-star hotel offering superb views of the lake, swimming pool and restaurant at Ghiffa, 10 minutes north of Verbania on the way to the Swiss border. Ghiffa is a pretty village, with a ferry stop, though the road on the west of the lake is very busy and difficult to cross. The hotel has its back on the road, its front facing the lake. Good value nonethe-

Hotel Ghiffa

less. Corso Belvedere 88, info@hotelghiffa.com, ☎ 39 0323 59285, www.hotelghiffa.com. €€€€

Cannobio

Hotel Pironi. A small hotel (only 12 rooms, some with lake view) in a restored 15th-century palazzo. Has the added charm of a vaulted cellar, which functions as a bar/tavern. Very colorful

Hotel Pironi's breakfast room

and a bit different. Parking available. Via Marconi, 35, info@hotelpironi.it, ☎ 39 0323 70624/70871, www.hotelpironi.it. €€€

Cannero

Hotel Cannero. 55 rooms, many with lake view. A beautifully furnished hotel with swimming pool, lake terrace and tennis courts. Good value. info@hotelcannero.com, ☎ 39 0323 788046, www.hotelcannero.com. €€€

Luino

Camin Hotel in Colmegna. Set in what was once an early 18th-century hunting lodge, on the edge of the lake and within a private park. Recently refurbished and with great lake views. Not to be con-

Hotel Cannero

fused with the Camin Hotel in the center of Luino town – which is under the same management but is a less attractive option. The Camin Hotel in Colmegna often ofers specials, including cookery courses, Italian language courses and golf packages. If you're interested, ask before booking. Via A.

Palazzi 1, camincol@tin.it, ☎ 39 03 32 51 08 55, www.camin-hotels.com. €€€

Swiss Lake Maggiore
Ascona

Hotel Piazza au Lac. Offers very clean, simple and well-priced rooms in what is a very expensive Swiss resort, all with an uninterrupted lake view. Book early enough and ask for a room on the third floor – these have little terraces. Lungolage Giuseppe Motta 29, welcome@hotel-piazza-ascona.ch, ☎ 41 (0) 91 791 1161, www.hotel-piazza-ascona.ch. €€€

Romantik Hotel Castello

Romantik Hotel Castello. On the lake front, this hotel has the added charm of a medieval tower. Rooms in the tower cost more. The restaurant here has a good reputation. Family-run and with the charm of a small hotel with comfortable facilities. castello-seeschloss@bluewin.ch, ☎ 41 (0) 91 791 0162, www.castello-seeschloss.ch. €€€€

Locarno

Hotel du Lac. Great location, clean and bright. A couple of steps from the lake. Most of the rooms have a view of the lake or Piazza Grande. Via Ramogna 3, ☎ 41 (0) 91 751 2921, www.du-lac-locarno.ch. €€€

Hotel Belvedere. Set above Locarno town, a refurbished turn-of-the-century hotel with superb views. All but a handful of the rooms have private balconies. Two restaurants, bar, swimming pool, health club. Via ai Monti della

Hotel Belvedere

Trinita, info@belvedere-locarno.com, ☎ 41 (0) 91 751 0363, www.belvedere-locarno.ch. €€€€

Garni Fiorentina. Small hotel with adjoining restaurant in the historic quarter of Locarno – la Città Vecchia. Comfortable, clean and a good budget option. No lake view. Some apartments with kitchens available too. Via St.Antonio 10, info@garni-fiorentina.ch, ☎ 41 (0) 91 751 99 14, www.garni-fiorentina.ch. €€

Promenade in Ascona, Lago Maggiore

RENTING A VILLA OR APARTMENT

If you're looking to rent an apartment on the lake, a local company, **Lago Holiday**, has a good selection and a website in English, www.lago-holiday.com. **Inter Home** has well-priced apartments around the lake, www.interhome.co.uk. In Baveno, near Stresa, there's the **Residenza Hortensia**, which offers small apartments to rent (open all year). They are under the same ownership as the Hotel Rigoli, www.hotelrigoli.com.

The American company, **Villa Vacations**, has villas to rent on Lake Maggiore, some with private lake access. www.villavacations.com.

Move and Stay has a couple of lovely villas to rent on the lake. www.moveandstay.com.

Papa Vero Rentals has villas on Lake Maggiore and Lake Orta, some with private dock and rowboat included. www.papaverorentals.com.

Campsites

There are plenty of campsites in the area – the local tourist offices will have information, though not all will be near the lake. Some that are near the lake are listed below.

Camping Residence Campagna (www.campingcampagna. it) and **Camping Riviera** in Cannobio are both sited in a very sunny location and both have direct access to the lake. www.riviera-valleromantica.com.

Locarno has a couple of luxury campsites with caravans to rent – **Camping Tamaro**, www.campingtamaro.ch, and **Camping Delta** at the end of the lake, www.campingdelta.com.

Youth Hostels

Locarno has a clean youth hostel for those on a budget. It's a short bus ride from the station. Take a look at **www. hostelsweb.com**. Via Verenna 18, Locarno, ☎ 41 (0) 91 756 1500, locarno@youthhostelch.

Verbania also has a youth hostel at Via alle Rose 7, ostello_ verbania@libero.it.

Agriturismo

If staying in the heart of a Ticinese vineyard attracts you, try **Fattoria l'Amorosa** near Gudo, halfway between Locarno and Bellinzona. Nine very attractive, fresh rooms, set in 8½ acres of vineyard and woods, complete with a herd of Galloway and Angus beef cattle. You can eat here too. info@ amorosa.ch, ☎ 41 (0) 91 840 2950, www.amorosa.ch. €€

Where to Eat

Arona

Ristorante Pescatori. On the lake shore, traditional food, predominately fish. In the summer you eat on the veranda. Reservations recommended. Closed Jan and Tues. Lungolago Marconi, 27, ☎ 0322 48312, info@ ristorantepescatori.it. €€

DINING PRICE CHART	
For three courses, excluding wine	
€	Under €20
€€	€20-€40
€€€	€41-€70
€€€€	Over €70

Ristorante Vecchia Arona. Small and welcoming, this restaurant specializes in excellent fish dishes but also has a good selection of meat offerings. Very popular, so reservations recommended. Closed Fri. Check direct for annual holiday closure. Lungo Lago Marconi 17, ☎ 39 0322 242469. €€

Baveno Il Gabbiano. A lovely, fresh interior in this restaurant and interesting, well-priced food. Closed Mon outside of the summer season and between Feb 15 and Mar 1. Via 1 Maggio 19, ☎ 39 0323 924496. €€

Cannero Il Cortile. This small hotel and restaurant in the heart of old Cannero is full of character and is popular with Swiss visitors (the border is a 15-minute drive away). Interesting menu, with summer eating in the courtyard. The interior is very small and not for those that like privacy when eating. Closed Wed (except July/Aug). Via Massino d'Azeglio 73, Cannero Riviera, ☎ 39 03237 87213. €€€

Lago Maggiore

EATING LIKE A LOCAL

Lake fish, such as trout, perch, trench, are frequently found in the restaurants around Maggiore. Polenta (corn meal) and risotto are staples, the polenta served with porcini mushrooms, hearty meat stews, local sausages or gorgonzola, depending on the season and the region.

Goat (capra) and mountain goat (camoscio) are common, and farther south, toward Lake Orta, you'll find local sausages and salamis. Fidighina is made from pork liver and other cuts of pork and beef and is served with polenta.

Don't think that only the French eats snails. Lumache, as they are called here, appear on many menus in the Ossola region and the valleys west of the lake.

There are many varieties of cheese to taste – Alpine cheeses, goat cheese and, from the Piemontese province of Novara, south of the lake, the famous Gorgonzola.

In Italy
Cannobio

Lo Scalo. Elegant and discrete, in Cannobio's main square on the lake. Closed Mon (open Mon evening July 15-Aug 15) and Tues for lunch. Reservations recommended. Piazza Vittorio Emanuele II 32, ☎ 39 0323 7480. €€€

Ristorante Sant'Anna. Outside of Cannobio, good choice of fish and meat, local and national dishes. Terrace and garden. Very reasonable prices and popular, so book ahead, especially in the summer. Closed Mon. Via Sant'Anna 30, ☎ 39 0323 70682. €€

Osteria Grotto Vinodivino. Two km outside of Cannobio, this is a nice choice if you have a car or bikes and are exploring the Valle Cannobino – the valley outside of Cannobio. Simple, local food, with salami and cheeses their specialty. Outside eating on traditional stone tables in the summer. Closed between 8 Jan and Mar, and closed Wed (except May-Aug). Booking recommended, as it is very popular – particularly with the Swiss and Germans! €€

Laveno Il Porticciolo. On the eastern shore of the lake, near Santa Caterina del Sasso. This restaurant and hotel is right on the edge of the lake, and there's a terrace for summer eating. Very interesting menu, with much of it fish. Reserve ahead. Via Fortino 40, ☎ 39 0332 667257. €€€

Laveno Il Porticciolo

Stresa

Piemontese. In the center of old Stresa, this is one of the best restaurants in the area, and the place to come if you want to taste Piemontese cuisine and wine. Run by the Belossi family, good service and a relaxed, friendly atmosphere. It claims never to close – but call ahead to avoid disappointment. Via

Mazzini 25, info@ristorantepiemontese.com, ☎ 39 0323 30235. €€

Il Triangolo. Simple and delicious food – lake fish a specialty. Very reasonably priced. Reservations recommended. Closed in Nov or Dec and Tues (except Aug). Via Roma 62, ☎ 39 0323 32736. €€

Taverna del Pappagallo. Popular pizzeria in the heart of old Stresa. Also a selection of pasta, risotto, fish and meat dishes. The terrace outside is nice. Very good prices and good cooking. Credit cards are not accepted. Via Principessa Margherita 46, ☎ 39 0323 30411. €

Taverna del Pappagallo

Albergo Ristorante Verbano. Located next to the hotel of the same name on this charming island, this is certainly one of the best locations around to wine and dine. Local dishes and, though there is a lot of fish, the menu is varied. Reservations very much recommended. Isola Pescatori, ☎ 39 0323 32534. €€

Verbania

Boccon di Vino. A trattoria, rather than a restaurant, with simple, unpretentious, great food. At lunchtime only cold food is served – think salads, cheeses, salami. In the evening, dishes might include pasta, lake trout, grilled meats. Very good value for money and a good atmosphere. Close Tues, Wed at lunchtime and in Jan. Via Troubetzkoy 86, ☎ 39 0323 504039. €€

Chi Ginn. Above Verbania (take a taxi) and well worth the ride. Sublime views, the best to be had, over Lake Maggiore (there's a terrace in the garden for summer eating) and very good Piemontese cuisine. Quiet, elegant and friendly service. Reservations recommended. Closed Tues and between Jan 7 and Feb 8. Via Maggiore 21, Bee, ☎ 39 0323 56326. €€

Osteria del Angolo. Friendly and relaxed trattoria. Short menu and good prices. Closed Nov and Mon. Reservations recommended. Piazza Garibaldi 35, ☎ 39 0323 556362. €€

Vineria Italia. Great location with views over the lake, this wine bar/restaurant is a good choice for those who love their wine as much as their food. Vicolo del'Arco 1, on the corner of Viale delle Magnolie. €€

In Switzerland

Ascona

Cinese Lungolago. A Chinese restaurant right on the lakefront. A good menu and with a lovely terrace overlooking the lake. If the weather is good, sit outside and watch the moon rise as you enjoy the thrill that comes with eating affordably in Switzerland. Via Moscia 4, ☎ 41 (0) 91 792 3440. €€

Nostrana. On the lakefront for pizza and pasta. Very popular, very busy but with professional service and a good menu. Children's meals available. Reservations not taken. Lungolago G. Motta. €€

Locarno

Cittadella. In the old town above Piazza Grande. Affordable pizza downstairs and pricier but good fish upstairs. Often busy and for some the tables downstairs may be a little too crowded for comfort. Via Cittadella 18, ☎ 41 (0) 91 751 58 85. €€€

Navegna. Take a 15-minute walk along the lake to this hotel/restaurant for lunch. The setting is delightful, the food very good – fresh pasta, meat and fish. Via alla Riva 2, Minusio, ☎ 41 (0) 91 743 2222. €€€

Balleno. Near the Giardini Jean Arp. A permanently moored boat, near a small public garden with sculptures by Jean Arp. Great location if the crowds are getting to you – the Balleno is a bar and restaurant serving snacks and simple pasta dishes. €

Contrada Pizzeria. Opposite the camera store, this small pizzeria does nice panini made from pizza dough and stuffed with vegetables or mozzarella and ham. The pizzas are pretty good too. Piazza Grande. €

Lago Orta

Lago d'Orta lies less than 30 km/18 miles west of Lake Maggiore, but seems a world away. Orta is a lake of tranquility and simplicity. There are no coach parties here, no back-packers or conference hotels, and in the town of **Orta San Giulio**, one of Northern Italy's must-see sights, there

aren't even any cars. It's also a lake that few people seem to have heard of. Many Italians claim not to have heard of it, and those of us who are regular visitors selfishly wish it could remain this way.

Location/Geography

Only eight miles long and two wide, Orta (like all of the lakes, it also has another name, Lake Cusio) is one of the smallest of the Italian lakes, and the only one entirely in Piedmont. It lies in the province of Novara, with Monte Motterone between it and Lake Maggiore. Balzac said this was a lake made to the measurements of man. Get up high and you can see where it begins and ends, and the proximity of the soft hills (not jagged cliffs or mountains) gives it an altogether different appeal compared to the other, grander lakes.

The Niguglia River drains the lake at its northern end, joining first the Strona River and then the Toce, which flows into Lake Maggiore.

Economy

Tourism, agriculture and industry. Around Omegna, the lake's principal town, are a number of well-known factories, including Alessi and Bialetti, the maker of the iconic stove-top coffee pot. Alessi, today a global name, set up his first factory here in 1921 and, for those interested in shopping, Alessi has a factory outlet here at Via Privata Alessi 6, Crusinallo di Omegna, ☎ 39 0323 868648.

A DELICATE BALANCE

A number of factories set up around the lake in the first half of the 20th century had serious environmental effects on the plant and animal life in the lake. In 1928, virtually all forms of life had disappeared and the lake was classified as sterile! Over the last 20 years in particular, considerable efforts have been made to recover the lake's delicate ecosystem.

The Climate

 Orta has a mild climate, similar to that of Maggiore. The early morning mist and the hazy sunshine that so often envelop the lake add to its renowned fairy-tale atmosphere. No surprise that the town of Orta San Giulio is a favorite spot for weddings. Best times to visit are spring (a week or so before Easter is when the season kicks in), summer and autumn. Winter can be damp and cold.

Getting Here

 You can take a train from Milan Central Station to Arona (journey time 50 minutes) and from here take a taxi. There are also trains leaving from Milan Porta Genova (journey time is a little longer). Distance from Arona to Lake Orta is 10 miles and the fare will be around €50.

The Domodossola-Novara branch line runs close to Lake Orta. The nearest station to the town of Orta San Giulio is Orta Miasino, two miles away. The train also stops at Omegna. The direct service is the one you want – not the trains that require a change in Arona or Sesto Calande. Check www.trenitalia.it for times.

The award-winning British company **Holiday Taxis** offers transfers to Lake Orta from Milan Malpensa or Linate, by car or minibus for up to eight passengers. One-way transfer by car is about €125. Online booking at www.holidaytaxis.com.

Driving here from Milan or Malpensa, you follow the A8, which connects with the A26 in the direction of Gravellona-Toce. Take the Arona exit and head for Borgomanero and then Gozzano – this last road is the SS229. Journey time from Malpensa is a little over an hour, traffic permitting.

Buses are a possibility – either from Lake Maggiore or from Domodossola or even Milan. The website, **www.vcoinbus.it**, has a great interactive map showing all the bus, boat and train connections on Lake Orta, Lake Maggiore and beyond. You need a little Italian to understand it though.

Lake Orta (Catherine Richards)

Practicalities

Tourist Offices

 The Tourist Office is on Via Bossi 11, next to the Municipio – the Town Hall, ☎ 39 0322 911972, turismo.orta.san.giulio@reteunitaria.piemonte.it.

Traveling Around

There isn't much of the lake to travel around, and its manageable size means that you see more visitors in rowboats than on any of the other lakes. A favorite activity for visitors seems to be rowing from Orta San Giulio to the lake's only island, San Giulio. The island looks so inviting, the distance so unthreatening... ask on the quay where the ferries and water taxis dock.

You can take a motorboat – with its pilot in nautical blue and white – from Orta San Giulio. A variety of excursions are offered, from a quick trip over to the island of San Giulio or a one down to Omegna for the weekly market. Check out **www. motoscafisti.com**. There are also larger ferries (though much smaller than on the other lakes) that run between the main points of interest on the lake.

Tours

Opuntia arranges half-day or full-day tours of the lake, Orta San Giulio and the island of San Giulio. There is an environmental emphasis. Tours can include tastings of local specialities. The website is primarily in Italian. For details, contact associazioneopuntia@ortaturismo.net, www.orta.net/opuntia

Viator, an American company, operates a five-hour coach tour of Orta, picking up in Stresa and Baveno, which is good if you're based on Lake Maggiore and don't have the time to stay over on Lake Orta. You can book online. Look on **www. viatour.com** under tours and then Lake Maggiore.

Viatour also offer a great tour up to the Alpine village of **Macugnana** at the foot of Monte Rosa – the second-highest peak in the Alps. Again, they pick you up from the Lake Maggiore area.

Markets

Omegna has an antique market on Thursdays

Orta San Giulio has a small market, mostly clothing, on Tuesdays

Gozzano has a Saturday market

What to See & Do

★★★Orta San Giulio

This is the must-see attraction on the entire lake, and one of most charming towns on any of the lakes in Northern Italy. A small, pedestrianized town – if you're arriving by car you have to leave it just outside the town – with no hint of conference hotels or crowds, Orta

Orta San Giulio (Catherine Richards)

San Giulio is frankly a relief, especially if you arrive here after Milan or a few days in Stresa.

You'll find **Via Bossi** easily enough, a narrow medieval street lined with delicatessans and tiny stores selling antiques, jewelry and crafts. It leads you past the terracotta-colored **Municipio**, or Town Hall, where summer weddings take place in the garden overlooking the lake, to **Piazza Motta**, the central square. Take a moment to wander into the garden of the Municipio. Its lakeside location and view of the island

Piazza Motta (Catherine Richards)

makes for some great photographs. The Tourist Office is here too.

Piazza Motta has been likened to a theater where all seats command a view of the Isola di San Giulio, the most beautiful of all the lake islands. At the far end of the piazza is the once-grand **Albergo d'Orta**. On the left are tiny shops and bars below a row of 17th-century houses painted in shades of yellow, the palest pinks and blues.

The tiny broletto or town hall, the Palazzo della Communità, is a delight. Built in 1582, it was once the seat of legislative power in this small community. On its frescoed exterior are coats of arms of some of the Bishops of Novara who governed the region almost continually until 1817.

The piazza is known affectionately as the **Salotto**, or the drawing room, perhaps because of the air of languid comfort here. A quick drink turns into a long, lazy lunch, a 15-minute pit-stop to check the guide book turns into two hours watching the world go by – and here it goes by in a boat. Small ferries chug between the island and the town, private taxi-boats (skippered by pilots dressed in nautical blue and white) join them, and every now and then tourists clamber into little wooden boats and row out to the island.

Santa Maria della Assunta
(Catherine Richards)

To the left of the Palazzo della Communità, the **Scalineta della Motta** leads up to the yellow-painted parish church of **Santa Maria della Assunta**. First built in 1485 as a thank-you by townsfolk who had survived the plague, the church was rebuilt in the 18th century. Its cool exterior, which avoids the worst excesses of Baroque, provides some relief from summer sun, but the Scalineta della Motta itself is the main draw, lined as it is with decorated or frescoed houses and palazzi built between the Middle Ages and the 18th century.

★★★ Isola San Giulio

The Island of San Giulio is named after the saint who founded the first church here who, as legend has it, arrived in Orta in the second half of the fourth century and asked to be taken across to the island. Given that the island was inhabited by dragons and snakes, his request was refused, and so Giulio took himself across, spreading his cloak onto the water and using his staff as a rudder. Once landed, he rid the island of the serpents and set about building a basilica.

Isola San Giulio (Catherine Richards)

Giulio hailed from the Greek island of Aegina and, along with his brother Giuliano, had built 99 churches before arriving in Orta. The **Basilica of San Giulio** was his hundredth, and his last.

The Basilica, Giulio's burial place, was restored in the 11th and 12th centuries, and contains some beautiful frescos dating from the 15th century that are attributed to Gaudenzio Ferrari. The greatest work of art, however, is the ornate grey-green marble pulpit (or ambo), carved from the stone at Oira, in the Ossola Valley. Though the Basilica dominates the island, there is room for a Benedictine monastery and some private villas as well, many of them originally the Canons residences. **Villa Tallone** acts as a venue for the **Festival of Ancient Music** in June, and in late September an English-language **Poetry Festival** is held by Welsh resident Gabriel Griffin.

DID YOU KNOW?

Lake Orta is drained by the Nigogli River, which because of the lie of the land between it and Lake Maggiore, flows toward the Alps, rather than away from them. It's the only river in Italy to do so and, as a result, the locals take pride in it. They have a saying: "The Nigoglia flows up and we make the rules."

★★★Sacro Monte

On the Sacro Monte

Orta's Sacro Monte was recently made a UNESCO World Heritage Site. Very much a feature of Northern Italy and Ticino in southern Switzerland, these holy mounts were intended to bring to life religious scenes through paintings, frescoes and life-sized painted wooden and terracotta statues. Inspired by the Sacro Monte in nearby Varallo with its 44 chapels, Orta's Sacro Monte, which depicts the life of St Francis of Assisi, was begun in 1590, and work continued for 200 years, until the final chapel – the 20th – was completed in the 18th century. It is certainly not to everybody's taste. The lifesize terracotta figures can be a bit alarming to the modern visitor. But the peace and tranquility of the Sacro Monte and the wonderful view of the lake, the island and the mountains beyond make this a must-see spot. If you time it

Statues on Sacro Monte

right, you may find yourself the only visitor up here, sharing the space with the maintenance men... and 379 terracotta figures. Come here in the late morning and then take lunch at the restaurant (see *Where to Eat*).

The German philosopher Nietzsche spent time here in spring of 1882, along with a young Russian named Lou Salomé, who was chaperoned by her mother and a mutual friend. One balmy afternoon both Salomé and Nietzsche spent a few hours alone together on the Sacro Monte... where it seems likely that a misunderstanding of a romantic nature occurred. In short, Nietzsche's feelings were not reciprocated, though clearly the experience affected him deeply, as a marked change can be seen in his work only months later.

★Santuario della Madonna del Sasso

If you have a car, take a trip up to this 18th-century church, on the opposite side of the lake from Orta San Giulio. In terms of engineering it is pretty impressive – it sits high up on a rocky outrop above the village of San Maurizio. The views

Madonna del Sasso

from here are great – right to the end of Lake Orta to Maggiore and beyond.

The sanctuary itself is bijoux, and the interior lovely, with some 18th-century frescoes and 17th-century painting. If you're driving, take the road that is intended for buses: only a couple of minutes longer but you drive right through the center of a lovely village – so sleepy that dogs feel comfortable snoozing in the road.

La Torre di Buccione

Toward the southern tip of the lake is **La Torre di Buccione**, all that remains of a medieval stronghold. In 1529, a colonel in Charles V's army demanded 4,000 gold crowns from the people of Orta. Thoroughly fed-up after years of tax demands, kidnapping and ransoms, the people of the Riviera fled to the island of San Giulio and prepared to revolt. Maria Canavesa, a local woman, ran to the tower with her son, in order to ring the bells as a signal for the revolt to begin. The revolt was successful, but Maria and her son paid for their bravery with their lives.

Omegna

The outskirts of Omegna can be off-putting, though persist, as the historic heart of the largest town on the lake (population 16,000) is very charming. The 13th-century Romanesque church of **Sant'Ambrogio** is worth a visit. There is quite a lot of industry around Omegna (Alessi, Bialetti and Lagostina are some of the biggest names).

Museums & Galleries

Fondazione Calderara in Vacciago, close to Orta San Giulio. A collection of modern art, mainly from the 1950s and '60s, displayed in the 17th-century home of artist Antonio Calderara. There are more than 300 pieces. Open between May 15 and Oct 15, 10 am-12 pm, 3-6 pm. Closed Mon. Entrance free with guided tours.

Museo Etnografico e dello Strumento Musicale e Fiato, Quarna Sotto, close to Omegna. The villages of Quarno Sopra and Quarno Sotto (upper and lower) have a long tradition of woodwork and are particularly famous for musical instrument making. The small museum will delight music lovers. The emphasis is very much on old manufacturing techniques. Open July-Sept, 10:30 am-12 pm, 3-7 pm. Closed Mon. If you want to visit outside of these months, call and set up an appointment, ☎ 39 0323 826001.

Museo del Ombrello e del Parasole. A museum dedicated to umbrellas and parasols. About 15 minutes from Lake Orta in the village of Gignese. Also easily accessible from Lake Maggiore. An incredible collection of more than 1,000 pieces from the 19th century to the present day. Photographs and memorabilia of the umbrella makers as well. ☎ 39 0323 20067. Open April 1-Sept 30, 10 am-12 pm, 3-6 pm. Closed Mon.

 Lake Orta is the setting for the **World Fireworks Championship** in August. The exact dates are confirmed each year. Fireworks manufacturers from all over the world compete for several days before crowds of up to 100,000. If pyrotechnics are your thing, this is not to be missed! www.fioridifuoco.it.

Adventures

On Horseback

 The **Fattoria del Pino** in Miasino offers riding lessons and tours in the area. Currently the property is up for sale, but check their website for up-to-date information. www.fattoriadelpino.it.

On Foot

 If you are interested in a six-day walking tour that includes Lake Orta, have a look at **Wilderness Travel**, www.wildernesstravel.com. Starting on Lake Como, taking in Lake Lugano, Lake Orta and finishing in Milan with experienced leaders and fairly moderate walking, you will be walking between three-five hours a day. The company **Country Walkers** offers a similar itinerary. www.countrywalkers.com.

Take a walk in the **Monte Mesma Natural Reserve**, in the hills on the eastern shore of Lake Orta. There are three protected areas here: Sacro Monte itself, Monte Mesma and the area around the Buccione Tower. At the top of Monte Mesma (576 m/1,890 ft) is the 17th-century **convent of Monte Mesma**. The cloisters are open Mon-Sat from 9-11:30 am. Check out the National Parks website for more information. www.parks.it/parco.sacro.monte.orta.

On Water

There are plenty of watersports available, many of them available at the campsites and hotels on the lake.

Water-skiing is popular here, particularly at the Omegna end of the lake. Contact **Dario Rossi** at Sci Nautico Cusio, at Via Zanoia 4, Omegna, sncusio@tin.it, ☎ 39 0323 61365.

For **sailing**, try the **Club Velico** in Pella, close to Orta San Giulio. You can take lessons here too. Ask at the Tourist Office or call Club Velico direct at ☎ 39 0328 453 8206.

Swimming is possible is on much of the lake. For children the safest areas are at the **Lido di Buccione** at Gozzano, **Omegna** and at **Pella**.

There's lots of **fishing** around Orta, in the **Laghetti di Bonte Bria** and the **Laghetti di Nonio**. For details regarding permits ask at the Tourist Office in Orta, ☎ 39 0322 911 937.

On Wheels

If you read Italian, pick up a copy of *Lago Maggiore e Lago d'Orta: Corsi in Bici, in Piedi, in Mountain Bike*. There are nine itineraries around Lake Orta for cyclists on city bikes and mountain bikes. Available from www.libreriadellosport.it or www.bol.it. Ask at the Tourist Office in Orta San Giulio about renting bicycles.

On the Rocks

There is some tough rock-climbing to be had on and around **Monte Mottarone**. Most of the climbing routes are in the Inferno Valley, reached from Omegna on the path that starts at a place called Brughiere di Crusinallo. Ask at the Tourist Office in Omegna. Ufficio IAT, Piazza XXIV Aprile, 17.

On the Golf Course

See *Lake Maggiore* for golf courses. The nearest ones to Lake Orta are the 18-hole **Golf Club Iles Borromees**, www.golfdesilesborromees.it and the nine-hole **Golf Club Alpino di Stresa**, www.golfalpino.it.

With Language

If you you'd like to learn a language during a homestay – you live with your tutor as part of the family – check out **Eurolingua**. They have a qualified Italian tutor in Omegna, and one in Borgomanero, between Arona on Lake Maggiore and Lake Orta. www.eurolingua.com. Look under One-to-One Homestays.

Where to Stay

It makes much more sense to stay in Orta San Giulio than Omegna, which has a nice enough historic center but none of the beauty of Orta San Giulio. Orta San Giulio is one of the prettiest towns on any lake in Italy. The tranquility is sublime and the view of Isola di San Giulio is one the best views you'll have on your trip. Guaranteed.

HOTEL PRICE CHART	
Double room with tax & breakfast	
€	Under €80
€€	€80-€130
€€€	€131-€180
€€€€	€181-€250
€€€€€	Over €250

Lake Orta

Villa Crespi

Some of the hotels below are open all year round.

Villa Crespi. Four-star. A stunning 19th-Moorish folly built by Lombardian merchant Cristoforo Crespi and remodeled in 1999. Situated just above the town, and with a superb restaurant. Not for the budget-conscious. ☎ 39 0322 911902, crespi@crespi.it, www.lagodortahotels.com. €€€€€

Albergo San Rocco

Albergo San Rocco. Four star hotel and restaurant, located in a 17th-century convent right on the lake. The restaurant also comes highly recommended. Via Gippini 11, ☎ 39 9 0322 911 977. €€€€€

Hotel La Bussola. Sited in an elevated position above the lake, with bright rooms, outdoor swimming pool and terrace. During the summer months on weekends you have to take half-board – either breakfast or dinner. Via Panoramica 24, ☎ 39 0322 911913, hotelbussola@yahoo.it, www.orta.net/bussola. €€

Hotel La Bussola

Albergo d'Orta. Three-star. Somewhat dated but comfortable and in a great position at Orta's central piazza overlooking the lake. Piazza Motta, ☎ 39 0322 90253, info@hotelorta.it, www. hotelorta.it. €€

La Contrada dei Monti. Delightful, reasonably priced small hotel, run by the same owners as the immaculate lakeside three-star Leon d'Oro. No lake view here, but somehow it doesn't matter. Via Contrada dei Monti 10, ☎ 39 0322 905114, www.orta.net/lacontradadeimonti. €€

Leon d'Oro. Recently renovated, great lakeside position. Has a nice restaurant too, with a terrace overlooking the lake and the island. Piazza Motta 42, ☎ 39 0322 911991, albergoleondoro@tiscalinet.it, www. orta.net/leondoro. €€

Leon d'Oro

Piccolo Hotel Olina. Full of character – more like someone's house in décor and atmosphere. Bright and fun. It also appears in a number of guidebooks so is very popular. Good prices for those with families or small groups. Via Olina 40, ☎ 011 800 220 62001 (toll-free from US), or from Italy, ☎ 39 0322 905532, danielanegri@yahoo.it or orta@email.it.

Piccolo Hotel Olina

Hotel Aracoeli. Bright, modern, very quirky and right near the lake. Showers big enough for two...and the lack of privacy from the room itself makes them suitable for the more adventurous visitor. Piazza Motta 34, ☎ 011 800 220 62001, 39 0322 905173, danielanegri@yahoo.it or orta@email.itportrait@email.it, www.orta.net/aracoeli.

Hotel Giardinetto

Hotel Giardinetto. Right on the lake with a view of Isola San Giulio. Family-run and family-friendly. Also has some apartments to rent, with access to all of the hotel's facilities such as their swimming pool and restaurant (good but expensive). Can arrange bicycle rental, windsurfing, horseback riding, tennis, golf and sailing, most within a very short distance of the hotel. Via Provinciale 1, Pettenasco, ☎ 39 0323 89118, hotelgiardinetto@tin.it, www.lagodortahotels.com. €€€

Renting a Villa or Apartment

Casa Vacanze Olina, the same organization that runs Piccolo Hotel Olina, has a number of houses and apartments around the lake. apartment@ortainfo.com, www.orta.net/cvo.

Lake Orta

Select Italy has properties on Lake Orta (and the other lakes too), including apartments and a villa that sleeps up to 10 people. http://selectitaly.com.

Holiday Homes at Lake Orta has a good selection of villas and apartments on or near the lake. Some of the apartments offer shorter stays – three nights instead of the usual week. holidayhomes@lakeorta.com, www.lakeorta.com.

Papa Vero Rentals has villas on Lake Maggiore and Lake Orta, some with private docking and a rowboat included. www.papaverorentals.com.

Camping

 Lake Orta is a good location for camping. The campsites are generally smaller than others on the bigger lakes. The road around the lake is that much quieter and the easy proximity to both the lake and the verdant hills and woods beyond make for a family-friendly vacation.

Camping Cusio is close to Orta San Giulio. Small and friendly. Motor homes to rent, a small swimming pool and a children's play area. cusio@tin.it, www.orta.net/cusio.

Camping Orta is near the lake, with a private beach, less than a mile from Orta San Giulio, and has space for 150 moor homes and tents. There are three bungalows and some motor homes to rent. All the usual facilities. info@campingorta.it, www.campingorta.it.

Camping Verde Lago is at Pettenasco, a mile or so before Orta San Giulio. Small, quiet (no dogs allowed) and set between the lake and the hills behind. You can rent RVs here, do any number of water sports, there are plenty of facilities for the kids, and in Pettenasco village, less than 100 m/100 yards away, there's a grocery store, pharmacy, restaurant and a tennis court. campingverdelago@campingverdelago.it, www.campingverdelago.it.

Where to Eat

Orta

 Orta San Giulio. In the hotel of the same name. Superb Mediterranean cuisine in a Michelin-starred restaurant. Don't turn up in sneakers and shorts. Elegant dress is expected. Closed Tues and Wed lunch except in very high season. Villa Crespi, www.slh.com/crespi. €€€

Albergo San Rocco. A renowned restaurant in one of Orta's best hotels. Regional and international cuisine, plus a great lakeside location. Again, try to avoid dressing too casually. Orta San Giulio, ☎ 39 0322 911 977, www. hotelsanrocco.it. €€€

DINING PRICE CHART	
For three courses, excluding wine	
€	Under €20
€€	€20-€40
€€€	€41-€70
€€€€	Over €70

Taverna Antico Agnello. Family-run, with a lot of charm, and very popular with visitors. Fish and local specialties. Also has a few rooms. Orta San Giulio, Via Olina 18, ☎ 39 0322 90259. €€

Ristorante Sacro Monte. As it sounds, a restaurant on the Sacro Monte. Family run. Local and regional cuisine, not expensive. Closed Tues, ☎ 39 0322 90220. €€

Ristorante Leon d'Oro. Fabulous lakeside location. Menu of fish, fresh pasta, salads. Orta San Giulio, Piazza Motta 42, ☎ 39 0322 911991. €€

Ristorante San Giulio. On the island of San Giulio itself. Might be a good idea to book ahead if you're dead set on eating here – it's the only restaurant on the island. There's a private boat in the evening to take you to and from Orta San Giulio. You come here for the superb location – the food is good but standard. Via Basilica 4, Isola Di San Giulio, info@ ristorantesangiulio.com, ☎ 39 0322 90234, www. ristorantesangiulio.com.

Lake Orta

EATING LIKE A LOCAL

Lake fish, polenta, a Piedmont staple, and a very local specialty – tapulon. This in fact comes from Borgomanero, some 15 km/nine miles from Orta. It's donkey, minced and with the addition of garlic, wine and herbs. Orta mortadella is a local specialty. The predominant grape is Nebbiolo. Some of the local wines benefit from a good few hours breathing.

Gozzano

Al Sorriso. No guidebook can fail to mention this, one of the best restaurants in Piemonte, and one of the most expensive. It has three Michelin stars – one of only three places in the entire country that ranks that high. Around five miles from Lake Orta in the tiny village of Gozzano. The restaurant also has eight rooms for overnight guests, in case you want to make the whole experience last a little longer. www.alsorriso. com.

Omegna

Da Libero. Lovely outside terrace for summer eating. Fish, polenta, risotto. Good food at good prices. Book ahead. Salita Beltrami 5, in the village of Fornero, five miles west of Omegna. ☎ 39 0323 87123.

Bars

For a glass of wine or a cocktail in Orta San Giulio, try **Ai Due Santi**, Piazza Motta 18.

Also in Orta San Giulio, check out **Al Boeuc** in via Bersani, 28. A tiny wine bar/taverna in a little street in the old town. Lots of charm.

Lago Lugano

Like Maggiore, Lake Lugano straddles both Italy and Switzerland, with the largest part of the lake, (since the 16th century), in Switzerland. Lugano probably derives from the Latin, lucus meaning wood, or sacred wood. In common with most of the lakes, Lugano has another name –

Ceresio, which is used frequently by the locals. The hills and mountains that surround the lake and Lugano City are stunning, and comparisons to Rio di Janeiro abound. There is an air of sophistication and money here, no surprise when you learn this is Switzerland's third most important financial center. There are a number of beautiful lakeside villages to discover (some accessible only by boat or on foot), some great walks and views to enjoy, and the city of Lugano itself is a surprise to many: an almost perfect blend of Italy and Switzerland, full of art galleries, chic stores, cobbled streets... and banks.

Location/Geography

 Lake Lugano has an area of 49 sq km/19 sq miles, and a maximum depth of 288 m/945 ft. Rarely much more than a mile and a half wide, the lake is around 36 km/22 miles in length, half the size of Lake Maggiore.

 Did you Know? Lugano is the only lake to have a bridge built across it. Between Bissone and Melide, in the Swiss part of the lake, it is so shallow that a dam was built to carry traffic and the Zurich-Milan trains.

Economy

 Finance, tourism, commerce, construction and light industry are the main economic sectors in and around Lake Lugano and, more specifically, Lugano City. Tourism alone employs about 38,000 people.

The Climate

 A very mild climate, with the highest temperatures in June, July and August (24°C/75°F on average in these months.) Rainfall is highest in May, June and Oct, while August is well-known for its temporali – the brief but intense summer storms. Pretty much anytime from May through to early October is a good time to visit: May/June for lovers of flowers, July/Aug for lovers of the heat, while Sept and early Oct often bring fresh, sunny days perfect for walking.

Getting Here

By Air

 Lugano has its own small airport at Agno, with connecting flights to Zurich, Geneva, Basle and a few other European cities. If you're flying into Zurich or Geneva, check out prices for the brief flight down to Lugano – there are often good deals available. To get from here to Lugano City, take a taxi (about 20 minutes, ☎ 00 41 (0) 91 605 2510) or the small shuttle bus, (www.shuttle-bus.com).

Many hotels also operate a shuttle service.

Travel from Milan's Malpensa takes 75 minutes. There is an hourly bus service throughout the year operated by Star Bus (www.starbus.info) – you must reserve online, though you pay on the bus in either Swiss francs or euros. A round-trip fare is €40/60 CHF.

At Malpensa Terminal 1, the bus leaves from parking bay no:19, near arrivals exit no:4. At Terminal 2, the bus leaves from in front of the bus parking lot.

From Lugano, turn right out of the station, walk 20 m/65 ft or so. The bus stop is opposite a bar/restaurant and is clearly indicated.

By Car

 Europcar car rental is at Lugano airport, with most well-known providers at Milan's airports and at Zurich.

By Train

 There's a regular half-hourly service from Milan's Central Station to Lugano – journey time 60 minutes. Check www.trenitalia.com for timetables and to book online. If you are coming from Zurich, there's an hourly service, which takes three hours. Book train tickets online at www.sbb.ch. For those who enjoy train travel, it's a great journey, and includes the Gotthard Tunnel, opened in 1882 and for many years the longest railroad tunnel in the world.

When you arrive in Lugano station, there's a funicolare to take you down to the city center. The fare is 1.10 CHF, though you can also pay the fare in euros, €.80.

A NEW TUNNEL

A second tunnel is currently being built through the Gotthard Mountain – the AlpTransit – which will function as an express route, mainly for freight trains, connecting northern Europe with the south. Journey time from Zurich to Milan will be cut to two hours and 40 minutes. The stretch through the Gotthard mountain will run for 35 miles – the longest rail tunnel in the world. It's possible to experience guided tours of four of the sites, including excavated tunnels. Two at Faido and Bodio are south of the existing Gotthard tunnel and easily reachable by train. Check out the website for more information. www.alptransit.ch.

Lake Lugano

By Bus

 Lugano (from Cassarate) is linked to Menaggio on Lake Como, making a visit to both lakes easy. Take the **SPT Linea** bus C12 from Menaggio or Lugano bus station, which takes an hour. You have to buy your tickets before boarding the bus. The **Swiss yellow post bus** has a daily departure. Reservations are compulsory. In both cases ask at the Tourist Office for timetables, tickets and points of departure, as information online isn't too clear.

 Author's Tip: If you're traveling with a lot of luggage and flying into or out of Geneva or Zurich, take advantage of Swiss Rail's Fly Rail Baggage service. Check the SBB site at www.sbb.ch for details. Do a search for Fly Rail to find the relevant information.

Getting Around

 The **Società Navigazione Lago di Lugano**, www.lakelugano.ch, arranges boat excursions and tours as well as regular services to the lake's main points of interest: Gandria, Morcote-Ponte Tresa, Porlezza and Capolago.

The same company has a regular bus service to Gandria, and to Campione d'Italia for the Casino, also stopping at the tourist attraction of Swiss Miniatur (see below for details on both). Check the website for the timetables. In Lugano City itself, walking is best, especially since the center is traffic-free. If you want to take a bus, have a look at the Lugano Tourism website, www.lugano-tourism.ch, and click on City Public Transportation. You can download a map of the bus routes from here.

To reach Ponte Tresa, just over the Italian border, from Lugano, there's a small train service – the **Ferrovie Luganesi** – which happens to run near the airport. Take this train to Magliaso for the cablecar to Monte Lema. The service is regular. Timetables can be found online at www.flpsa.ch. Click on Orario.

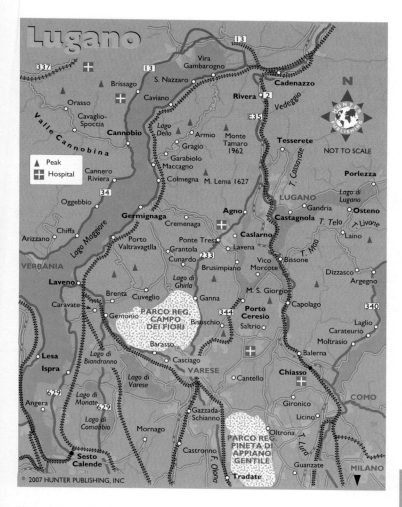

Water Taxis

If you don't want to hire a boat yourself, you might want to make use of a watertaxi, especially if you're heading to some out-of-the way restaurant or village along the lake. **Ambra Taxi** has a good website that clearly indicates prices and routes. You can book online too. info@lugano-lake-taxi.ch, www.ambrataxi.ch.

Practicalities

Currency

 Switzerland uses the Swiss Franc, though the majority of places in Lugano (and Locarno and Bellinzona) accept euros. However, if you intend to travel around Ticino, it's advisable to have some Swiss francs.

Tourist Offices

 Lugano Tourism, Riva Albertolli-Palazzo Civico, 6901 Lugano, info@lugano-tourism.ch, ☎ 41 (0) 91 913 3232, www.lugano-tourism.ch.

Mendrisiotto Turismo, Via A. Maspoli, Mendrisio, info@mendrisiottotourism.ch, ☎ 41 (0) 91 646 5761, www.mendrisiottotourism.ch.

Malcantone Tourism, Piazza Lago, Caslano, info@malcantone.ch, ☎ 41 (0) 91 606 2986, www.malcantone.ch.

 Tip: If you are staying in Ticino for three days or more, consider buying the **Lugano Regional Pass**. At 72 CHF for three days, or 96 CHF for seven days, you get to travel for free on Lugano's buses and most of Lugano's cablecars, get 50% off the cost of trains between Lugano and Locarno, cablecars between Lugano and Locarno, ferry prices on Lake Maggiore, and buses and cablecars in Locarno. Buy it at the railway station, Tourist Office or at some hotels. For more information have a look at www.utp.lugano.ch.

Tours

Lugano Tourism offers a number of tours in and around Lugano. A walking tour of the city is free, as is a walking tour of the city's architectural higlights and its park and gardens. Other tours (a fee is charged) include the Hermann Hesse Trail (the German author lived here for a number of years), Gandria and Val Verzaska, near Locarno. Check www.lugano-tourism.ch for more information or call ☎ 41 (0) 91 605 2643.

You can also download a leaflet that includes further tours offered by Lugano Tourism. If you're looking for help deciding what to see, where to go and where to stay, a local company, **Ticino Tours**, arranges vacations and tours within Ticino, primarily around Lake Lugano and Lake Maggiore. Run by an British-Swiss couple, they can help with walks, treks and watersports, as well as cultural and gastronomic tours. info@ticinotours.com, www.ticinotours.com.

Markets

- Tues and Fri morning, Piazza della Riforma, Lugano.
- Saturday, all day, Ponte Tresa.

What to See & Do

★★★Lugano City

Lugano is an almost perfect blend of Swiss efficiency and Italian lifestyle – with an emphasis on style. The most important city in Ticino, and the third-biggest financial center in Switzerland, Lugano is a surprise to many. Its location is certainly one of the biggest draws, since the views to be had from any number of mountains that surround

Lake Lugano (Catherine Richards)

Lake Lugano

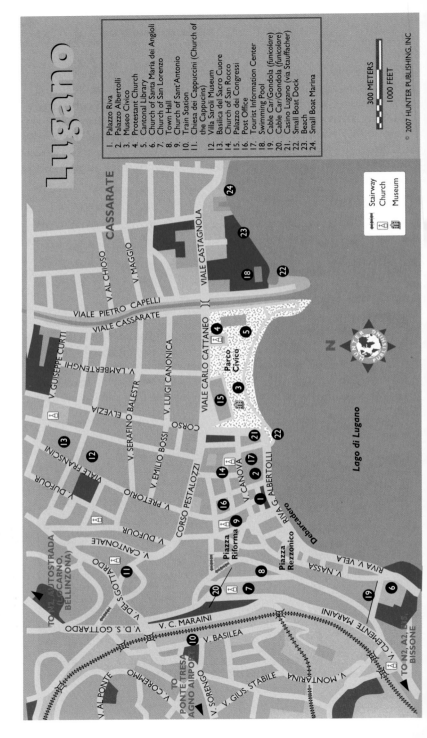

Lugano

1. Palazzo Riva
2. Palazzo Albertolli
3. Museo Civico
4. Protestant Church
5. Cantonal Library
6. Church of Santa Maria dei Angioli
7. Church of San Lorenzo
8. Town Hall
9. Church of Sant'Antonio
10. Train Station
11. Chiesa dei Cappuccini (Church of the Cappucins)
12. Villa Saroli Museum
13. Basilica del Sacro Cuore
14. Church of San Rocco
15. Palazzo dei Congressi
16. Post Office
17. Tourist Information Center
18. Swimming Pool
19. Cable Car/Gondola (funicolare)
20. Cable Car/Gondola (funicolare)
21. Casino Lugano (via Stauffacher)
22. Small Boat Dock
23. Beach
24. Small Boat Marina

Stairway
Church
Museum

300 METERS
1000 FEET

© 2007 HUNTER PUBLISHING, INC.

CASSARATE

Lago di Lugano

the city are fabulous. Known too for its parks and gardens, Lugano is the kind of place you stroll around, taking a cable car or funicolare, enjoying a glass or two of local Merlot and fabulous views.

If you wish, Lake Lugano is also the perfect place to enjoy being active: hiking, trekking, tennis, swimming, paragliding or cycling. Sports and well-being are highly developed here, with the Tourist Office producing a large quantity of information on guides and trails – much of it free.

Visitors will notice that prices seem more Swiss than Italian: Lugano the city and Lugano the lake are not cheap. The biggest shock in my view are restaurants. Eating out doesn't come cheap here (the same is true for Ticino in general): you can spend twice as much as you would a few miles south in Italy. Wine, though locally produced and some of it excellent, is also shockingly expensive. When eating out, expect to pay at least 50 CHF for a reasonable bottle of the local Merlot. Twice as much if you're looking for something memorable.

If you balk at the idea of blowing the price of a hotel room on a bottle of wine (the restaurant markup is huge), order Italian wine when eating out and pick up a couple of bottles of Ticinese Merlot from an entoteca (wine store). In the center of Lugano, try **La Bottega del Vino** (Via Pessina 13), or **Enoteca Nonsolovino** (Via Balestra 15a).

There are not as many churches or monuments to see in Lugano as you might expect in a city this size, but the unassuming church of **Santa Maria degli Angioli** (1499-1510) is well worth a visit. Its plain façade gives way to a richly-frescoed interior. Many of the frescoes are by Bernardino Luini, including the enormous *Crucifixion*.

Luini fresco

Lake Lugano

BERNARDINO LUINI

Bernardino Luini was a prolific Lombardian artist, who may have been a student of Leonardo da Vinci. He is known for his soft palette, and for the emotive quality of his work. There is a lot of his work to be seen throughout Lombardy and Ticino in Switzerland, while the Louvre in Paris and the Uffizi in Florence also contain examples.

San Lorenzo, Via Cattedrale, below Lugano station, is Lugano's cathedral, a parish church in the ninth century, with a 15th-century bell tower. Much of the cathedral was renovated in the 18th and 19th centuries. The interior contains a number of frescoes, the oldest dating from the 13th century, and a 15th-century baptismal font.

San Lorenzo

Lugano has a number of good art galleries. The **Museo Cantonale d'Arte**, Via Canova 10. Open Weds-Sun, 10 am-5 pm, Tues 2-5 pm. It has a good collection of 19th- and 20th-century work that includes paintings by Renoir, Degas and Paul Klee, as well as art from the late Gothic period. The **Museo d'Arte Moderna**, Riva Caccia 5, www.mdam.ch, is open Weds-Sun 9 am-8 pm. It hosts exhibitions of important 20th century artists – Francis Bacon, Chagall, Egon Schiele – as well as contemporary artists.

Villa Favorita, Via Riviera 14, Castagnola, is open Easter-October, Fri-Sun 10 am-5 pm. Dating from the 17th century, the building belonged to Baron Heinrich von Thyssen-Bornemisza, and was the home of his incredible collection of Old Masters. After his death, 800 works were loaned to Madrid and Barcelona (his wife was a former Miss Spain)

Villa Favorita

although the villa retained the Baron's superb collection of European and American modern art. The villa is approached through the splendid lakefront gardens. Take time out to enjoy them. You can walk to the villa along the lake (around 30 minutes). Take a boat or take Bus 1.

The **Museo delle Culture Extraeuropee** is housed in Villa Heleneum, in Castagnola, a little beyomd Villa Favorita. It contains an interesting collection of objects from Oceania, Asia and Africa. Open Tues-Sun, 2 pm-7 pm. The gardens of the villa are very attractive. Entrance is free. They are open 6 am-11 pm summer, 6 am-9 pm winter. Get here by Bus 1, on foot or by boat.

TAKE A HIKE

From Villa Favorita or Villa Heleneum, join the **Sentiero di Gandria** footpath, through the Parco degli Ulivi. The park is at its best in May and June, when the olive trees, cypresses, laurels, pine trees and pomegranates are joined at ground level by a blanket of wild herbs and flowers. Sitting at the base of Monte Brè, the **Parco degli Ulivi** enjoys a semi-tropical microclimate, with endless sunshine. An hour or so on the footpath and you reach **Gandria**, a small village that seems to rise straight out of the lake. It's inaccessible to cars (though you can get pretty close) and one of the loveliest areas of Lake Lugano.

Back in the city, **Piazza della Riforma** is Lugano's central piazza, the venue for the Estival Jazz concerts in July, home to the 19th-century town hall (the **Palazzo Civico**) and a

Lake Lugano

great place to stop for a coffee (you'll pay for the location) and watch the world go by.

The highlight of Lugano City are the views you get from a number of distinct mountain tops, all reachable by funicolare or cable car.

Monte Brè

At 960 m/3,150 ft, and known as Switzerland's sunniest mountain, Monte Brè can be reached from Cassarate, to the east of the city center (Bus 1 or 11). A funicolare takes you up to the summit for fabulous views, a restaurant and the interesting village of Brè. The funicolare runs every 30 minutes between mid-Mar and October, with limited service in the winter. If you're thinking of coming here at lunchtime, the restaurant offers a simple three-course meal and a round-trip ticket for not much more than the cost of the ticket itself – around €27. Call to book: ☎ 5 41 (0) 91 9941 350, www.montebre.ch.

 Tip: You can rent mountain bikes at Monte Brè and take one of two trails down to Survigliana. Prices for a day's rental are around €20. Look under Services on the Monte Brè website or e-mail info@montebre.ch.

★★Monte Generoso

At almost twice the height of Brè, it offers unparalleled views over Ticino, over the Lombardy plain to the Apennines, and of the Alps, including the peaks of the Matterhorn and the Monte Rosa group. A small cog-

The view from Monte Generoso (Ticino Tourism)

wheel railway takes you up in 40 minutes, and once there a short walk of 10 minutes takes you to the peak (1,704 m/5,590 ft). There's an ugly-looking restaurant at the top, and hostel facilities if you want to spend the night at the top – dorms, a room for four and double rooms. To inquire, call ☎ 41 (0) 91 630 51 11. You catch the Monte Generoso train at Capolago, on the south arm of the lake. Take the 9:20 boat from Lugano or train to Capolago-Riva S.Vitale.

★★Monte San Salvatore

Yet another peak from which to admire the view (915 m/ 3,000 ft). This time the funicolare leaves from Lugano's Paradiso suburb, west of the central railroad station. There are a couple of restaurants at the top, one of which is self-service. The funicolare leaves every 30 minutes and takes 10 minutes to climb to the peak. You can check the timetable at www.montesansalvatore.ch. To get to Paradiso take the train one stop from the central station or Bus 2.

TAKE A HIKE

Why not walk to Monte San Salvatore, either from Paradiso or take the funicolare to the intermediate stop of Pazzallo. Starting from here the distance is only around one and a half miles, the rise around 500 meters. Even the moderately fit could manage this in less than an hour. Much of the path is through woods.

★Serpiano

From the tiny village of ★★**Brusino Arsizio**, take the cablecar up to Serpiano (600 m/ 1,968 ft). If you're feeling lazy, sit on the restaurant terrace and enjoy the view over to Morcote, and up the east side of Lake Lugano to the city. Otherwise, there are a number of easy

Brusino Arsizio

walks through woods, or take a longer walk (1½ hours) up to **Monte San Giorgio** (1,096 m/3,595 ft), a UNESCO World Heritage Site. You can stay up here too, at the **Hotel Serpiano** (about €200 for a double room, www.serpiano.ch).

When you come back down, head into the tiny lakeside village of Brusino Arsizio for a wander or pitstop. Here you will find tiny fishermen's houses, superb views over to Morcote and silence. A charming place. The **Osteria della Posta** serves food, and the shockingly painted yellow **Casa Sole** next door is a bargain spot to stay (see *Where to Stay* for details).

 There are five UNESCO World Heritage sites in Switzerland – and two of them are in Ticino. One is the castles at Bellinzona, and the other, Monte San Giorgio. San Giorgio is regarded as the single best fossil record of marine life from the Triassic period – that's 245-230 million years ago.

★★Monte Tamaro

At an elevation of 1,961 m/6,433 ft, Monte Tamaro is a few miles north of Lugano toward Bellinzona, at a place called Rivera-Bironico. Take the small cable-cars up to Alpe Foppa for great views of the pre-Alpine land-

Monte Tamaro cable-car

scape, the Alps and, weather permitting, Lake Lugano and Lake Maggiore. Monte Tamaro makes for a great day out, especially if you're traveling with kids. Halfway up the mountain is an Adventure Park, suitable for adults and kids, but, best of all, at the peak is the **Alpine Coaster Bob**. info@montetamaro.ch, ☎ 41 (0) 91 946 2303, www.montetamaro.ch.

Also at Monte Tamaro is the ultra-modern church of ★★**Santa Maria degli Angeli**, designed by internationally-renowned architect Mario Botta, who hails from Ticino. He was the architect responsible for the renovation and restructuring of Milan's La Scala opera house. Very controversial when it was first built in the 1990s, the church is a stunning example of contemporary religious architecture, and a must for those who have more than a passing interest in architecture and design. There are some pretty fabulous views to be had from here too.

★★★ Gandria

Santa Maria degli Angeli

One of the lake's must-see spots. Rising straight out of the lake, this small village of higgledy-piggledy houses, wooden

walkways and cobbled alleyways has tremendous charm and, in the summer season, tremendous numbers of tourists to boot. The restaurants and bars mostly sit right on the lakeside, affording lovely views. If you want to walk here,

Gandria

you can take the **Sentiero di Gandria** footpath (see above), which begins near Villa Favorita, east of Lugano City. The walk can take anywhere from one to 1½ hours. Boats serve Gandria fairly regularly. If you come by car (though not recommended as car-parking is very limited) you have to park five minutes outside of the village.

★★ Morcote

Once a fishing village, Morcote is one of the most popular destinations on the lake's southern shores. Undeniably attractive, with the 14th-century **Capitano Tower** and the very

Lake Lugano

Morcote (Catherine Richards)

fine church of Santa Maria del Sasso, Morcote has cobbled streets, pretty houses, and cafés, with their boardwalk-type terraces over the lake. Unfortunately, it gets very crowded between May and September, and also suffers from heavy traffic, so go early or later in the day. The church of **Santa Maria del Sasso** was founded in the 13th century and contains some interesting Renaissance frescoes. The views from here, and the cemetery, are fabulous. Take the boat to Morcote (first service at 9:20 from Lugano, arrives 10:30), or the bus from Lugano (Via San Balestra, line 31). Also at Morcote is the **Parco Scherrer** (open daily, mid-Mar to Oct, 9 am-5 pm, to 6 pm in July and Aug), at the foot of Monte Arbòstora. Designed by Hermann Arthur Scherrer in 1930, the park is both

Santa Maria del Sasso
(Catherine Richards)

Mediterranean and Asiatic in style, with sculptures, reduced

reproductions of temples and villas and a great collection of plants and trees. A relaxing place to wander.

There are more than 400 steps to the church of Santa Maria del Sasso, making it inaccessible for those with disabilities or difficulty walking.

★★Vico Morcote

Nearly a mile farther up the hill, Vico Morcote has all the charm of Morcote and none of the crowds. With a resident population of under 300, tranquility is pretty much guaranteed. There are a couple of places

Vico Morcote (Catherine Richards)

to eat here, the rustic **Osteria al Bocc**, which serves Ticinese and Lombardian dishes, and the **Bellavista**, which has a reputation for great dishes, great views and reasonable prices (by Swiss standards). Consider staying here too, for its peacefulness, those great views and the reasonable prices (Strada da Vigh 2, ☎ 41 (0) 91 996 1143, ☎/fax 41 (0) 91 9961288). If you're not intending to walk up from Morcote, there are infrequent buses (a handful a day) from Morcote Piazza Grande (Line 40) or you can drive here.

Campione

A little piece of Italy within Switzerland: politically as well as culturally. It's an Italian enclave, known primarily for its **Casino**. There isn't much going on here, but this is the place to go if you want to try some gambling. It's part of Italy, so there are no border checks. Open from 12 pm to 4 am daily. Get here by boat or bus from Lugano.

In the village of Montagnola, 10 minutes outside of Lugano, there's a museum dedicated to **Herman Hesse** (☎ 41 0 91 993 3770, www.hessemontagnola.ch), writer, poet and painter, who spent nearly half of his life here. It was here that he wrote *Siddhartha*, *Narcissus and Goldmund* and *Steppenwolf*. Just above the station in Lugano, on Via

Lake Lugano

Sorengo, take the yellow post bus to Montagnola, or catch it at the terminus in Via Balestra, in the city center.

A little farther north from Lugano is the pretty village of **Ponte Capriasca**. The church contains a mid-16th copy of Leonardo's *Last Supper* – where all the apostles are named. Not a woman among them!

Kid-Friendly

Swissminiatur

In nearby Melide, there is **Swissminiatur**, which is fun if you're with young kids and pretty educational if you've always wanted to see Switzerland but don't have the time on this trip. It has 120 models of the best of Swiss architecture: cathedrals, castles, town halls, and 3,500 m/11,500 ft of railroad track – all miniaturized. The scale is 1:25. It gets crowded with tour groups so skip it if you're looking for peace and quiet (www.swissminiatur.ch, open mid-Mar to end Oct, 9 am-6 pm).

At the west of the lake, toward Ponte Tresa there are a couple of other spots that kids might appreciate. the **Alprose Chocolate Factory** at Caslano – complete with a chocolate fountain – allows visitors to take a short tour of the factory (www.alprose.ch). In nearby

Zoo al Maglio residents

Magliaso there's the small **Zoo al Maglio**. Over 100 animals, including lions, puma, tigers, and rare monkeys and gibbons are here, near the river Magliasina. You can picnic too. Open year-round. (☎ 41 (0)91 606 1493).

If **minigolf** is more your thing, there's an 18-hole course at Caslano, complete with electric cars for small kids and trampolines for all but the heaviest! (Via Golf 1. Open Mar-Sept 1:30-6 pm or from 10 am Sun, closed Mon and Tues. June-Aug open daily 10 am-11 pm).

FREE

★★★**Estival Jazz** is a well-respected jazz festival that's held in the Lugano's Piazza Riforma in the first week of July. Previous lineups have included Buddy Guy, Van Morrison, Yes, Jethro Tull, Yellowjackets, Al Jarreau, Randy Brecker. It's open-air, it's crowded (best not to take small kids) and, incredibly, it's free! There's a great atmosphere in the city at this time.

Italian Lake Lugano

Porto Ceresio

★★**Porto Ceresio** is a quiet, pretty lakeside village, with fine views over the lake to Morcote and along the two arms of the lake. There are three daily boat runs here from Lugano, with twice-daily return trips. **Ponte Tresa**, favorite supermarket-stop for local Swiss (prices can be up to 40% cheaper) is attractive enough, and is the jumping-off point for trips to Miglieglia and the cable-car to **Monte Lema** – another peak with outstanding views and great walking/biking trails. Boats serve Ponte Tresa, also reachable (a more regular service) on the **Ferrovie Luganesi**, www.flpsa.ch, a small train that essentially operates as a commuter service for all the workers and school kids commuting to Lugano City.

Lake Lugano

Mendrisiotto

This is the region south of Lugano lake, toward the Italian border. A lovely area to explore, mainly for its countryside of rolling green hills (a softer landscape than in the north of Ticino) and vineyards.

Mendrisiotto

Canton Ticino has more than 2,800 acres of vineyards and over 200 wine producers. At least 80% of the wine produced is Merlot. In 2006 Ticino celebrated 100 years of Merlot production, and over the last few years the reputation of Ticinese wines has grown, with many winning awards internationally. In Mendrisio, acres of land is given over to vines, and many of the vineyards are open for visits. Contact Mendrisio Tourism for a list of local wineproducers

DID YOU KNOW?

The Mendrisiotto people are known as momo by their fellow Ticinesi, and are renowned for their friendliness, warmth and sense of humor.

Both **Monte Generosa** and **Monte San Giorgio** lie in the region, as does the **Broggia Gorge Park**, www.parcobroggia. ch, an area rich in flora, fauna and fossils, and a great place to walk, cycle or picnic. The **Muggia Valley** is another place to delight walkers. It's a Pre-Alpine valley that contains nine historic villages. The Mendrisio Tourist Board has suggestions for hikes in the valley. Check out www. mendrisiotourism.ch, and look under Nature Parks.

Adventures

Asbest Adventures are Lugano-based, and offer an enormous range of activities: climbing, canyoning, diving, mountain-biking, paragliding, skiing and snowboarding – even photography. Contact them at info@asbest.ch, ☎ 41 (0) 91 966 11 14, www.asbest.ch.

On Foot

 Lugano, and Ticino in general, is perfect for walkers, trekkers and hikers. The Tourist Board has three suggested treks around Lugano. Look on **www. lugano-tourism.ch** under *Activities* for *Routes and Excursions*. The Tourist Office also leaflets describing 28 walking trails in and around Lugano. Contact them at info@lugano-tourism.ch, ☎ 41 (0) 91 913 32 32.

As a general rule, the mountains around Lugano have websites with suggested trails or treks.

 Pick up a copy of *Walking in Ticino* by Kev Reynolds, published by Cicerone Guides, 1992. ISBN 1-85284-098-6. More than 75 of the best walks in Ticino's valleys.

If you want to try some Nordic walking – increasingly popular in Europe – contact **Sport & Turismo**. Twice a week, on Tues and Thurs they organize a Nordic walk near Lugano. Minimum two people. Cost ranges from about €25, which includes the sticks and a coffee! ☎ 41 (0) 91 924 9653.

On Wheels

 Lugano railroad station has bikes to rent – mountain bikes, countrybikes and even three bikes for kids. Reserve in advance to avoid disappointment. If you read German, you can book online at www.sbb.ch; if not, contact **Lugano station** on ☎ 41 (0) 51 221 5642. Cycle helmets (complete with hygienic liners) are available free of charge. Most of the bigger hotels have bikes to rent or contact the Tourist Office.

For mountain bike rental, contact **Sport & Turismo** who organizes accompanied mountains bike trails and rent out the bikes. They're located near Melide. About €30 per day, ☎ 41 (0) 91924 9653.

Lugano Tourism, www.lugano-tourism.ch, has details on 42 mountain bike trails in the Lugano area. You can download trail maps and do a search based on level of difficulty and elevation difference. On their website, look under Activities and select Mountain Bike.

For renting a scooter, contact **Gerosa Motocicli** on Via Canonica 7, Lugano, ☎ 41 (0) 91 923 5636, or try **Cagiva Motor** on ☎ 41 (0) 91 985 1170.

On the Golf Course

 Golf Club Lugano, with 18 holes, is five miles from the city of Lugano in Magliaso. It's a popular course, so book ahead. Cost is around €60 for weekday play. info@golflugano.ch, ☎ 41 (0) 91606 1557, www.golflugano.ch.

In Italy, **Varese** has a beautifully-located golf club (views over Lake Varese) at Luvinate. 18 holes. The clubhouse and restaurant is in a restored Benedictine monastery. info@golfclubvarese.it, ☎ 39 0332 229 302, www.golfclubvarese.it.

On Water

 If you'd like to do some **water-skiing**, contact **Club Ski Nautico Ceresio**, at the Hotel du Lac, eva. barr@gmail.com, ☎ 41 (0) 79 691 6601.

Boat Center Palace offers **water-skiing** and **wakeboarding** as well as **speedboats** for hire and **water taxis**. See www.boatcenterpalace.com.

For **wakeboarding** on Lake Lugano (and at Vira Gambarogno on Lake Maggiore) contact **Cecco Torenas**, ☎ 41 (0) 76 383 6656, www.ceccotorenas.ch.

Club Nautico Lugano, between Lugano City and Melide, offers **water-skiing**, **windsurfing** and has **motorboats** for rent, ☎ 41 (0) 91 649 6139.

To rent a **speedboat** (some don't need licenses), contact **Boat Center Palace** at www.boatcenterpalace.com.

For **diving**, contact **Lugano Sub**, info@luganosub.ch, ☎ 41 (0) 91 994 3740, or **Corallo Sub** at Club Nautica Sassalto, ☎ 41 (0) 91 606 3195.

For sailing, contact **Club Nautico Lugano**, Via Calloni 9, ☎ 41 (0) 91 994 12 56.

If you don't want to **swim** in the lake, try the **Lido** at Via del Lido, Lugano. With an Olympic-sized swimming pool, a 25-m/ 82-ft heated pool and two pools for kids, it's no wonder it's extremely popular. There's a restaurant and bar here – the latter stays open until 1 am Thurs-Sat in the summer.

The **Lido di San Domenico** is in a beautiful spot, on the Sentiero di Gandria near Villa Heleneum. Direct access to the lake. Also try the **Lido at Conca d'Oro**. A 23-m/75-ft pool right on the lake and a number of trampolines to keep the kids happy. At **Riva Caccia**, right below the Museum of Modern Art, there's a bathing area right on the lake.

Contact the Tourist Board (www.lugano-tourism.ch) for a list of beaches and safe swimming areas on the lake, and for a list of restaurants with lake mooring if you've rented a boat.

In the Air

For **paragliding** (parapendio in Italian), the **Pink Baron** in Capolago, organizes courses. info@pink-baron.ch, ☎ 41 (0) 91 648 3088, www.pink-baron.ch.

For **tandem flights**, check out www.paragliding-ticino.ch. If you look under biposto there is a list of all licensed pilots who offer tandem flights, where they fly from, and whether they speak English. Each pilot has contact details.

On the Tennis Court

There are a good number of tennis courts in the area. A couple of the best-known are:

TC Lido, info@tclido.ch, www.tclido.ch, and **TC Lugano 1903**, lumani@ticino.com.

The Tourist Board will have a list of courts and clubs in the area. Many of the bigger hotels have courts.

On Horseback

For riding lessons and/or trekking, contact the **San Giorgio Stables** at Origlio, ☎ 41 (0) 91 966 5212. Also in Origlio is the **Scuderia Hubertus**, ☎ 41 (0) 91 945 4595. In Cureglia there's **Scuderia del Tiglio**, ☎ 41 (0) 91 966 8971. In a place called ★★**Alpe Vicania**, there's a

Lake Lugano

riding school offering a range of equestrian activities, including group lessons, private lessons or treks through the beautiful countryside. Lessons for kids too. Jessica Stamm, ☎ 41 (0) 79 613 0450, www.alpe-vicania.ch (in Italian).

With the Language

 Amerispan arranges intensive Italian courses in Lugano. Do a homestay program or organize your own accommodation; four hours of lessons a day. Minimum length of a course is two weeks. info@amerispan. com, www.amerispan.com.

Eurolingua Insitute offers something similar, with a choice of accommodation to suit most people. Minimum two weeks. www.eurolingua.com.

Where to Stay

 The Swiss do luxury very well indeed, and there are a good number of luxury hotels all around Lake Lugano. Wellness, spa treatments, health and beauty facilities, gourmet dining and fabulous lake views are to be had in return for a sizeable amount

HOTEL PRICE CHART	
Double room with tax & breakfast	
€	Under €80
€€	€80-€130
€€€	€131-€180
€€€€	€181-€250
€€€€€	Over €250

of money. There are, however, a good number of reasonably-priced hotels around the lake, and the tourist board has a very easy-to-use guide that is available online.

 Tip: You can download the Tourist Board's accommodation guide from the Internet at www. lugano-tourism.ch. Look under Accommodation and then Hotels.

The cheapest other options, aside from camping and hostels, are restaurants with rooms – both in the Italian and Swiss parts of the lake. It goes without saying that booking ahead is highly advisable from May-Sept (and holiday periods such as Easter). Northern Swiss and Germans love the Swiss canton of Ticino and, in the summer, cities like Lugano and Locarno are very popular. In fact the population of Ticino (300,000) doubles in size in the summer months, swelled by visitors. If you plump for a budget option, double-check that credit cards and euros are accepted – if this is how you wish to pay.

Lugano

Terrace at Grand Hotel Eden

Grand Hotel Eden. Highly-rated luxury hotel in the Riva Paradiso district of Lugano City. Superb views – particularly from the terrace. It has all the facilities and service you would expect in a hotel of its kind. 120 rooms. ☎ 41 (0) 91 985 9200, welcome@edenlugano.ch, www.edenlugano.ch. €€€€

International Au Lac. Near the lake in the city center, on Lugano's chic shopping street. Underground parking, swimming pool, restaurant/bar and terrace. Very convenient if you are staying only a couple of nights in Lugano and want to be close to the stores, restaurants and boat docks. Not luxury but very comfortable. If your budget stretches to it, take a room with a lake view. Via Nassa 68, ☎ 41 (0) 91 922 7541, www.hotel-international.ch. €€€€

Grand Hotel Villa Castagnola. Another luxury spot with fabulous views. Set in a large park,

Hotel International Au Lac

with indoor pool, tennis courts, and lido on the lake. Beautiful interior and excellent restaurant. The hotel also has apartments for stays of three months or more. Viale Castagnoa 31, ☎ 41 (0) 91 973 2550, info@villacastagnola.com, www.villacastagnola.com. €€€€€

Parkhotel Villa Nizza. More affordable comfort here. Family-owned, a 10-minute walk to the lake and located at the foot of Mount San Salvatore. Lovely views over the city and the lake. Swimming pool, garden, and

Parkhotel Villa Nizza view

restaurant. Décor not so great, but it's charming – the hospitality and views more than make up for any shortcomings. Make use of the shuttlebus the hotel arranges or take a taxi. Getting here involves a bit of walk uphill from Lugano station or Paradiso. €€€€

Fischer's Seehotel. On the Sentiero di Gandria, right on the lake, so great for those seeking a bit of peace and quiet. Rooms are decidedly simple, though you pay for the view. Sentiero di Gandria 10, ☎ 41 (0) 91 971 5571. €€€

Montarina. Great value here, a hotel/hostel just below the station, with good views, a garden and a swimming pool. Keep costs down by sharing bathrooms (a private bathroom costs extra). Free parking. A choice of rooms, including some with air-conditioning, and larger rooms/dorms for groups or families. Via Montarina 1, info@montarina.ch, ☎ 41 (0) 91 966 7272, www.montarina.ch. €

Hotel Stella. Just above the station, a fresh, clean hotel with good prices. Swimming pool and pretty garden. The owners are art collectors, which makes the interior more interesting than most. ☎ 41 (0) 91 966 3370, info@hotel-stella.ch, www.hotel-stella.ch. €€

Lugano Dante Swiss Quality Hotel. In the historic heart of Lugano (so no lake view), this hotel offers value in an otherwise very expensive city. No restaurant, but within seconds of many. Very close to the funicolare station, so it's convenient if you're traveling with a lot of luggage. Parking available, though not free. Piazza Cioccaro 5, ☎ 41 (0) 91 910 5700, info@hotel-luganodante.com, www.swissqualityhotels.com. €€€

Hotel Dellago. Modern interiors, lots of color, extra facilities like hi-fi and a complimentary coffee tray (very unusual in European hotels).

Lounge at Hotel Dellago

Many rooms have terrace and/or lake view. If your budget permits, try the Panoramic Room – with a private hot tub overlooking the lake. Good website with images of all the rooms. Nice seafood restaurant and bar, with lake terrace. In Melide. ☎ 41 (0) 91 649 7041, www.hotel-dellago.ch. €€€€

Gandria

Locanda Gandriese Ristorante. One of the few places to stay in Gandria, right on the lake (as is most of the village). Book ahead here for simple rooms (there are only four) in a traffic-free village. If you can't get a room, eat lunch here. ☎ 41 (0) 91 971 4181, locanda@pacchin.com. €

Antica Ristorante. Four rooms here, so book ahead. No frills – but you're on the lake in traffic-free Gandria. Nighttime tranquility virtually guaranteed. Open all year. ☎ 41 (0) 91 971 4871. €

Miralago Ristorante. Five simple rooms here right on the lake. Book ahead if you want any chance of getting a room. ristorante.miralago@bluewin.ch. €

Morcote

Hotel Morcote /Della Posta Ristorante. Another restaurant with rooms. Great views over the lake, and good prices. If you are looking to be traffic-free, be warned that the lake road runs between you and the lake. This shouldn't be much of a problem at night. ☎ 41 (0) 91 996 1127, info@hotelmorcote. com, www.hotelmorcote.com. €€

Battello Ristorante. As above, the restaurant in the lovely Morcote, though remember that Morcote can suffer from traffic during the day. Fresh, bright rooms, though they only have only four doubles. ☎ 41 (0) 91 996 1260. €€

Vico Morcote

Just above Morcote, far quieter and with great views, is the **Hotel Bellavista**. Good value rooms, some with lake views, and a very good restaurant (see *Where to Eat*). Hard to get to on public transport, though. There are nine double rooms, three suites with terraces and an apartment. Mar-Dec 1. Strada da Vigh 2, Vico Morcote. Book via www.ticinohotel.ch or call ☎ 41 (0) 91 996 1143. €€

Swiss Diamond Hotel. Sheer luxury here, with excellent rooms, many having a lake view. Not one but three restaurants, a piano bar, swimming pools and good health and beauty facilities. Five miles from the city of Lugano, easily reachable by car or boat. ☎ 41 (0) 91 735 0000, info@swissdiamond-hotelcom, www.swissdiamond-hotel.com. €€€€€

Swiss Diamond Hotel

Bogno/Valcolla

Locanda San Lucio

Locanda San Lucio. Northeast of Lugano City, 1,000 m/3,280 ft up, immersed in the countryside. Very close to a riding school and a good jumping-off point for walks and bike trails. Nine rooms, three suites, all simply but tastefully decorated. The Locanda is also a restaurant. Too difficult to reach if you don't have a car. ☎ 41 (0) 91 944 1303, info@sanlucio.ch, www.sanlucio.ch. €€

Brusino Arsizio

Casa Sole. A little fishing village on the lake, facing Morcote. Simple rooms with views either over the lake or toward Monte San Giorgio. Very near the cable-car for Monte Serpiano and a beautiful village where everything seems very, very small. ☎ 41 (0) 91 996 2344, info@casasolebrusino.ch, www. casasolebrusino.ch. €€

Hotel Chalet San Giorgio. This restaurant/pizzeria has two rooms to rent. Right on the lake, moments from the Italian border, and moments from the cable-car for Serpiano. Superb views across to Morcote. ☎ 41 (0) 91 966 2155. €€€

Miglieglia

Casa Santo Stefano. Two restored Ticinesi houses in Miglieglia (710 m/2,329 ft elevation), run by a Swiss couple, who also organize seminars, yoga and tai-chi workshops and art courses. You can rent rooms or the entire house (great for large groups). Simply and tastefully furnished. Good spot for exploring Monte Lema. Around 10 miles from Lugano City. ☎ 41 (0) 91 609 1935, info@casa-santo-stefano.ch. €€

Bed and Breakfast & Apartments

Rental property in Brusino-Arsizio

You can download an apartment and villa guide from **Lugano Tourism** (www.lugano-tourism. ch), or check their website and click on Accommodation. **Interhome** has a selection of properties to rent around Lake Lugano, in both the Italian and Swiss areas. www.interhome.com.

Residence Ville Lago Lugano. Attractive apartments on the lakeshore, in a residence (specially built holiday complex). In Porto Ceresio in the Italian part of the lake. Via Casa Mora 6, ☎ 39 033 291 7004.

Camping

Lake Lugano is well-served with campsites – check out the list on the Tourist Office website, www. lugano-tourism.ch, and click on Accommodation. Some of the campsites between Melide and Capolago are horribly close to the freeway, though they don't mention it on the websites or in their information.

Campeggio ai Bosconi Caslano is really small, has an RV for rent (yes, seemingly just one) and is on the lakeshore. www.campeggiaiboscони.ch.

Camping Golfo del Sole is near Agno. 57 pitches, direct access to the lake, with a small, pebbly beach. Via Rivera 8, info@golfodelsole.ch, www.golfodelsole.ch.

Also in Agno is **Camping La Palma**, with more than 200 pitches and a reasonable range of facilities. Via Molinazza 21, Agno, ☎ 41 (0) 91 605 2561.

Some 10 miles from Ponte Tresa, toward Luino, is the **4x Camping Tresiana**. Next to a river (the Tresa), the campsite has a swimming pool, children's playground, caravan and tent rental. ☎ 41 (0) 91 608 3342, mail@campingtresiana.ch, www.camping-tresiana.ch.

Hostels

Lugano has two youth hostels: the Oasis, a little over a mile from Lugano City center, and one at Figino, on the western arm of the lake. Both are suitable for families, and both are open from Mar to mid- or late Oct.

The **Oasis** is family-owned, and is set in a beautiful garden with palm trees, swimming pool and play area for the kids. A number of family rooms and doubles/triples. Breakfast is provided, but not lunch or dinner. There are, however, kitchen facilities. A family of four staying in the same room can expect to pay around €100. ☎ 41 (0) 91 966 2728, lugano@ youthhostel.ch, www.luganoyouthhostel.ch.

The hostel in **Figino** is also attractive, set in nice grounds and five minutes to a bathing area on the lake. A family-friendly place. It's a member of Hosteling International (if you're not a member, you can buy daily membership at the hostel). Breakfast provided, dinner also available, including

BBQs in the grounds. A family of four in the same room can expect to pay €100 a night. ☎ 41 (0) 91 995 1151, figino@youthhostel.ch, www.youthhostel.ch/figino,

Where to Eat

Don't assume that locals eat only pasta. And avoid, at all costs, tourist-type places with menus as long as your arm and a hundred different kinds of pasta. Neither Italians nor Swiss-Italians eat pasta sauces made from 27

DINING PRICE CHART	
For three courses, excluding wine	
€	Under €20
€€	€20-€40
€€€	€41-€70
€€€€	Over €70

different ingredients and half a pitcher of cream. Though pasta is certainly eaten, and regularly too, in common with much of northern Italy, risotto and polenta are considered the staples here.

Swiss Lake Lugano
Alpe Vicania

Ristorante Vicania

Ristorante Vicania. Sublime setting, 610 m/ 2,000 ft up, in a protected reserve above Morcote and Vico Morcote. After a superb lunch on the outside terrace, take a 20-minute walk to the Morcote Castello through the vineyards. Fabulous views over the lake and beyond. You need a car to get up here. Closed Mon and Tues from Mar-June, Mon from July through Oct, ☎ 41 (0) 91 980 2414, www.alpevicania.ch. €€

Bissone

Ristorante Ticino. Regional food – especially lakefish – in an historic property full of character. You can stay here too.

Lake Lugano

Room rates are around €90 for a double. Bissone itself is a very attractive village by the edge of the lake. Closed Wed. Piazza Borromini 21, bertolina.reisen@bluewin.ch, ☎ 41 (0) 91 649 5150. €€€

TRY LUNCH!

You may be shocked at the prices when eating out in the Swiss part of the lake. But lunch is often an affordable option. Many of the hotels with renowned restaurants (and beautiful terraces with lake views) offer fixed-price lunch menus with a couple of courses. Same food, same view at half the price! If you have hired a boat, or want the experience of taking a water taxi to eat, Lugano Tourism, www.lugano-tourism.ch, has a list of restaurants that are on the lake with mooring.

Brusino Arsizio

Ristorante Chalet San Giorgio. Restaurant and pizzeria, just outside the tiny lakeside village of Brusino Arsizio. If you have a boat, you can moor it directly in front of the restaurant. Their terrace is right on the lake – a beautiful location. Via Cantonale. Closed Mon lunch in the summer, all day Mon other times. ☎ 41 (0) 91 996 21 55. €€€

Campione

Ristorante da Candida. Renowned restaurant with French/Italian cuisine (emphasis on the French), run by a husband-and-wife team. Always busy for dinner so book ahead. Closed Mon evening and Tues lunch. Via Marco de Campione 4, ☎ 41(0) 91 649 7541. €€€€

Caprino

Grotto Moderno Caprino. Great bar and restaurant in the tiny hamlet of Caprino, right opposite the Gulf of Lugano. A good selection of fixed-price menus, or just have a beer and a sandwich. Not the easiest place to get to (which means you leave the crowds behind), but take a water taxi, www.ambrataxi.ch, or the (irregular) ferry service, www.lakelugano.ch. €€

Grotto dei Pescatori. Also in Caprino, a more traditional place, with the same sublime views over to the Gulf of Lugano. Given the location, prices are reasonable. Regional, traditional fare. It's small, so book ahead, especially on weekends and in the height of the summer. For getting here, see above. ☎ 41 (0) 91 923 9867. €€

Caslano

Locanda Esterél. A lovely place, sometimes described as a little paradise, in Caslano on the western arm of the lake. Italian/French cuisine. Also a hotel. Closed Mon. Via Cantonale, ☎ 41(0) 91 611 2120, esteral@bluemail.ch. €€€

Castagnola

Villa Castagnola. This luxury hotel has a couple of fine restaurants, with superb views. At the **Arte Restaurant** you sit right at the lake's edge; in **Le Relais** restaurant, you sit on the terrace and enjoy a stunning view. Not cheap, but a lovely experience. A menu degustazione (tasting menu) will cost around €70. The Artè Restaurant is closed Sun and Mon. Viale Castagnola 31. Reserve a table online at www.villacastagnola.com, or call ☎ 41 (0) 91 973 2555. €€€€

Lugano

Ristorante Villa Principe Leopoldo. For serious foodies, this restaurant, under Chef Dario Ranza, is internationally renowned. It's in the hotel of the same name, which is a villa built for the Austrian Prince Leopoldo in 1926. Even lunch will

Ristorante Villa Principe Leopoldo

be expensive, though some things are worth the money. In Collina d'Ora overlooking the lake. Note: you cannot walk here easily – take a taxi. ☎ 41 (0) 91 985 8855, leopoldo@relaischateaux.com, www.leopoldohotel.com.

Lake Lugano

Ristorante Al Portone. Family-run place with an excellent reputation. A chance to experience elegant, modern Ticinese/Italian cuisine. Menu degustazione, and a fixed-priced lunchtime business menu at about €40. Closed Sun and Mon, and for the month of August. Viale Cassarate 3, ☎ 41 (0) 91 923 5511, www.ristorantealportone.ch. €€€€

Ristorante Movenpick Parco Ciani. A bit of a Swiss institution, this Movenpick restaurant is set in the Palazzo dei Congressi, overlooking the green of the Ciani Park. Big choice of pasta, salads, fish and seafood dishes. Vegetarian options available in the evening. The Swiss love their Movenpicks, so it's often busy. ☎ 41(0) 91 923 86 56, restaurant.parcociani@movenpick.com. €€€

Antica Osteria del Porto

Antica Osteria del Porto. Simple, fresh interior, with Mediterranean/regional cuisine. Located not too far from the center of Lugano near the Cassarate River. Also a wine bar, open throughout the day for a glass of wine with a plate of cheese or salami. Closed Tues. Via Foce 9, ☎ 41 (0) 91 971 4200, www.osteriadelporto.ch. €€€

Osteria dal Caprino. Come here for regional cuisine, traditional Ticinese cooking prepared with imagination and flair. Risotto with Merlot, cured meats, and, of course, goat. Closed Wed. Via Carona 28, calprino@ticino.com, ☎ 41 (0) 91 994 1480. €€€

Enoteca Giardino. Just above Lugano station. An enoteca with a good restaurant and an attractive, cozy interior. With a good choice of meat and fish, the dishes are Italian-inspired. Closed Sun. Piazzale Besso 1, ☎ 41 (0) 91 966 1677. €€€

La Tinera. In the heart of Lugano, a friendly, relaxed atmosphere, and good prices at this basement trattoria. Simple hearty food, but it often appears in guidebooks so you may

have trouble getting a table! Closed Sun. Via dei Gorini 2.
☎ 41 (0) 91 923 5219. €€

> **Tip:** If you're looking for a low-priced self-ser-
> vice place in the center of Lugano, head to the
> restaurant in **Manor**, the department store.
> Popular with workers who go here for lunch
> (go later!), you'll find branches of the store,
> complete with restaurant, all over Switzer-
> land. Freshly cooked meals – fish, meat, soup,
> good salad bar, fruit. A good choice if you're
> with kids; they can eat, you have a drink. Or
> vice versa. On Salita Chiattone 10, just south
> of the funicolare. 3rd floor. €

Massagno

Antica Osteria Gerso. Simple (though not particularly
cheap) French/Italian cuisine. Booking recommended as it's
very popular. Nice atmosphere. Closed Sun and Mon.
Piazzetta Solaro 24, ☎ 41 (0) 91 966 1915. €€€

Grotto della Salute. Traditional Ticinese "grotto"-style restaurant, in a nice location shaded by trees. Some great
regional dishes and seasonal specialities, with a casual,
relaxed setting. Via Sindacatori 4. ☎ 41 (0) 91 966 0476. €€€

Sorengo

Ristorante Santabbondio

**Ristorante Santab-
bondio**. A lovely place,
part of the Relais Gour-
mands group. Husband-
and-wife team, Mediter-
ranean-inspired cuisine
(and interior), beautifully
presented. Terrace for
summer eating. Closed
Mon, Sun dinner and Sat
lunchtime. Via Fomelino
10, santabbondio@relaischateaux.com, ☎ 41 (0) 91 993 2388.
€€€€

Lake Lugano

S. Pietro di Stabio

Ristorante Montalbano. Regional dishes with inspiration. The restaurant is set on the ridge of a hill, surrounded by vines, very close to the Italian border at Stabio. A good choice if you're exploring the southern part of Ticino. Closed Mon, Sun dinner and Sat lunchtime. Via Montalbano 34c, ☎ 41 (0) 91 647 1206. €€€

Taverne

Motto del Gallo. Vico Morcote

Ristorante Bellavista. Come here not only for the good food but for the unparalleled views across Lake Lugano from the terrace. You can stay here too, in reasonably priced rooms. Closed Mon and Tues at lunchtime. ☎ 41 (0) 91 996 1143, info@bellavistavicomorcote.ch. €€€

Vacallo

Ristorante Conca Bella

Ristorante Conca Bella, Michelin-starred place very close to the Swiss border near Chiasso. About 20 km/ 12 miles from Lugano. If you don't want to blow your budget, come for lunch and try the daily menu. For three courses it's €40. Concabella is also a hotel with reason-ably-priced rooms. Closed Sun and Mon. Via Concabella 2, Vacallo, ☎ 41 (0) 91 683 7474, www.concabella.ch. €€€€

Italian Lake Lugano

Porto Ceresio

La Trattoria del Tempo Perso. Traditional regional cooking, with lots of fresh pasta, risotto, soups, lake fish and regional specialties from Northern Italy. Small outside terrace and pretty, fresh interior. Closed Wed. Close to the ferry stop in Piazza Bossi 17, ☎ 39 0322 917 136. €€

Grottos

Throughout the region of Ticino there are "grottos," very char-acteristic of the region, and often very charming. Traditional grottos are stone-built, with granite tables outside, often, though not always, deep in the countryside. These are sum-mer places to eat. All grottos close in the winter, reopening around Easter time. The name grotto derives from the Italian word for cave. In the past fresh food was kept in holes or cracks in the rocks to keep them cool. Many of the older places are very small, with no seating inside, sometimes with food being prepared on wood-fired ranges, as there is either no electricity or simply a generator. Food served is invariably regional: cheeses, salami, polenta and hearty beef stews, goat, rabbit or, in the season, local game such as wild boar. Snails, (lumache) are not uncommon. Wine is usually local Merlot, traditionally served in a boccalino, a small pottery pitcher-like cup.

As a general rule, the simpler the place, the cheaper the food – but be warned that this is not always the case. Some so-called grottos are restaurants with restaurant prices. The tradi-tional grottos are open all day, and are good places to stop for a drink and a snack of local cheese and bread. At night they can be charming and intimate, with dining outside by candlelight, surrounded by trees and the chirping of grasshoppers. Be warned that some of the small places, the most rustic, will not take credit cards or euros. Be sure you have Swiss francs. In the Lugano area, try **Antica Grotto Fossati** at Meride. It was recommended to me by an Italian taxi driver, who spoke very favorably of the quail that is served in season.

Grotto Grassi in Tremona (Via ai Grotti) seems as authentic as they come. Sit under a canopy of trees and enjoy simple Ticinese food. Great views of Lake Lugano. At Balerna (Via Tarchini 53) there's the **Grotto dei Tigli**, near the little church of St. Anthony. Trees and vines overhead, granite tables and checkered tablecloths. For those with a car, try the grotto at **Eremo San Nicolao**, a mile above the village of Somazzo under Monte Generoso. The grotto is part of the her-mitage. The views over the Mendrisiotto and the Alps are sub-lime.

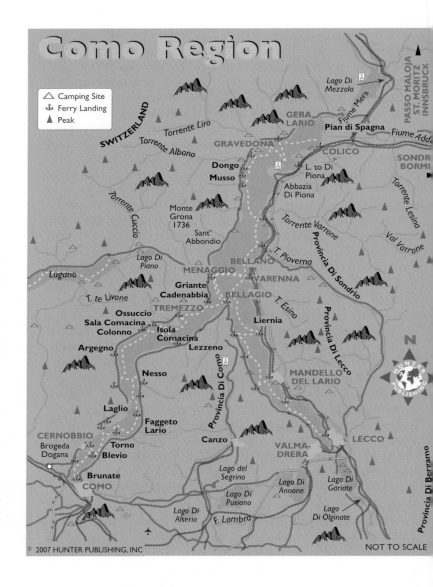

Como Region

- △ Camping Site
- ⚓ Ferry Landing
- ▲ Peak

SWITZERLAND

Torrente Liro
Torrente Albano

Lago Di Mezzola
Fiume Mera
PASSO MALOJA
ST. MORITZ
INNSBRUCK

GERA LARIO
Pian di Spagna
Fiume Adda

GRAVEDONA

COLICO
SONDR
BORMI

Dongo
Musso

L. to Di Piona
Abbazia Di Piona

Torrente Cuccio

Monte Grona 1736
Sant' Abbondio

Torrente Varrone
Provincia Di Sondrio
Torrente Lesina
Val Varrone

Lugano

Lago Di Piano

BELLANO
T. Pioverna

MENAGGIO
VARENNA

T. te Livone

Griante
Cadenabbia
TREMEZZO
BELLAGIO
T. Esino

Ossuccio
Sala Comacina
Colonno
Isola Comacina
Lezzeno

Liernia

Argegno

Provincia Di Lecco

Nesso

Provincia Di Como

MANDELLO DEL LARIO

N

Laglio
Faggeto Lario

Canzo

VALMA-DRERA

LECCO

CERNOBBIO
Brogeda Dogana
Torno
Blevio

Lago del Segrino

Lago Di Annone

Lago Di Gariate

Provincia Di Bergamo

Brunate
COMO

Lago Di Pusiano

Lago Di Alserio
F. Lambro

Lago Di Olginate

© 2007 HUNTER PUBLISHING, INC

NOT TO SCALE

Lago di Como/Como Town

There is always something alluring about Lake Como, perhaps the most beautiful of Italian lakes.

With many hours of sunshine throughout the year, it is an ideal vacation spot, but even in the rain Como exudes romance, serenity and an air of luxury. This is due in part to the number of exquisite 17th- and 18th-century villas that line its shores, but also to the num-

ber of chic Milanese who keep weekend homes here. "This lake exceeds anything I ever beheld in beauty" penned Shelley, who knew a thing or two about lakes. An impressive list of poets, writers and composers have found inspiration here, including Wordsworth, Byron, Stendhal, Rossini, Verdi and Puccini. A touch of modern-day glamour comes in the shape of actor George Clooney who has recently extended his Como estate by purchasing another two properties here.

Though you could be happy doing very little in Como, as the third-largest lake in Italy, it offers excellent water sports. Entirely surrounded by mountains, the area is also a favorite with walkers, offering everything from gentle strolls to Alpine hikes. In the summer season, when Lake Como becomes swamped with visitors, and the campsites around the lake are heaving, you can still find some peace by heading away from the lake up into the hills. For the experienced hiker, the walk to the summits of Monte Grona and Monte Bregagno, at 2,000 m/6,500 ft, will be rewarded with spectacular views across to Lake Lugano in Switzerland, Lake Como, Milan and the Po plains, the Valtellina and the higher Alps. For those seeking a less energetic trip, Como offers lush gardens, pretty lakeside villages, and plenty of sun-filled terraces on which to doze or sip chilled white wine.

Location/Geography

Como lies about 40 km/25 miles north of Milan, and only a few km from Switzerland. The Como region is divided into a number of different zones with a total population of about 543,000, while the city of Como itself has a population of 84,000. The lake is the third-largest in Italy after Lake Garda and Lake Verbano. It is also the deepest in Europe, and has been inhabited since prehistoric times. There is even some talk of a creature akin to the Loch Ness Monster in the lake – but don't let that put you off as it has rarely (if ever) been seen!

Cut into the foothills of the Alps and shaped like an upside-down Y, each branch of the lake is roughly the same length – 26 km/16 miles – with Colico to the north, Lecco to the southeast and Como town at the tip of the southwest branch of the lake.

DID YOU KNOW?

The lake is entirely surrounded by mountains, the highest being Monte Legnone (2,609 m/8,557 ft). There are 37 rivers flowing into the lake and only one outlet, the Adda River, which flows out through Lecco and onward into the Po River.

Economy

The areas of Como and Lecco were among the first to be industrialized in Italy and, along with Lombardy, are among the richest and most industrial in Italy. About 50% of the working population is employed in industry – with textiles, engineering, furniture and fittings predominating. For centuries Como has been known for its production of wool and high quality silk. Como still produces 80% of the silk made in Europe. The other 50% of the workforce is employed in sectors such as tourism and transport. Agriculture employs only about 1% of the workforce.

The Climate

The climate is usually mild and sunny in the Como region, even subtropical in some areas, with lush greenery and palm trees. The gardens along the sunnier shores of the lake boast a rich and varied flora, including citrus trees, camelias, azaleas, rhododendruns, wisteria, even bougainvillea. It escapes both the humidity and the terrible summer heat that can cripple Milan. The average temperature in July and August is around 29°C/66°F. January and February are the coldest months and snow at this time is not uncommon. Rainfall is not uncommon either, especially in the Pre-Alpine zone, though clear winter days with lots of sunshine are one of the attractions.

The lake itself is subject to a variety of weather conditions and, though this can make for some great sailing and windsurfing, inexperienced sailers need to pay attention as the winds can change very quickly. The best months to visit and from April through to the end of October, each month having its own character.

History

Como town is often overlooked by visitors who use it simply as a base from which to explore the lake. That's a great pity as the town is well worth a visit. For those who expect their Italian towns to be living museums, Como may disappoint at first glance . Lombardy is the richest region in Italy, so there's a lot of business and industry in the area around Milan and Como. But this is not Turin or Detroit. There are no huge chimneys belching black smoke into the Lombardian sky, no muddy brown haze sitting on top of the town. Drive past the superstores on the outskirts of Como, through the scruffy suburbs and within minutes you're in Como town: small, very attractive, with some fine architecture, a beautiful duomo, quaint shopping streets and all in a perfect setting.

Como's history dates from 196 BC, when it was founded by the Romans, for whom it had huge strategic importance. Como – or Larius, as it was called – served as an essential gateway, connecting the Po Valley with the northern regions of Europe, and over the years was subject to numerous invasions and from the north and the south. Julius Caesar sent 500 Greek slaves of noble birth to Como, in an effort to gentrify the city – this air of faded nobility being something that still clings to Como and its lake.

In the 12th century Como fought against Milan, though in the mid-14th century it fell under Visconti rule, and later, in 1451, under Sforza domination. From here on in, Como's history was that of Milan. It fell under Austrian rule, then Spanish, and even, for a brief period, French rule – all of which can be seen in the city's architecture. Finally, in 1859, Como became part of the kingdom of Italy.

Como is as famous for the villas along its lake as it is for the lake itself, and Como residents and visitors have been building their palaces and summer retreats since Roman times. Some of the villas that line the shores of the lake today date from the early 16th century, though most were built in the 17th and 18th centuries. Many of these villas and their gardens are open to the public. (See *What to See & Do.*)

Famous Como Residents & Visitors

Pliny the Younger (62-115 AD), a Roman senator, was born in Como. He was raised by a close family friend, his uncle, Pliny the Elder, governor of Bithynia-Pontus (109-111), and he authored an historically important collection of letters. Pliny the Younger left Como when he was only 14, but he inherited land here on the death of Pliny the Elder during the eruption of Vesuvius. He returned to build two villas here.

One was higher up at Bellagio, which he called Tragedia; the other, lower down in Lenno, he called Comedia. "Each villa," he said, "seems more attractive to the occupant by contrast with the other."

Alessandro Volta (1745-1827), pioneer in electrochemistry and inventor of the battery who gave his name to the "volt." Born in Como, Volta became professor of physics at the University of Pavia in 1779. By 1799

Alessandro Volta

he had developed the voltaic pile, a forerunner of the electric battery. Napolean was so impressed he made him a count in 1801. You can visit the Neo-Classical Tempo Voltiano on the shores of Como, which has a small collection of Volta's letters, apparatus and personal objects (see *Museums*). As a child, Volta said nothing until the age of about seven or eight. It was only when he voiced his dislike of a particularly bitter drink that his family knew he was able to speak.

Leonardo da Vinci

Leonardo da Vinci spent some time around Lake Como and tried in vain to find the source of the Fiumelatte at Bellagio. He wrote in his notebook: "Opposite the castle Bellaggio there is the river Latte, which falls from a height of more than 100 braccia from the source whence it springs, perpendicularly, into the lake with an inconceivable roar and noise. This spring flows only in August and Sept."

Virgil, who called Lake Como simply "our greatest" lake, is among the many writers, poets and composers who have found inspiration here. Though there were many writers before the 18th century who appreciated the beauty of the region, it was Romanticism that made Como more than just a lake and the

Virgil

trading and communication route out of northern Italy. The Romanticists were concerned with the spiritual influence of nature on their lives and on their souls, and their movement was partly a backlash against the Rationalism of the 18th century.

Percy Shelley and his wife **Mary** – created the Villa Pliniana in Torno. Byron was a guest here, as was the writer Stendhal, and the composer Rossini (he composed *Tancredi* here). Robert Browning came, Goethe, Tchaikovsky, Rossini. Later, American writer Edith Wharton stayed here, finding relief from the horrors of English-style horticulture, which had swept over Lombardy like a "tidal wave," she fumed, destroying traditional Italian gardens, many of which

Shelley

were centuries old. Though the fashion for English gardening was responsible for the remodeling of many established Italian gardens (and clearly wasn't to Ms Wharton's taste), the fashion was responsible for some of the loveliest gardens along the lake.

Villa Pliniana

Gabriel Faure, the French composer, loved the lake, **Lizst** stayed here in exile after an ill-fated love affair and penned his homage to Dante and Beatrice – *Dante Fantasia* – on the shores of Bellagio. **Manzoni**, the Italian writer of the 18th century, set his classic novel, *I Promessi Sposi*, in and around Lecco and the lake. Among 20th-century visitors and residents are **Versace**, whose family still has a villa on the

Gabriel Faure

lake, **George Clooney**, and a host of European celebrities and actors.

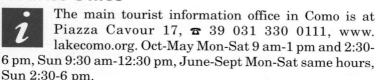

Practicalities

Tourist Office

 The main tourist information office in Como is at Piazza Cavour 17, ☎ 39 031 330 0111, www. lakecomo.org. Oct-May Mon-Sat 9 am-1 pm and 2:30-6 pm, Sun 9:30 am-12:30 pm, June-Sept Mon-Sat same hours, Sun 2:30-6 pm.

A smaller tourist information counter can be found at Como Train Services.

Tours

Bellagio & Lake Como Tour Guides. Recommended Italian/British tour guides, registered and with good local knowledge. ☎ 039 031 951151, 039 335 5923768 (cell), www.bellagio. co.nz/guides.

Guide Turistiche di Como. Guided tours of Como and the region by registered guides. A professional association with suggested itineraries on their website You can book online too, though be careful because you apparently can't cancel by telephone. ☎ 39 031-817096, info@guidecomo.it, www. guidecomo.it.

What to Pack

 From Oct through to Mar, don't forget your umbrella and warm, rainproof clothing. The winters can be sunny but cold, so bring suitable clothes. There is often snow from December too. Bring a sweater year-round for the evenings as the lakeside can feel cool at night.

Internet Café

 There's free Internet service at the town hall, **Comune di Como**, via V. Emanule II, 97.

Public Holidays

September 7-15 – Como Baradello medieval festival. Also called the Lario Boat Festival. Boats in procession on the lake, with heraldry and bunting representing the medieval communes of the lake.

End September at Chiavenna (15 km north of the end of the lake) – Traditional foods eating in the caves –the natural clefts of the rock faces.

The Tourist Agency website has a calendar of events, listing all types of festivals, exhibitions, concerts, food fairs and the like happening in Como and the surrounding area. Currently it is only available in Italian. On the homepage select Cultura e Tempo Libero then select Calandario degli Eventi'. www.commune.como.it.

Getting Here

Train

 There is a frequent **train** service to Como from Stazione Centrale in Milan and from Switzerland. These trains stop at Stazione San Giovanni, Piazzale San Gottardo, a short bus ride (#4 or #7) or 15-minute walk from Piazza Cavour. The trains are fast and reasonably priced. Journey time 40 minutes. Operated by Trenitalia.

Trains from Malpensa or Milano Nord arrive in Como Nord Lago, right on the lake near Piazza Cavour, though this trip involves a change at Saronno. Operated by Ferrovie Nord. Journey time 50 minutes to one hour.

There is a third station in Como, Como Borghi, which is a short walk south of the town center. These trains serve the local area.

Treni Italia, ☎ 39 39 89 20 21, www.trenitalia.com.

Ferrovie Nord, ☎ 39 031 30 48 00, www.ferrovienord.it.

Tip: If you're intending to travel around by train when in Italy, seriously consider going first class. In Italy, the price difference between first and second class is far less than in other countries. Italian trains can get really busy, and in the summer on popular routes you sometimes run the risk of having no seat at all. You can book your tickets online before you leave home, and pick them up at the station. Check the excellent American site **www.raileurope.com** for more information regarding booking, passes, and fly/drive combinations.

Bus

 From Malpensa, buses arrive in Piazza Cavour or Piazza Matteoti, with a journey time of 50 minutes. They are generally operated by SPT, www.sptlinea.it. If you are flying into Bergamo, SPT has a service to Como. Journey time is about an hour and 50 minutes. SPT, ☎ 39 031 24 72 47, www.sptcomo.it/tpl/default.asp.

Car

 Driving from Milan is quick – as little as 30 minutes if the traffic is light and you like driving quickly! The road gets very busy Friday as Milanese head out of Milan for the weekends and Sun evenings as they all come home again. Sun lunchtime can be busy too as the Milanese leave the city for lunch. For central Como, exit at Como Sud, which is the first exit you come to. If you are heading for the west of the lake, you can continue to Como Nord which is another seven km/4.2 miles. Parking is difficult in Como, though if you're lucky your hotel might have its own parking lot. You might ask if the hotel can recommend somewhere to park or, failing that, you will have to find somewhere outside of the city center.

Getting Around

On Foot

 Traveling around in Como town, walking is best. It's a small city, the sights are centrally located and the shopping area is virtually a pedestrian one. I say virtually, as in Italy cars or scooters can appear from nowhere, turning a pedestrian zone into a through street – albeit momentarily. Parking is always a problem and you are advised to leave the car in the hotel lot if you're lucky enough to have one, or park the car outside the city center.

For wonderful views, take the funicolare up to Brunate – there are hiking trails that begin here too (more on this in *Hiking*) The funicolare station is in Piazza dei Gasperi, to the right of Piazza Cavour along the lake, and runs every 30 minutes from 6 until 10:30 pm. The trip up to Brunate is fast – six minutes and 30 seconds with a maximum gradient of 55% – making this particular funicolare unique in Europe.

By Bus

 If you want to take a bus in the Como area, online timetables are available at **www.sptlinea.it**. These give timetables for bus trips farther afield too, though the site is in Italian.

By Boat

 Getting around on Lake Como involves boats of course. **Navigazione Laghi** operates an extensive network of ferries and hydrofoils, including a fast service from Como to Colico, at the north of the lake. They have a website with current timetables for services on Lago Maggiore, Garda and Como at www.navigazionelaghi.it, ☎ 800 551801 (toll-free).

Boats can be rented on the lake too, either bare, if you have a licence, or crewed. Bare boats eight m/26 ft long can be rented from as little as €60 a day. Check out **Sailing Days**, Piazza Vittoria 28, Como, ☎ 39 031 301623, www.sailingdays.it. If you like the idea of a smaller boat or even a motorboat, contact **Canottieri Domasao**, Via Antica Regina, 36 22013 Domaso. A pilot's licence is not necessary, though you have to know how to handle the craft. Members of the club take priority, but it's also open to non-members. www.canottieridomaso.it.

Rent-a-Boat at Dongo, ☎ 39 380 843 5253, www.rentland.it, also rents out boats that don't require a nautical license. Prices vary depending on the size of course but a 40 HP boat big enough for six people can be rented for around €175 a day. An hour costs about €65.

Lake of Como Tourist Consortium promotes a variety of cruises on the lake, including weekend dinner and dance cruises in the summer season, ☎ 39 0341 289041, www. lakeofcomo.info.

By Air

 If the idea of a trip over the lake in a seaplane sounds fun, contact **Aero Club Como**, Viale Masia, 44 22100 Como, ☎ 39 031 574495, info@aeroclubcomo. com.

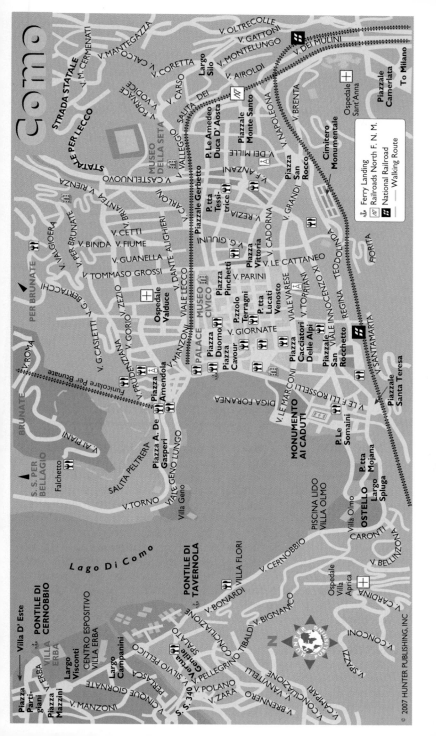

Como

© 2007 HUNTER PUBLISHING, INC

Legend:
- ⚓ Ferry Landing
- Ⓝ Railroads North F. N. M.
- National Railroad
- — Walking Route

Lago Di Como

To Milano

STRADA STATALE

VIALE PER LECCO

S.S. PER BELLAGIO

PER BRUNATE

BRUNATE

Places:
Villa D' Este, Piazza Partigiani, Piazza Mazzini, VILLA ERBA, Largo Visconti, CENTRO ESPOSITIVO VILLA ERBA, Largo Campanini, PONTILE DI CERNOBBIO, PONTILE DI TAVERNOLA, Villa Flori, OSTELLO, Largo Spluga, P.tta Mojana, PISCINA LIDO VILLA OLMO, Villa Olmo, Piazzale Santa Teresa, MONUMENTO AI CADUTI, P. Le Somaini, DIGA FORANEA, Piazza A. De Gasperi, Piazza Amendola, Falchetto, Villa Geno

Streets:
V. ERBA, V. MANZONI, S. S. 340, PERLASCA, V. PELLEGRINO TIBALDI, Genale, V.SILVIO PELLICO, Vertua, V.CONCILIAZIONE, V.POLANO, V.ZARA, V.BRENNERO, V.VANVITELLI, CONCILIAZIONE, V.BIGNANCO, V.CERNOBBIO, V.BONARDI, CARONTI, V.BELLINZONA, V.CARDINA, V.CONCONI, V.SPAZZI, V.CIAPPARI, V.TORNO, SALITA PELTRERA, VIALE GENO LUNGO, V.ROMA, V.AI PIANI, V.G. BERTACCHI, V. VIA GIOERA, V. PER BRUNATE, V.G.CASLETTI, V. GORIO, V. ZEZIO, V. PRUDENZIANA, V. CETTI, V. BINDA, V. FIUME, V. GUANELLA, V. TOMMASO GROSSI, V. DANTE ALIGHIERI, VIALE LECCO, V. MANZONI, V. BRANTA, V. RIENZA, V. CASTELNUOVO, V. CARLONI, V.VALLEGGI, SALITA DEI, V. FORNACE, V. VODICE, V.M. CERMENATI, V. MANTEGAZZA, V. CALCAGNO, V. CORETTA, CARSO, V. OLTRECOLLE, V. GATTONI, V. MONTELUNGO, V. AIROLDI, V. DEI MILLE, V. NAPOLEONA, V. BRENTA, V. F. ANZANI, V. REZIA, V. GRANDI, TEODOLINDA, REGINA, V. SANTAMARTA, FIORITA, V. CADORNA, V. G. GIULINI, V. PARINI, V. GIORNATE, VIALE VARESE, V. TORRIANI, VIALE INNOCENZO XI, V. LE FELLI ROSSELLI, V. LE MARCONI, VIALE ROCCHETTO, V.LE CATTANEO, Largo Silo

Piazze:
P.le Amedeo Duca D' Aosta, Piazzale Monte Santo, Piazza San Rocco, Piazzale Camerlata, P.tta Tessitrice, Piazzale Gerbetto, Piazza Pinchetti, Piazza Vittoria, Pzzolo Terragni, P.tta Lucati Venosto, Piazza Duomo, Piazza Cavour, Piazza Cacciatori Delle Alpi, Piazzale San Rocchetto, PALAZZO MUSEO CIVICO, Ospedale Valduce, Ospedale Sant'Anna, Cimitero Monumentale, Ospedale Villa Aprica, MUSEO DELLA SETA, Funicolare Per Brunate

N

Shopping

 There is always a Saturday market in Piazza San Fedele – sometimes antiques, sometimes local crafts and sometimes a bit of both. In the summer and once a month there's a Sunday craft market along the lake. Check with the local Tourist Office for details. A general market takes place around the perimeter of Como town every Saturday.

SILK

Como produces 80% of Europe's silk and has been doing so since the 14th century when silk worms were first imported. There are boutiques in the center selling high-quality silk merchandise along with a few factory outlets. Scarves, ties and shirts all make good buys.

Mantero, Via San Abbondio 8, Como, ☎ 39 031 321510, supplies the big fashion houses in Paris and Milan.

Binda has an outlet at Viale Geno 6, Como, ☎ 39 031 3861629.

Frey is located at Via Garibaldi 10, ☎ 39 031 267012. They also have a factory outlet outside of Como at Viale Risorgimento 49/51 in Mornasco.

Como is not known as a shopper's paradise, though serious shoppers would have (and should have) done their buying in Milan. However, the center of Como and Via V. Emanuele has some lovely pedestrian shopping streets and, with medieval origins, they twist and turn, full of small boutiques selling beautiful clothes, bags, household goods, glass, underwear, and gelati. If you're there in the winter, I recommend a pre-dinner stroll on a Saturday night, with the shop lights blazing, the bars and cafés full of people drinking creamy hot chocolates and cappucinos. The tiny streets will be thronged with chic Italians, some shopping and other seeing and being seen. If that doesn't make you feel good, the knowledge that over the border in Switzerland the shops closed at 5 pm and the town centers are now dark and empty certainly will!

La Tessitura is close to the center of Como town. It has a big selection of clothing for men and women plus accessories. Beautiful stuff – and a café too. Viale Roosevelt 2/A, www.latessitura.com.

What to See & Do

Como Town

The **Duomo** is one of Como town's finest buildings. Begun in 1396 by the Maestri Comacini, it was finally finished in 1740 with the addition of Filippo Juvarra's enormous dome. Spanning four centuries, the Duomo is a blend of Gothic, Renaissance and Baroque styles. Of particular interest are the early statues of Pliny the Elder and Pliny the Younger on either side of the portal by the Rodari brothers, Tommaso and Jacopo (c. 1500).

Duomo

Duomo doorway detail

There are a number of 16th- and 17th-century tapestries from Ferrara in Italy and from Flanders, 16th-century paintings by Luini, Lanino and Ferrari and some very early items rescued from the demolition of the Basilica di Santa Maria Maggiore, which once stood on the site.

PLINY THE ELDER & YOUNGER

Pliny the Elder and Pliny the younger were both Como-born. Pliny the Elder was a first-century AD Roman statesman and natural history writer. He died in AD 79 while studying the eruption of Vesuvius, which killed thousands. Pliny the Younger, his nephew, was with him at Misenum, across the bay of Naples, before he died. He wrote detailed accounts of the eruption and his uncle's death to Tacitus the Roman historian. Pliny the Younger inherited his uncle's estates around Como on his death, and built not one but two villas from which to enjoy the lake.

Basilica of San Carpoforo

Another building well worth seeing is the **Basilica of San Carpoforo**, one of the earliest Romanesque structures in Como. Reputedly built on the site of a temple dedicated to Mercury, and where the first Christians in Como worshipped in the fourth century, the basilica has a beautifully simple interior with an unusual raised presbytery. The bell tower and the apse date from the 12th century.

The **Basilica of Sant'Abbondio** dates from the 11th century and was built on the site of the early Christian church of Saints Peter and Paul. It has two bell towers and an interesting semi-cylindrical apse. There are some very lovely

Basilica of Sant'Abbondio

frescoes on the interior of the apse which combine local and Tuscan styles.

A very interesting example of a church – because of its age and the fact that it doesn't look very much like a church – is the **Church of San Giacomo**. Though it has been heavily modified and altered over the years, it dates back to the 11th century, though the present façade dates from 1585. Until the 16th century the Church of San Giacomo was the largest in Como. Its interior consists of paintings and frescos from the 18th century.

The **Basilica of San Fedele** dates from the 12th century and has an unusual trefoil interior, though the façade and bell-tower date from around 1900. The **Sanctuary of Annunciata** dates from the end of the 16th century and has an impressive interior. Equally impressive is the 14th-century wooden

Basilica of San Fedele

cross and the 17th-century chapel containing the bones of plague victims.

> ### FEDELE
>
> Fedele was a Roman soldier who was persecuted and imprisoned for his Christian faith. Along with Carpoforo (see the Basilica di San Carporforo) and other Christians, he escaped and headed towards Como. Carporforo and his followers were captured and executed in Como, while Fedele made it as far as Sondrio, south of Como, and was executed in 298 AD. His remains were brought to St Eufemia in the 10th century.

The **Church of San'Agostino** is the only example of an ogival Cistercian church in Como. It dates from the 14th century, was enlarged in the 17th and 18th centuries and finally restored in 1900. There are some examples of 14th- and 15th-century frescos here.

Medieval Como

There are some impressive medieval structures in Como, one of the best being **Porta Torre**, a defensive tower built in 1192 by Barbarossa after the 10 Years war with Milan. Barbarossa used the original Roman design to construct three walls around the town with fortified turrets in the corners and gates in the center of each wall. The Porta Torre is the gate that remains. Two towers still stand: Torre Gattoni and Torre Vitali. There used to be a moat that ran outside of the walls. Today it's a road and is the site of a thrice-weekly street market.

Porta Torre

Baradello Castle

Baradello Castle is on Via Castelo Baradello, just southwest of the city. It was erected in 1158 by Barbarossa to protect the city against attacks by the Milanese from the Brianza plains. The castle itself was reinforced by the Viscontis in the 14th century, but demolished by the Spanish in the 16th century. What remains is the well-preserved tower, 35 m/115 ft high, quadrangular in shape. You can visit the inside of the tower and you get a good view of the city from this spot. ☎ 39 031 592805, open Thurs, Sat, Sun and public holidays from 2:30-6 pm.

Following his defeat by Visconti in 1277, Napo Torriani and his family were captured, put into a cage at Baradello Castle, and left there. Not content with putting him in a cage, Visconti had Torriani himself hung on a wall inside the cage! He died 19 months later.

THE MASTERS OF COMO

The Comacine Masters or the Masters of Como have been called the most important Masonic guild in Europe – a Masonic guild being a group of master builders, masons, sculptors, stonecutters and architects. There is evidence that the history of the Comacine guild lay in Rome, in the Roman collegia that was suppressed by the Barbarians. If this is the case, the skills and methods practiced during the Roman Empire did not die out in the Dark Ages but were continued by the craftsmen and artists in the Comacine guilds of Como. It seems clear that St. Augustine took with him Masonic masters on his way to England in AD 597, and in this way architectural and sculptural knowledge passed from Italy into Germany, France, Spain and England.

Rationalist Como

In the years between World War I and II, Como was the center of modern Italian architecture, and as a result the town has some fine examples. The most influential architect at this time was **Giuseppe Terragni**, a founder member of the Fascist Gruppo 7 and an Italian Rationalist. Rationalism was a reaction against Neo-Classicism and all things impractical and extraneous. Modern materials such as concrete, glass and plastic were used, all produced locally in Lombardy at the time. Terragni and his brother opened their studio in 1927 and much of his best work is in Como, the best examples being the **Casa del Fascio**, the **Santeria Kindergarten** and the **Novocomum**, an apartment block. The Casa del Fascio is an elegant semi-cube with a focus on space and light. Other Rationalist masterpieces well worth seeing are **Casa Cataneo** by Cesare Cattaneo, Via Regina 41 (☎ 39 031 510173), the **Casa Frigerio**, the quietly beautiful war memorial **Monumento di Caduti** and the **Fontana** – an incredible exercise in balance, with its large circles resting on concrete spheres. If you drive into Como from Como Sud, you pass the Fontana; it serves as a kind of roundabout.

After four years in Yugoslavia and Russia during World War II, Terragni returned to Como in 1943. He was a mental and physical wreck. Sadly, he died later that year.

Suggested Walks

 The layout of the streets and roads in this part of the city follows exactly the Roman layout of nearly 2,000 years ago.

From Piazza San Fedele to the Teatro Sociale – the Heart of the City. This walk begins in Piazza San Fedele, which has been the historic center of Como since Roman times. Though there is not much in the way of Roman remains left in Como, archaeologists believe that much of it is buried below your feet – including the Forum. The early Christian church St Eufemia, from the sixth century, stood on the site of the Basilica San Fedele, which dates from the 12th century. (for details see above)

The piazza itself was the hub of medieval Como. A corn market was held there and it also functioned as the unofficial dividing line between the nobility, who lived to the east of the square, and the middle class, who lived to the west.

Palazzo Natta

From the west corner of the piazza walk into Via Natta where you can find **Palazzo Natta**, dating from the late 16th century and attributed to one Pellegrino Tibaldi. The Natta Palace even has the cloister of Santa Eufemia in its garden. Entry is through Via Indipendenza, which runs parallel. The palazzo has recently undergone extensive renovation, particularly of the frescos and plaster work. A Roman theater once stood in Via Natta.

A right turn off this street takes you into Via Adamo del Pero, into Via Bonanomi and then Via Tatti, and finally to Via Vitani. **Via Vitani**, named after one of the more powerful of the warring Como families, is one of the most interesting streets in the heart of Como. It is certainly one of the oldest, dating from the Middle Ages and complete with frescoed houses.

From Via Vitani you turn into Via Muralto, and then see the impressive Duomo (for details and information see above) and the Broletto. The **Broletto**, formerly known as the Palace of Reason and used originally as the town hall, was enlarged in 1215, though the original structure was earlier. It was remodeled again in 1435 and was altered yet again in 1477 when the Duomo was being enlarged. It is not precisely symetrical because there were so

The Broletto

many changes made to accommodate the Duomo. In addition to the local ceremonies that are held here, these days the Broletto is used as a conference and art exhibition center. To the left of the Broletto is the **Church of San Giacomo**, dating back to the 11th century (see above). The interior is less interesting than its façade, however.

Walking around the Duomo, to where the apses open out, you come onto Via Bellini and the classical **Teatro Sociale**. Built in 1813, the theater is surprisingly large. It used to have an arena at the back of the complex, which was used for outdoor performances. The interior is beautiful, was painstakingly restored recently and for those wanting a coffee or a brief rest, the Teatro Sociale also has a café and restaurant.

The Villas of Como – a Walk to Villa Olmo: This begins in the public gardens, running alongside the soccer stadium and the lake front. Situated nearby is the **Tempo Voltiano** (see below) and also Terragni's war memorial to the soldiers of Como killed in the Great War. It's a very imposing structure, though was not so well received when first erected in the 1930s.

Two hundred years ago this area along the lake was considered outside of the city and was mainly pasture land. With the 19th century and Como's increasing popularity, a number of rich families – those who didn't want to stray too far from the city of Como – built their country villas on the land, six in all.

Continuing on and once past the rowing club and the landing area for seaplanes (unique to Como) you enter the area known as the Borgovico. The first villa you come to is **Villa Musa** –not Neo-Classical but Art Deco in style – and the second is **Villa Carminati**, considered to be the best example of Neo-Classicism in the Borgovico. The architect was F. Soave.

Then comes **Villa Saporiti**, which is also known as La Rotonda. It has a beautiful 19th-century interior, unaltered and quite typical of the style in Lombardy at that time. The staircase by Cagnola is well worth a look. Today the villa, built in

Villa Saporiti

1793, is owned by the local government. It has played host to numerous illustrious guests, including Napolean, who stayed here in 1797.

The next villa is **Villa Gallia**, erected in 1615 by one Marco Gallio, who happened to be the nephew of Cardinal Tolomeo. The villa was actually built on the site of a much earlier villa, and the site of Como's earliest museum. These days the local council

Villa Gallia

owns the building, hosting cultural events and exhibitions there.

Continuing over a foot-bridge, you come to the smaller, less elaborate but no less elegant **Villa Parravicini**, and then to **Villa Canepa**. The most interesting feature of this villa is that the main part of the house is raised onto caryatids – sculpted female figures that serve as supports. The next and

Villa Parravicini

penultimate stop **Villa Mondolfo**, a graceful Empire-style building with two wings linked by a central terrace.

Then you arrive at ★★**Villa Olmo** – one of most beautiful villas on Lake Como, and with a park open to the public.

Villa Canepa

Villa Olmo was commissioned by Innocenzo Odelscalchi (a relative of Pope Innocent XI) and designed by the noted Ticinese architect Simone Cantoni in 1797. It was named after an ancient elm tree, which no longer exists.

Villa Olmo makes a good spot for a discrete picnic lunch. You certainly can't beat the view!

Successive owners enlarged and

Villa Olmo

added to the villa, resulting in an enormous property with a magnificent entrance hall, ballroom, a chapel, Italianate gardens, an English park and a 19th-century theater that seats 90. The interior is richly frescoed and decorated. Today it is owned by the Como council, who use it for conferences and exhibitions. It is also the home of the Alessandro Volta Center of Scientific Study, which hosts many international events. Like many of the villas on the lake, it has received a host of illustrious guests in its 200 years, including Napoleon and Garibaldi. (Open 9-12 and 3-6 pm. Closed Mon.)

 When the villa was owned by the Raimondi family, Giuseppe Garibaldi, a frequent guest, had an ill-fated and highly controversial love affair with Georgina Raimondi. A hasty marriage took place followed by an even hastier termination of the marriage-and bitter accusations all round!

The Alessandro Volta Walk: Como City & Brunate:
This begins, like the last walk, in the public gardens, running alongside the soccer stadium and on the lake shore. The first point of interest is the **Tempo Voltiano** in Viale Marconi (see below). Not an old structure but elegant, it was built in 1927 to commemorate the centenary of Volta's death, and functions also as a museum. Heading back into the town center, you come to **Piazza Volta**, a large open piazza named after the scientist and with a statue of Volta by Pompeo Marchesi. Turn right out of the piazza onto Via Garibaldi, and then left into Via Volta. Four blocks down Via Volta on the left-hand side is the birthplace of Volta, beautifully painted in soft ochres and reds. Unfortunately, it is not open to the public, but houses the offices of some local companies. Also in Via Volta, just before Volta's birthplace is the 16th-century **Odelscalchi Palace**, which, though unrelated to Volta himself, is worth a look. In the parallel street, Via Diaz, you can find the small church of **San Donnino** where Volta was baptized and you can even see the baptismal certificate.

The rest of the walk involves the funicolare to Brunate. The funicolare station is in Piazza dei Gasperi, to the right of Piazza Cavour along the lake.

Just above Brunate, in a place called San Maurizio, is **Faro Voltiano**, the Volta lighthouse that was built in 1927 to commemorate the centenary of the scientist's death. The beam from the lighthouse can be seen from 30 miles away and is a fitting symbol for Alessandro Volta's invention of the battery.

San Maurizio, at 2,972 ft, is about 500 ft above Brunate. There is a local minibus service that can take you from Brunate to San Maurizio, but the walk is very manageable for those who are reasonably fit. The views from this point are spectacular. Take a camera and a picnic lunch.

In September 1933, Albert Einstein was in Como. Of Volta and the voltaic pile (the first battery) he declared "The pile is the foundation of all modern inventions."

Brunate to Monte Ballanzone (4,711 ft). This walk begins in Brunate, which you can reach by funicolare (see above). Head for San Maurizio, 500 ft above Brunate and the location of the Volta Lighthouse (see above).

From San Maurizio the asphalted road goes on up to the **Capanna C.A.O**, a restaurant/bar/center, run by the Club

Alpina Operaio, and the **Sanctuary of Santa Rita**, which is the smallest in Europe. The views are breathtaking: to the right is Brianza, to the left is Lake of Como, to the north, the Alps and Switzerland. This is a steep walk and not for those who are unfit.

 When hiking in these regions you are never far from an Alpine hut, known as a **baite**, dispensing food and serving as a place to rest. Between Brunate and Monte Bolettone, you'll find five: Rifugio Cao, Baita Carla, Baita Bondella, Ristoro Boletto e Rifugio del Bolettone.

You can continue walking to **Mount Bolletto** (4,054 ft), **Mount Bollettone** (4,320 ft) and **Mount Ballanzone** (4,710 ft). Depending on your walking speed you could reach Mount Boletone in two hours and Ballanzone in about three hours. You need to be fairly fit to get the best out of this walk. The lush greenery, the purity of the air, the flora and fauna, the silence and the views make this a memorable experience.

Museums

Tempo Voltiano, Viale Marconi, Como, is a Neo-Classical building dedicated to Alessandro Volta (1745-1827), the famous physicist. Displays include Volta's scientific apparatus, letters, documents and his first "pila." (April-Sept 10 am-12 pm and 3-6 pm, Oct-Mar 10 am-12 pm and 2-4 pm. Closed Mon.)

 The "voltaic pile" invented by **Alessandro Volta** consisted of discs of copper and zinc separated by discs of paper or cardboard (soaked in salt water). Attached to the top and bottom of this "pile" was a copper wire. When Volta closed the circuit, electricity flowed through the pile. This first battery was later refined by other scientists, and the French emperor, Napoleon, made Volta a Count for his discovery.

Museo Didattico di Seta, the Silk Museum, Via Vallegio 3, Como, tells the story of the silk industry in Como. (Open 9 am-12 pm and 3-6 pm, closed Sun and Mon, ☎ 39 031 303180, www.museosetacomo.com.)

Civico Museo Archeologico Giovio (Archeological Museum), Piazza Medaglie d'Oro Comasche, Como. (Tues-Sat 9:30 am-12:30 pm and 2-5 pm, Sun 10 am-1 pm. Closed Mon. ☎ 39 031 271343.)

Pinacoteca Palazzo Volpi,Via Diaz, 84, Como. (Open Tues-Sat 9:30 am-12:30 pm and 2-5 pm, Sun 10 am-1 pm. Closed Mon. ☎ 39 031 269869.)

Museo Storico di G Garibaldi, Palazzo Olginati, Piazza Medaglie d'Oro, 1, Como. For those interested in the history of Italy and Garibaldi's campaign for independence. Housed in the same building as the Archeological Museum. (☎ 39 031271343.)

Outside Como Town

Museo del Cavallo Giocattolo, the Toy Horse Museum, Via Tornese 10, Grandate (just outside Como). A little different, this museum has a unique collection of toy horses. There are more than 500 of them, dating from as far back as 1700. Free entry. (10:30 am-12:30 pm and 3-7 pm Tues to Sat. Closed Sun and Mon. ☎ 39 031 382038 and 031 382912, www. museodelcavallogiocattolo.it.)

Museo del Legno, Wood Museum, Riva R1920 center, Via Borgognone 12, Cantù (Como). Another interesting museum reflecting the history of industry and craft, such as carpentry and wood-turning. More than 600 displays of machines and tools for working with wood from the last 300 years. Free entry. (☎ 39 031 7073353.)

The Villas

You can't talk about Como without talking about its villas – there are many of them lining the shore of the lake, some sumptuous or ostentatious, some elegant, some privately owned. Others are hotels or owned by the local government or foundations such as the Rockefeller Trust. It comes as no surprise to learn that today celebrities continue to keep homes on Lake Como.

★★**Villa Olmo**, Via Cantoni, Como. Beautiful 18th-century villa on the lake designed by the Ticinese architect Simone Cantoni. Open to the public, along with its classical gardens. Napolean stayed here, as did Garibaldi and Marshal Radesky.

Villa Olmo

Permanent exhibition of the works of Futurist architect Antonio Sant'Elia (1888-1916). Open daily 8 am-6 pm. Closed on Suns and public holidays. Walkable from Como town.

★★**Villa Carlotta**, via Regina, 2, Tremezzo. One of the most beautiful villas on Lake Como. Began life in the 18th century and was remodeled into a Neo-Classical villa in the 19th century. The villa was bought in 1842 by Princess Marianne of Prussia, who gave it to her daughter Carlotta on her marriage to Prince George of Sax-Meiningen – and so the villa was renamed.

Villa Carlotta (D.A.BI.Mar)

A fine interior, with paintings, furniture and sculpture by Canova, plus 40 acres of gardens laid out by the Dukes of Sachsen-Meiningen and containing some very rare specimens. (Open 9 am-6 pm from April to Sept, 9-11:30 am and 2-4:30 pm from Mar to Oct. ☎ 39 034 441011 and 034 440405.)

Villa d'Este, Cernobbio. One of the grandest hotels in the world (see below under *Where to Stay*). The hotel dates from 1873, but the villa started life in 1568, built by Cardinal Tolomeo Gallio. The grounds are exquisite too, with a floating swimming pool (which doesn't so much float as sit on top of the lake). ☎ 39 031 3481, info@villadeste.it, www.villadeste.it.

★★**Villa del Balbianello**, between Sala Comacina and Lenno, is exquisite, with an equally lovely garden, set on a promontory known as "the hump." Originally a 17th-century structure built on the site of a medieval monastery, it was purchased by Cardinal Durini in 1787. It was presented to the Italian Environmental Foundation by Count Guido Monzino – an explorer who reached the North Pole in 1971. Film buffs might like to know that the final scene in *Star Wars* was filmed in the magnificient gardens here.

On Tues, Sat, Sun and holidays you can reach the villa on foot from Lenno; from the boat landing

Villa del Balbianello

stage it's about a mile. On the other days, the villa can only be reached over the water from the landing stage at Sala Comacina. Between 9:45 am and 3:15 pm there's a motorboat every 30 minutes. ☎ 39 034 45 6110.

Villa Pliniana

★★ **Villa Pliniana**, Torno. One of the earlier villas on the lake, dating from the latter half of the 16th century. It has an almost melancholic air and a touch of romance in its history. One owner, Prince Emiliano Barbiano of Belgioioso, had an eight-year romance with Anna Berthier, Princess of Malpaga, and the Duke of Plaisance's wife. Guests over the years have included Napoleon, Rossini, Bellini and the poet Byron.

Villa Passalacqua, Cernobbio. Late 18th-century villa where Bellini once stayed (see page 235).

★★**Villa Serbelloni** (not to be confused with the Grand Hotel Villa Serbelloni). Built on the site of Pliny the Elder's villa. Guided tours twice daily. The villa is set in 50 acres of parkland and has a breathtaking view of the lake and the mountains beyond. Tours of the garden take place April-Oct on Tues-Sun at 11 and 4 pm. ☎ 39 031 950204.

Grand Hotel Villa Serbelloni, Bellagio. Owned by the Bucher family. Dating from the 19th century the hotel enjoys a wonderful location on the promontory that juts out into the lake. Italian-style gardens with subtropical and Mediterranean plants. An impressive

Grand Hotel Villa Serbelloni

former guest list too, including Churchill, Al Pacino, Robert Mitchum and J.F. Kennedy.

★★**Villa Melzi**, Bellagio. Count Francesco Melzi d'Eril built the Neo-Classical villa in 1808-10. It had one of the very first English gardens on the lake, and is well worth a visit, particularly in spring. Only the gardens are open to the public. (Open April-Sept from 9 am to 6:30 pm, Mar and Oct from 9 am to 12:30 pm and 2 to 4:30 pm. ☎ 39 031 951281.)

Villa Monastero, Varenna. Built in the late 16th century and now a convention center. Originally the villa was a Cistercian convent, founded in 1208 by survivors of the destruction of the Isola di Comacina. The magnificient grounds and some rooms in the villa are open to the public. (Open April to Nov 1st every day, 9 am to 6 pm. ☎ 39 034 1830129.)

Around the Lake

Cernobbio

Cernobbio is the first lakeside village after Como town, and the beginning of a series of wonderful villas which has made this part of the lake so famous. The most well-known villa here is also one of the most famous luxury hotels in the world: **Villa d'Este**. Cernobbio has a beautiful lakefront – the oldest part of the town – and is the third-largest town on the lake, with a population of 7,000. Villa d'Este is unfortunately not open to the wander-ing public. **Villa Erba**, the other imposing villa in Cernobbio, was once the home of Visconti, the famous Italian film director. Now the villa is a conference, exhibi-tion and events cen-ter. Rock concerts are often held in the

Villa Erba

summer in the beautiful grounds, which are open to the pub-lic between May and October on Saturdays, 2-6 pm, and on Sundays, 10 am-6 pm. Visits to the interior of the villa are by appointment only. ☎ 39 031 3491.

★★★Bellagio

Bellagio (APT del Comasco)

Even the name sounds beautiful... bella... and indeed this is considered one of the most beautiful villages in Italy, though how anyone could choose I do not know. The views here are sub-lime. Gabriel Fauré, the French composer, described Bellagio as "a diamond contrasting brilliantly with the sap-phires of the three lakes in which it is set."

Situated on the headland that divides the lake into two branches, Bellagio feels almost Mediterranean, with its palm trees, geraniums and bouganvillea, its cobblestones, cafes and medieval alleyways. **Villa Serbelloni** is here (see *Villas*, above) as is ★★**Villa Melzi d'Eril**, with its archeological museum and gardens. Also well worth seeing is the 12th-century church of **San Giacomo**. Like all popular destinations, Bellagio gets very busy in the summer and the prices are higher than in less touristy spots.

There are many marked trails that take you up out of Bellagio into the hills behind. Two hours will take you to **Monte San Primo** and a breathtaking view!

Careno, halfway between Como and Bellagio (APT del Comasco)

★★Isola Comacina

This is the only island on Lake Como and, until the 12th century, had been continuously inhabited since prehistoric times. As a result the island is considered one of the most archaeologically important in Lombardy. From a Roman stronghold, it passed to the Goths and then the Byzantines, and then to the Longobards in 588 AD. During the 10-Year War of 1118-1127, the island sided with Milan against Como. As a result, the people of Como ransacked the island, burning and destroying all. Architectural investigations suggest there were seven churches on the small island, a number dating from the Paleo-

Isola Comacina

Christian period. Related to this find is the suggestion that some of the Greek slaves of noble birth that Julius Cesar sent to Como may well have lived here. You can get to the island by the private boat service from the village of Sala Comacina.

REMEMBERING THE DESTRUCTION

The last week of June, the local festival of San Giovanni (the oldest in the Como area) is held on Isola Comacino. Mass is said in the ruins of the S. Eufemia basilica, there's a costumed procession and fireworks later at night. The festival remembers the destruction of the island by the Comaschi (the residents of Como) in 1169 as a punishment for its alliance with Milan during the 10-Year War (1118-1127).

Lenno

A small, tranquil village, chiefly know for the **Villa del Balbianello** (see *Villas*, above). The church of **Santo Stefano** and its baptistery is interesting, as is the **Abbey of Acquafredda** above the town, which dates from the 12th century. There are a couple of restaurants, a lakeside promenade, and at night it's very quiet, but you are near enough to Cadenabbia and Tremezzo if you want to find more bars or nightlife. The little church of **Sant'Andrea and Casanova** is from the 11th century, though it has been repeatedly restored. Its bell tower is a particularly noteworthy. The olive trees that grow here were introduced by the Greeks, who were brought here by the Romans.

Near Lenno in Giulino, on the morning of April 28th, 1945, Benito Mussolini his mistress Claretta Petacci were executed at Via XXIV Maggio. Conserved intact is the room in which they spent their last night at the house of Giacomo De Maria, in Via Riale 4.

★★Tremezzo

Villa Carlotta (APT del Comasco)

A very popular resort, Tremezzo gives its name to this part of the lake: "the Tremezzina." The climate here is superb, allowing all manner of plants to thrive: olives, oranges, palms, jasmine and even the equatorial rubber tree. **Villa Carlotta** is at Tremezzo, probably the most famous villa on the entire lake and equally famous for its garden (see *Villas*, above). The town has classic arcades and steep streets. At Rogaro, a hamlet in the hills behind Tremezzo, there is the **Black Madonna**, taken from Switzerland or Germany during the Lutheran reforms.

Menaggio

On the western shore of the lake, Menaggio was very important commerically and strategically to the Romans, who built Via Regina here in 196 AD. The town wasn't discovered by

Menaggio (Catherine Richards)

tourists until the late 19th century, however, though since then they have never left. It's a particular favorite with the English and Germans, and many of the villas above the town have non-Italian owners. Menaggio is bigger than many of the other towns on the lake and is livelier in the evenings as a result. It's very attractive, however, without being too much or *troppo*, as the Italians would say. There are fewer crowds than in Belaggio – or perhaps, being bigger, it absorbs them better. This, and its location, make it worth a visit. The imposing ruined castle dominates the town. The parish church of **Santo Stefano** is worth visiting, Baroque in style though built on the site of a much earlier church. **San Carlo**, dating from the 17th century also should be seen.

Gravedona

Gravedona

On the northwest bank of the lake, Gravedona was a fortified town of some importance in Roman times. From the 10th through to the 14th century it was part of the Duchy of Milan and, because it sided with the Milanese during the 10-Year War in the early 11th century, the citizens of Como ransacked the town and destroyed much of it, as they did the Isola di Comacina. Gravedona is full of character, with narrow alleyways that end at the lake, and houses that seem to lean against one another. There is a wide sandy beach, an open-air lido and three tennis courts to use near the lake.

In 1522 Gravedona became the capital town of the Tre Pievi Republic of the Lario which included Sorico and Dongo. The republic made its own laws, it coined money and was recognized for the craftsmanship of its goldsmiths. The most famous leader of the Republic, Francesco Ser Gregori, who lived in the 15th century, kept Tre Pievi autonomous even under Visconti and Sforza rule.

During the Spanish domination, however – the darkest period for the Como region – Gravedona was handed over to Cardinal Tolomeo Gallio of Como. **Palazzo Gallio**, designed by Pellegrino Tibaldi in 1583, was commissioned by Cardinal Tolomeo Gallio and is now owned by the local council. Gallio, 25 years earlier, had also commissioned Villa Serbelloni.

Santa Maria del Tiglio

The church of **Santa Maria del Tiglio**, complete with octagonal bell-tower, is the best example of Lombard Romanesque architecture in the Alto Lario region (the north of the lake.) Built on the site of a fifth-century building, the church is from the 12th century, its façade with layers of black and white stone. Inside there's a 12th-century wooden crucifix, a sixth-century mosaic floor and medieval frescos.

Opposite Gravedona atop a premontory on the northeastern shore of the lake is the exquisite ★★**Abbazia di Piona**. Founded by the Clunaisci friars in the 11th century, and built on the site of the seventh-century church of Saint Nicholas, the abbey has a beautiful 13th-century cloister, a bell tower rebuilt in 1700 and the church itself has 13th-century frescoes in the Byzantine style. Today, the abbey belongs to the Cistercian brotherhood. (Open 8:30-11:45 am, 2:30-5:30 pm daily. ☎ 39 0341 94 03 31.)

★★Bellano

This town has preserved its medieval character and, though bigger than Varenna (with a population of 3,400), it feels tranquil and a world away from some of the other villages along the lake, which can get very full in the season. Before passing to the dukes of Visconti and Sforza, Bellano (which means "war zone") was part of the Archdiocese of Milan, and was a favorite summer residence of Milanese bishops. The church of

Santa Marta has some interesting artwork and the church of **SS Nasario and Celso** is worth a visit. The latter dates from the 14th century and is attributed to Giovanni di Campione, though, as with

Bellano

many of the churches and villas in Europe, it is built on the site of much earlier structure. The dome, the vaults and the apse were altered in 1567. At night, during the summer, Bellano's lakeshore can be lively with music from the bars and restaurants along the shore.

THE GORGE OF ORREDO

For hundreds of years visitors to Bellano, near Varenna, have written about the Gorge – chasms and caves cut into the rocks by the Pioverna River. The noise of the water and the atmosphere is enough to inspire even the most reluctant tourist to compose a ditty. Locals used to tell children that a house nearby was nothing less than the devil's house – *Ca del diavol*. Scary stuff! Open April 1-Sept 30, daily 10 am-7 pm Oct 1-Mar 31, open weekends and holidays, 10 am-12:30 pm and 2-7 pm. Groups can have daily access in this period with prior booking. Contact info@comune.bellano.lc.it.

Tip: Why not walk from Bellano to Varenna, or vice versa. The paths are well-worn, generally easy on the ankles, and you get beautiful views of Bellagio and Menaggio on the other side of the lake. It's about eight miles and at a comfortable pace will take three hours to complete. There are some hills involved.

Varenna

Varenna

Opposite Menaggio is Varenna, built on a rock at the foot of a mountain and rivalling Bellagio as the most attractive town on the lake. The fact that it doesn't get quite as busy as Bellagio gives it an added advantage.

Varenna originated in the fifth century, and you can still see the original Roman layout of the town in places, a geometric design that allows wonderful views of the lake. It was here that the residents of the Isola Comacina came when their island burned in the 12th century. The reds, terracottas and yellows of its houses, its mild climate and the olive and cypress trees make you wonder whether you aren't, after all, in Liguria. **Villa Monastero**, from the 13th century and originally a Cistercian monastery, has beautiful gardens open to the public. See **Villa Cipressi** as well, with its lovely terraced garden.

Varenna was known for its marble: black "Varenna marble." Nearby is the shortest river in Italy – and one with the most enticing name: *Fiumelatte* (River of Milk). Leonardo da Vinci was quite perplexed by the river as he and countless others failed to find its source. It runs for only 250 m/820 ft; this and the degree of descent create its white, milky appearance. Like many hotels and restaurants in the area, even this closes in the winter (it dries up in the middle of October and reappears suddenly in the second half of March).

The poet E.W. Longfellow wrote about Bellagio and Verenna:

> *I ask myself is this a dream?*
> *Will it all vanish into air?*
> *Is there a land of such supreme*
> *And perfect beauty anywhere?*
> (Cadenabbia 1872)

Near Varenna

Try not to miss the **Sanctuary of Lezzeno** near Varenna. Built in 1690, two years after a miracle took place in 1688, when Bartolomeo Mezzera, passing by his own chapel, saw a plaster relief of the Madonna "crying tears of blood." That was officially recognized as a miracle, and the sanctuary still attracts many religious pilgrims.

Vezio Castle, on a hilltop above Varenna and with great views over the lake, dates to about 1300. In common with

View from the main tower of Vezio Castle (Filippo Besana)

many structures in the area, it is associated with Queen Teodalinda, a medieval ruler of Lombardy. Complete with drawbridge, the castle's setting, the views across the lake and its history make it well worth seeing. On certain days the castle dungeons are open. The hamlet of **Vezio** is historically interesting too. Its origins may be Ligurian-Celtic or even Etruscan.

Adventures

Multi-Adventures

 The **CavalCalario Club** offers a big selection of activities around Bellagio-horseback riding, canyoning, mountain-biking, kayaking, trekking and even paragliding for first-timers! You go up with an experienced paraglider and get to enjoy the experience without worrying too much about technique. cavalcalarioclub@ tiscalinet.it, www.bellagio-mountains.it.

Windsurfing, canoing, sailing, mountain biking are all offered by **TaboSurf**, which is right on the end of the lake at Gera Lario. You can take lessons and rent boats, canoes or mountain bikes. A mountain bike for a day will cost about €25. TaboSurf, Via Prato del Vento, 22010 Gera Lario, www. tabosurf.com.

On Water

The **Como Diving Center** is at Viale Geno 14, Como, ☎ 39 031 300 544.

Those of you wanting to water-ski on the lake can contact **Gli Eschizzibur**, in Viale Geno, Como, ☎ 39 031 306127, or the **Como Water-Skiing Center** in Cernobbio. Located between Villa d'Este and the Versace villa, the center offers water-skiing and canoes for rent. They also have guided mountain biking and rock climbing in the area. Contact Nicole Lucini-Flavio, ☎ 39 0335 6829850 or 031 342232.

Canottieri Domaso also has water-skiing and boarding lessons by reservation. Water-skiing for 30 minutes costs around €60. www.canottieridomaso.it.

For all things connected with sailing, try **Circolo Vela Annje Bonnje**. They offer pilot's licences, sailing courses and boat rental. Viale Perlasca 4, ☎ 39 031 301419, www.annjebonnje. it.

Nautica Domaso has a week-long course for the nautical licence. ☎ 39 0344 85355, info@nauticadomaso.it, www. nauticadomaso.it.

Pensa Aqua Sport rents out kayaks and rowboats below the Royal Victoria Hotel in Varenna between June and Sept. They also conduct their own guided tours of the Lario triangle by boat. ☎ 39 0341 804260, c.dallume@virgilio.it.

Lake Como and the smaller lakes are well-stocked with fish, such as lucci, trout, corregone, and black bass. A local company called **Fishing Land** offers fishing for periods of days or weeks in the season, between March and October/November. Piazza Trieste, Gravedona, ☎ 39 034 489 273, www. fishingland.it.

The **Lake Como Tourist Consortium** also has information on fishing in the area. Contact info@lakeofcomo.info or ☎ 39 0341 289 041.

There are some smaller lakes in the region where you can fish without a licence. You simply pay an entrance fee for the lake. **Circolo La Geretta** has two lakes with a maximum depth of 22 m/72 ft and with gravel bottoms. Trout, chars, pike, perch, carp and sturgeon can be caught. Via Cascina Gera 5, Eupilio, ☎ 39 031 642 254.

On Foot

 Check out **Lombardia and Assorifugi**, an excellent organization specializing in guided treks and hikes throughout the region. Many of these treks take a number of days. www.rifugi.lombardia.it.

 Also contact the **Tourist Office of Lake of Como**, www.lakeofcomo.info.

Suggested Walks

Tremezzo to Rifugio Boffalora: From Tremezzo there is a bus to Argegno, and from there you can take the funicolar to Pigra. From Pigra you hike. The **Intelvi Valley**, through which you pass, is lush and beautiful, connecting Lake Como with Lake Lugano in Switzerland. It's full of small hamlets and villages and is good for the walker. In the winter the valley is known as a ski resort. The Alpine refuge **Rifugio Boffalora** is at a height of 1,250 m/4,101 ft, and offers lodging, food and drink. It's open between May 15th and Oct 15th – though it's a good idea to double-check with the tourist board that it is indeed open. If you stay overnight here you can continue the next day to Mount Galbiga.

From Rifugio Boffalora to Mount Galbiga: Starting from the Rifugio Boffalora, an hour's walk following a narrow mule trek takes you to Mount Galbiga. The Rifugio Galbiga (1,696 m/5,563 ft) is open only in August, so make sure you have sufficient water and food with you if you're there at other times. Mount Galbiga is one of the highest mountains of Valle Intelvi and from here there are stunning views of Lake Lugano, Lake Como, Lake Del Piano and of the Lepontine Pre-Alps.

From Menaggio to Monte Grona: From Menaggio take the bus C13 to Breglia. At Breglia the red and yellow trail signs to Rifugio Menaggio begin.

The **Rifugio Menaggio** (1,400 m/4,593 ft) is situated on the southern slope of Monte Grona (1,736 m/5,695 ft) and affords spectacular views of Lake Como and the surrounding mountains. Another 15 minutes from the Rifugio there is a well-known viewpoint called "Pizza Coppa." From here, the view stretches across the whole of the Menaggio Valley including Lake Piano and Lake Lugano.

The Rifugio Menaggio

At the Rifugio, meals and accommodation are available. Open every day during the summer months and during the rest of the year on Sat and Sun, ☎ 39 0344 37282.

For experienced hikers the Rifugio Menaggio is the

starting point for various hikes in the Pre-Alps, including the three-day Alta Via del Lario hike. From here, the summit of Mount Grona takes another hour and it's not an easy hike.

> **Warning:** Never attempt a hike like the ones above if you are not well-prepared. Every year volunteers have to rescue tourists, lost thousands of feet up, dressed in shorts and sandals, some suffering from hypothermia or exhaustion. Enthusiasm is no substitute for a compass, a map and the right clothing.

Lago di Piano: The small Lake Piano, situated in the Val Menaggio between Lake Como and Lake Lugano, is a protected natural oasis and a breeding place for many types of water birds. This is a very easy, flat trail that would be suitable for children. You pass **Castel San Pietro** on the trail, a medieval fortified group of houses near Brioni.

To get here from Menaggio, take the C12 bus to La Santa. You can return from Piano di Porlezza, also on the C12.

In Nature

Keen **bird-watcher**s might enjoy an afternoon at the nature reserve on the northern tip of Lake Como, in the area known as the **Pian di Spagna**. The name refers to the camps of occupying Spanish troops in the 17th and 18th centuries. A large marshy area (where malaria was common until the 19th century), it is now one of the few humid areas in an Alpine country. Many species of migratory birds stop off here or nest, including the reed warbler and the mute swan. Depending on the season, you may be lucky enough to have snow-capped mountains as a backdrop.

Golf

The Como region has a large number of golf courses, many with lovely views over the lake or the plains. The majority are open to non-members and some are open year-round, though it is advisable to confirm that before arrival.

Villa D'Este Golf Club, Via Cantu 13, 22030 Montorfano. 5,585 m/6,106 yards, par 69. The Villa d'Este Golf Club lies beyond Montorfano Lake, with 18 holes in a very natural landscape. Closed between Nov and Feb. www.golfvilladeste. com.

Monticello Golf Club, Via Volta 4, 22070 Cassina Rizzardi. 6,376 m/6,971 yards, par 73; 6,056 m/6,621 yards, par 72. It's 10 km/six miles from Lake Como. Open year-round, closed Mon. ☎ 39 031 928055.

Menaggio and Cadenabbia Golf Club, Via Golf 12, 22010 Grandola ed Uniti. It was originally founded by an Englishman, a Mr Wyatt, who had retired to the area above Menaggio after colonial service in India. The course was redesigned in 1965 by the club president Antonio Roncoroni. It still feels like an English golf club in part, though in a very Italian setting. segreteria@golfclubmenaggio, www.menaggio.it.

Carimate Golf Club, Via Airoldi, 22060 Carimate. Situated on the estate of the Hotel Carimate (see *Where to Stay*). 18 holes.

On Horseback

 Bellagio Mountains, otherwise known as CavalCalario Club, offers horseback riding in the area around Bellagio. cavalcalarioclub@tiscalinet.it, www.bellagio-mountains.it. In the Pian di Spagna nature reserve, on the northern tip of the lake, there is a **Equestrian Center** that offers lessons and guided horseback excursions through the nature reserve. Via della Torre 7, 22010 Sorico, ☎ 39 (0) 344 84500, info@centroippicodellario.it, www. centroippicodellario.it.

Polo might be the sport of kings but you don't have to be royalty to enjoy it. **Polo Holidays** (based in Canada) arranges vacation trips to the very impressive polo stables in the province of Lecce, near Como. www.poloholidays.com.

On the Soccer Field

 How about watching a **soccer/football game**? Depending on the season, you can buy a couple of tickets for a home game at the stadium in the center of Como next to the lake. It must rank as one the best locations for a stadium, with a fantastic view of the lake if the action on the field doesn't appeal. It's a very small stadium –a capacity of 10,000 or so. Tickets cost between €27and €50.

> **Warning:** Italian football fans can get raucous after a match – lighting firecrackers and flares. If you don't want to get caught up in the celebrations, make sure you don't hang around too long after the game.

In the Kitchen

The **International Kitchen** offers three-day cooking courses in Varenna, with accommodation at the Hotel Royal Victoria. The package includes two lessons with local chefs in their restaurants, sightseeing, tours of local markets and cheese makers. Also offers a similar course where you stay at the Villa d'Este. www. theinternationalkitchen.com.

With Wine

The Tourist Consortium (Coordinamento Turistico Lago di Como) can organize wine-tasting tours of the area. Contact them on ☎ 39 0341 289041, info@ lakeofcomo.info. They are by far the most helpful organization if you need information.

With Language

You can learn Italian at **International House** in Lecco, www.ihteamlingue.com, though Lecco itself is not the most attractive of towns, and you may wish to stay farther along the lake or in Como.

With Art

American artist **Jerry Fresia** offers painting workshops in Mazzegra Azzano with a method handed down from the great Impressionist painters. For those who really want to learn how to paint, ☎ 39 0344 43068, jerryfresia@hotmail.com, www.fresia.com.

Diane Willis runs **Paint in Italy**, offering workshops and "art adventures" in Bellagio in July and August. ☎ 39 212 308-5040, paintinitaly@aol.com, www.paintinitaly.com.

In the Theater

Como is home to the **Teatro Sociale di Como**, with a great variety of performances including opera and classical concerts. You stand a better chance of getting ticket here than you do at La Scala in Milan! The theater itself first opened its doors in 1813, and is well worth seeing even if you don't want to experience a performance of *La Traviata* or *L'Amore delle Tre Melarance*. The interior is beautiful. Ticket prices range from a mere €10 to €70 for the best seat in the house. You can book online too at www.teatrosocialecomo.it.

In the Casino

If you have some energy left you could visit the casino at **Campione d'Italia**. This is a tiny Italian enclave on Lake Lugano, completely surrounded by Switzerland. You can use euros or the Swiss francs in Campione d'Italia, and remember to take your passport as you will be traveling into Switzerland before re-entering Italy. It's about 22 km/12 miles from Como town and nine km/5.4 miles from Lugano. The casino opens at 3:30 pm and closes at 2:20 am.

Where to Stay

There is a good range of accommodations in Como and on Lake Como, but remember that in the north of Italy prices are higher than you would pay in other regions. Many hotels, particularly those on the lake, are closed in the winter (between Nov

HOTEL PRICE CHART	
Double room with tax & breakfast	
€	Under €80
€€	€80-€130
€€€	€131-€180
€€€€	€181-€250
€€€€€	Over €250

and Feb/Mar in many cases). For those hotels on the lake, always specify if you want a room with a view to avoid disappointment. These will naturally be more expensive. If you're on a budget, consider camping, a B&B, an agriturismo or – an under-appreciated option – a restaurant with rooms. Listings below.

Como

Due Corti

Due Corti. A few steps from the lake (but no lake view) and seconds from the historic heart of Como. Completely refurbished over the last few years, complete with stone walls, atmospheric lighting and antiques. This hotel has the atmosphere of a place smaller in size, though it has 65 rooms, a swimming pool, an excellent restaurant and two bars. Some apartments with kitchens also available. Piazza Vittoria 12, 22100 Como, hotelduecort@virgilo.it, ☎ 39 031 3132811. €€€

Hotel Quarcino. A clean, refurbished hotel with air-conditioning. Two stars, so it's basic, but a convenient location near the lake. Ask for a room overlooking the garden. Very close to a church and the bells start early – not a good choice if you like sleeping late. Via Salita Quarcino 4, 22100 Como, ☎ 39 031 303934, www.hotelquarcino.it. €€

Piazzolo. Centrally located – 160 yards from the Duomo and family-owned. One star with 10 rooms, bathrooms en-suite and with telephone. Has its own restaurant. Via Indipendenza, 65 22100 Como, ☎ 39 031 272186. €€

Albergo Terminus. Restored 19th-century building seconds from Piazza Cavour. Intimate restaurant with terrace overlooking the lake for al fresco eating. The fabrics used in the bedrooms, largely local Como silk, will not be

Albergo Terminus

to everybody's taste, though the Junior Suite with its views of the lake is very elegant. Lungo Lario Trieste, 14, 22100 Como,

☎ 39 031 329111, info@albergoterminus.it, www.
hotelterminus-como.it. €€€€

Brunate

Hotel Ristorante Falchetto

Hotel Ristorante Falchetto. A three-star hotel and restaurant, recently restored. Great for those who want to be away from traffic and the noise of the city. It's up in Brunate and involves taking the funicolare for those without a car. Stunning views over the lake. Salita Peltrera 37, ☎ 39 031 3365033, hotel@falchetto.net, www.falchetto.it. €€

Argegno

Villa Belvedere. Halfway between Como and Menaggio. Old-fashioned family-run villa right on the edge of the lake. 16 rooms, all en-suite. Restaurant. No frills here, but friendly people, frescoed ceilings and a pretty terrace. via Milano 8-

Villa Belvedere

Argegno, ☎ 39 031 821116, http://utenti.lycos.it/villa_belvedere. €€€

Locanda Sant'Anna. A restaurant with very pleasant, simple rooms, on the way to Menaggio. You're away from the road here – a car is needed to reach the place. Good prices, nice restaurant, charming cantina where you can taste wine or have an aperitivo. The suite has views over the lake and is worth the extra few euros. Via per Schignano 1, ☎ 39 031 821738, locandasantanna@libero.it, www.locandasantanna.net. €€

La Griglia. Well-known restaurant with 11 bright, clean rooms at a good price. You need a car to get up here, but you escape the crowds and traffic on the lake. Good deals for half-and full-board. Only one room has views of the lake. ☎ 39 031 82 1147, infoweb@lagriglia.it, www.lagriglia.it. €€

Bellagio

Hotel Bellagio. New hotel in the center of Bellagio. Two stars. Some rooms have superb views over the lake. Guests can use the swimming pool, tennis courts and restaurants at the Bellagio Sporting Club. Salita Grandi 6, 22021 Bellagio, ☎ 39 031 950424, hotelbellagio@virgilio.it, www. hotelbellagio.it. €€€

Silvio. Restaurant and hotel, with great views, great food and great prices. Appears in all the guidebooks so book very early to get a room. It's above the village of

Hotel Bellagio

Bellagio. Getting to and from the village involves walking along a very busy road. Take a taxi if you don't like the thrill of Italian traffic. Via Carcano 12, ☎ 39 031 950322, info@ bellagiosilvio.com, www.bellagiosilvio. com. €€

Silvio

Moltrasio

Hotel Ristorante Posta. A family-owned place, in a convenient location (good if you're without a car), moments from the lake in a very pretty spot. A selection of room sizes here includes triples and a couple of quads. Prices are very good. A road passes between the hotel and the lake, but the rooms are air-conditioned and have sound-proof windows. Their restaurant is well-known and the deals for half- or full-board are worth considering. Do NOT confuse this with the Hotel Posta in Como! Piazza San Rocco 5, ☎ 39 031 290 444, info@hotel-posta.it, www.hotel-posta.it. €€

Montorfano

Sant'Andrea Golf Hotel. Ten minutes outside of Como. Very attractive golf hotel with 18-hole course, swimming pool and tennis court. 11 rooms and restaurant. Via Como 19, Montorfano, info@santandreagolfhotel.it, ☎ 39 031 200221, www.santandreagolfhotel.it/home.htm. €€€

Varenna

Hotel Du Lac. Small early19th-century hotel, with four stars. Beautiful location and lovely rooms, some with stunning views. Pretty terrace, meeting room for business guests, even a log fire in the chillier months. Via

Hotel du Lac

del Prestino, 4-Varenna (LC), ☎ 39 0341.830238, info@ albergodulac.com, www.albergodulac.com. €€€

Cernobbio

Villa Flori. Two km from Como, set in its own grounds and with stunning views across the lake. 45 rooms, most with lake views. Restaurant with lakeside terrace for summer eating. ☎ 39 031 33820, info@hotelvillaflori.it, www.hotelvillaflori-lagodi-como.com. €€€€

Villa Flori

Carimate

Castello di Carimate, deluxe room

Castello di Carimate. Fifteen minutes or so outside Como toward Milan, this is especially for golfers and those who have always wanted to stay in a real castle! Dating from the 12th century, it has four stars and 58 rooms. Set in its own park and with an 18-hole golf course, plus an outdoor swimming pool and restaurant. Also has its own shopping arcade. Piazza Castello, 1, 22060 Carimate, ☎ 39 031 79179, hotel@castellodicarimate.com, www.castellodicarimate.com. €€€€

Cernobbio

Villa d'Este. A world-famous five-star hotel with beautiful rooms and an impressive history. Dates from the 16th century. Set in 10 acres – complete with helipad should you need it. Excellent restaurant. Via Regina, 40 22012 Cernobbio,

Villa d'Este

☎ 39 031 3481, info@villadeste.it, www.villadeste.it. €€€€€

Bellagio

Grand Hotel Villa Serbelloni

Grand Hotel Villa Serbelloni. Five-star deluxe hotel. Painted ceilings, glittering chandeliers, gilded furniture, a beautiful setting, and Italianate gardens. A luxurious experience. Former guests include Winston Churchill, JF Kennedy and Al Pacino. Via Roma,1 22021 Bellagio, ☎ 39 031 950216, inforequest@villaserbelloni.it, www.villaserbelloni.it. €€€€€

Bed & Breakfasts

Bellagio

Alla Torretta. Attractive Edwardian villa, family-owned. Also a pizzeria/restaurant. Child-friendly with swings in the garden and facilities such as a microwave in the breakfast room. There's also an apartment available. Via Nuova 3, ☎ 39 031 951272 and 339 7434147, info@allatorretta.com, www.allatorretta.com. €€

Blevio

Villa Edera. Three km north of Como. Two rooms with en-suite facilities and nice views. Via Caronti 15/a, ☎ 39 031 419201. €

Como

In Riva Al Lago. Very basic, but fairly cheap and a central location. Not all rooms have en-suite facilities. Above a bar owned by the same family. Piazza Matteotti, 4, ☎ 39 031 302333. €

Renting a Villa or Apartment

There are plenty of apartments and accommodations where you can cook for yourself to rent on Lake Como and in Como city.

The **Lake of Como** website has a very good selection under "Holiday Houses," www.lakeofcomo.info.

Villa Passalacqua. For those of you who want to make this a once-in-a-lifetime event. A luxurious villa that'll have you wanting to invite George Clooney over for dinner. With a villa like this, he'll probably accept. www.thevilla-passalacqua.com/home.html. €€€€€

Villa Passalacqua

Palazzo del Borgo. Centrally located apartments and studios. Good prices. Piazza S. Teresa 5, Como, ☎ 39 031 575222, www.intouritalia.it. €€

Holiday Lettings. A good organization based in the UK, which allows you to rent directly from the owners. They have a number of properties in the Como area. www.holidaylettings.co.uk.

Villa Vacation. Another UK-based organization with a good selection of properties in the Como area. You deal direct with the owners. www.villa-vacation.com.

Villa Vacations. This time a US-based company with a very good selection of properties on all the lakes. www.villavacations.com.

Meridian Villas. A selection of exclusive villas and more affordable apartments on Lake Como. www.meridianvillas.com.

Vacation Rental By Owner has a number of properties in the Lake Como area. As the name suggests, you deal direct with the owner. www.vrbo.com/vacation-rentals/europe/italy.

Parker Villas. A well known and well organized site with a good selection of properties to rent. Not all large villas; lots of small apartments too. www.parkervillas.com.

Hostels

Como

Villa Olmo Como. A Hostelling International hostel, which requires membership. Very cheap (about €13 each a night) and they serve food. There are family rooms available. Only for those seriously watching their budget, however, and not for those celebrating an anniversary (single-sex dorms). Gets mixed reviews. Open Mar through early Nov. Via Bellinzona 2, ostellocomo@tin.it, ☎ 39 031 573800.

Menaggio

La Primula. Gets great reviews. Good food, great location, very cheap (about €13 a night each) and good facilities, including family rooms. Open Mar through early Nov. Via 1V Novembre 106, menaggiohostel@mclink.it, ☎ 039 0344 32356, www.menaggiohostel.com.

Camping

 A good option if you're on a tight budget, want to relive your youth or are traveling with kids. Clearly not an option if you are looking for rest, relaxation and early nights, however. Pick up a copy of *Italian Camping and Caravanning*, published by the Touring Club of Italy, for reviews of websites around this and other lakes. (ISBN 8836529631.)

Sorico

La Riva. In the north of the lake between Colico and Gera Lario. A fairly simple, green site. Rated three stars. Via Poncione, 3 22010, ☎ 39 0344 94571, www.campinglariva.com.

Au Lac du Como. You can rent bungalows here, rooms, flats and mobile hooms. Rated three stars. Via C.Battisti 18, ☎ 39 0344 84035, www.aulacdecomo.com.

Dongo

Camping Magic Lake. Rated two stars. Via Vigna del Lago, 60 Dongo 22014. €21 (two people and one tent). ☎ 39 0344 80282.

Menaggio

Santa Maria Rezzonico Camping Sole, ☎ 39 0334 50089.

Agriturismi

One of the best ways to have an Italian adventure is to experience agriturismi – to have a farm vacation. Farm getaways are well established in Italy, and there are many available in the Como region. Some of the properties are large, including castles, or vineyards, with their own restaurants, stores selling farm produce, and many rooms for guests and/or apartments to rent. Others are much simpler affairs, with only a couple of rooms. Born out of necessity – when a crisis in agriculture forced farmers and small-holders to think of alternative ways to make a living – agriturismo properties all serve local food, much of it grown or raised on the property, and their aim is to give you an authentic Italian experience. Some have facilities such as swimming pools, and most can provide bikes for rent, or can give advice on trekking or hiking. For practical reasons, many properties do not rent rooms for one night only and, because of their location, many of the properties are not easily accessible by public transport. On the other hand, if you have your own transport, are looking to really get away from it all and to experience something a little different, an agriturismo holiday might well be for you.

The **Lake of Como** website has a selection under "Farm Holidays," www.lakeofcomo.info.

There are a number of websites with similar-sounding names, specializing in agriturismo getaways. One such site is www.agriturismo.it.

Where to Eat

The Food of Lombardy & Como

 As with many of the regions in Italy, the cuisine of Lombardy varies from one locality to the next, partly because of the influence of neighbouring regions, but also because of the difference in climate. Risotto al Milanese, osso bucco, minestrone, polenta, bresaola, costoletta milanese, gorgonzola, and minestrone are all renowned Lombardian dishes and cheeses. Even panettone, the cake traditionally served at Christmas, is Lombardian. Around the lakes, fish dishes feature, as you might expect. Trout, perch, trench are all common. Simpler food can be found too – hearty dishes of meat and polenta or rice.

REGIONAL CUISINE

Como Lake

Pesce in Carpione – Various fish fillets, fried and then marinated in an aromatic marinade.

Lavarelli alla Salvia – Fillet of whitefish lavarets cooked in butter and sage.

Luccio in Stufato – Pike stewed in red wine.

Baccala in Umido – Stewed, dried saltcod. Often served with polenta.

Missultin – Shad, a lake fish, dried and then pressed into special tins called "missolte."

Como Valley & Mountain

Polenta Taragna – Maize meal and buckwheat cooked with butter and cheese from Valtellina.

Polenta Cunscia – Maize meal cooked with butter, garlic and sage.

Gnocchi alla Lariana – Gnocchi made with flour, eggs, milk and herbs. Served with fresh cheese, tomato sauce or with a meat sauce.

South of Como

Cassoela – A rich pork and cabbage casserole, traditionally served in the winter.

Stufato d'Asino con le Cipolle –Donkey braised in red wine and onions.

Polenta e Osei –Polenta served with small birds! These days sometimes lacking the small birds.

 Local Wines: Chiaretto is a light red wine from Bellagio, **Domasino** a sparkling light wine from Domaso, and the villages of **Rogaro**, **Griante** or **Carlazzo** also produce their own light wines. Brianza is home to **Bianco Secco di Montecchia**, a dry white wine much praised by the poets Maggi and Carlo Porta.

There are many good restaurants in and around Como to suit all tastes and budgets. Having said that, prices are higher in Lombardy for food than they are in many other regions in Italy so don't expect to dine out for $15 and still have change for a gelato. In many

DINING PRICE CHART	
For three courses, excluding wine	
€	Under €20
€€	€20-€40
€€€	€41-€70
€€€€	Over €70

cases it's a good idea to phone ahead and reserve, especially in the summer and on Friday and Saturday night or Sunday lunchtime. In the north of Italy, people start to eat lunch between 12:30 and 1:30 pm and dinner starting at 7:30 pm. Remember that Como may be a resort, but it isn't New York, and expecting service at 10:30 pm may be one expectation too many. If you want to eat late, ask what time the last orders are taken – usually 10 pm, though in some cases a bit earlier. In a standard Italian restaurant you are perfectly free to order as you like – don't feel obliged to have a three-course meal if you don't want to. If you don't want a secondi (the meat or fish main dish) and prefer to eat only a plate of pasta (the primo) and a dessert, then do so. You can have an antipasto and a primo, or two primi – any combination you like. The worst that can happen is that the staff will think you have strange eating habits!

AS THE LOCALS SAY...

- *El ris el nas in l'acqua e vör murì nel vin.* Rice is born in water but wants to die in wine.
- *La cazzola senza cudich, l'insalata senza aj, l'è istess d'una spusa senza bagaj.* Cazzuola without cotiche, and salad without oil, is like a wife without children.
- *L'è mej la pulenta a cà sua che pitanza in cà di olter.* Better to have polenta at home than a dish at another's house.

Argegno

La Griglia. A lovely place set above the lake in Località Sant'Anna. Family-run, with garden and terrace for summer eating. Lake view. Lombardian dishes. Except for July and Aug, closed Tues. Book ahead. ☎ 39 031 82 1147, infoweb@ lagriglia.it, www.lagriglia.it. €€

Bellagio

Silvio. Above Bellagio village. It's an uphill hike along a busy road so you might be better off taking a taxi. Very popular restaurant (and hotel) in the Ponzini family for four generations. The fish couldn't be fresher – all caught that day by

Silvio

Cristian, Silvio's son. The cuisine is local, mostly lake fish as you would expect, with fresh homemade pasta, and polenta/risotto dishes. The views across the lake are wonderful, especially from the terrace. Reservations strongly recommended. Via Carcano 12, ☎ 39 031 950322, info@bellagiosilvio.com, www.bellagiosilvio.com. €€

Bistro del Ritorno. Up the hill from the lakefront. Cheap and cheerful place with a good selection of pizza, light meals, pasta, and salad. Friendly owner. Good for a simple and unpretentious lunch. A tiny terrace for summer eating. Via E. Vitali 8, ☎ 39 031 951915. €

Bellano

Pesa Vegia. Small, with great food and lovely location. The terrace is extremely pretty. Very reasonably priced, with half-bottles of wine (not as common as you might think), superb selection of cheeses, a menu for kids and an excellent menu degustazione

Pesa Vegia

(fixed-price menu). Highly recommended. Closed Sun evening and Mon, except Aug. Piazza Verdi 7, ☎ 39 034 181 0306, info@pesavegia.it, www.pesavegia.it. €€

CROTTI

Something worth seeing in this area are the crotti – literally "the caves." Carved into the rock or built of stone, these were originally intended to keep things cool – latter day fridges – but many have been converted into osterie. Some of these are more or less authentic. Sometimes they look like caves and other times not at all. Some of the better-known are the **Crotto Bongiasca** at Pianello Lario, the **Crotto dei Platani** in Brienno, and the **Crotto del Misto** in Lezzeno. Many of these crotti are restaurants serving traditional local dishes. Similar caves, many, many more in fact, are found over the border in Italian Switzerland. Here they are known as "grotti" and serve simple, traditional dishes.

Carate Urio

Fiorini. In a lovely village on the lake, with plenty of things to see after a leisurely lunch, this restaurant serves local cuisine. Lake fish predominates. Great prices and a terrace with a verandah. You can stay here too. It's cheap (€), simple and all rooms have a lake view. Closed Wed. Piazza Minoletti 1, ☎ 39 031 400 149, fioronirist@tiscali.it. €€

Como

Crotto del Lupo, five km/three miles outside the center of Como, heading in the direction of Como Nord and Switzerland. Large country-style restaurant, with efficient and friendly service. Very popular with the locals – so book ahead on the weekend. The menu is a must for meat lovers. Lots of hearty recipes from the region and elsewhere, with some unusual meats to boot (like l'asino). The traditional antipasti are very good and they have a terrace for summer eating. Take a taxi or car to get here. Via Pisani Dossi 17, Cardina, ☎ 39 031 570881. €€

Al Giardino. Not central but in a residential part of town, 15 minute's walk from the center. A 19th-century villa with a lovely interior. Family-run, with relaxed service (often by the owners' daughters) and mainly food of the region. The incredible display of cheeses, prosciuttos and salamis as you enter the restaurant is quite something. Don't come here if you're dieting. Last time I was here I ate four courses! Nice wine list too. In the summer you eat on the terrace. Via Monte Grappa 52, ☎ 39 031 265 016. €€

Antica Trattoria da Angela. A little outside the city center, this is a nice place that serves modern cuisine based on traditional dishes. A varied menu, but lake fish predominates. Known centuries ago for its food, it has a warm, relaxed atmosphere, a good wine list and reasonably priced food. Via Ugo Foscola 16, ☎ 39 031 304 656. €€

I Due Monti. Excellent value, especially the "fixed price menu." Nice atmosphere, friendly service. Good for an economical lunch. Via Lambertenghi 24. €

Cernobbio

Trattoria del Glicine. Lovely place, good service, great food. Innovative cuisine for those who love their food, and it comes at a good price here. Closed Mon. Via Carcano 1, near Piazza Santo Stefano, ☎ 39 031 511 332. €€

Isola Comacina

Locanda del Isola Comacina. It's a beautiful and unusual location: a restaurant on the lake's only island and, aside from the restaurant, it's uninhabited. A boat takes you to the island from Sala Comacina. Fish and local cuisine, but no menu. You eat what they bring until you can eat no more! Closed from Nov until Mar. ☎ 39 0344 56755. €€€

Pesa Vegia

Moltrasio

Ristorante Posta

Ristorante Posta. A family-owned place, in the center of Moltrasio. A convenient location (especially if you're without a car), moments from the lake in a pretty spot. The dining room is elegant, though relaxed, and there's a terrace with trees for summer eating. ☎ 39 031 290 444, info@hotel-posta.it, www.hotel-posta.it. €€

Sala Comacina

Taverna Bleu. Right opposite Comacina Island, this hotel/restaurant is in a fabulous spot – you couldn't get much closer to the lake without swimming. Family-run, serving local dishes prepared with the freshest of ingredients. Many fish dishes, cheese, cured meats and pasta.

Taverna Bleu

You can stay here too – the hotel has three stars. Around €€ for a double room. Closed Tues. Via Puricelli 4, ☎ 39 034 455107, tavernableu@tin.it. €€

Pubs & Bars

There are many bars in the center of the city and most of the bigger hotels have bars open to non-residents.

Nightlife

Many hotels have discotheques and late bars open to non-residents and some campsites have bars and discos. There are also a number of lido discos set up for the local youth that operate along the shores of the lake in the summer. These are generally not for anyone over the age of 17.

Lake Como is not known for its wild nightlife, however, and if that's what you are looking for you will be better of in Milan. Kicking back and watching the sun go down seems to be the preferred evening activity for many of the lake's visitors. After a day spent hiking, sailing or soaking up the sun, who can blame them?

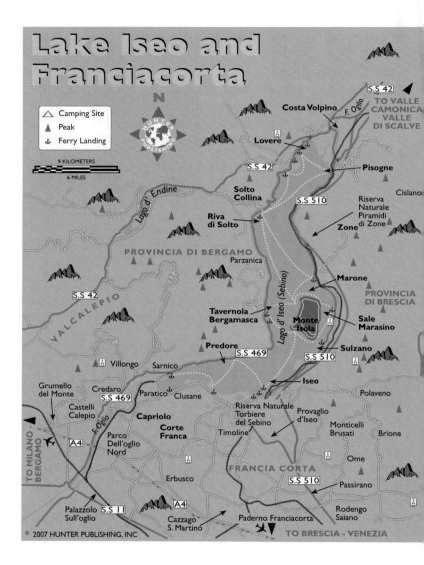

Lago d'Iseo

Lake Iseo is the fourth-largest lake in Lombardy but is little known outside of Italy. It lacks the glitzy sophistication of some of the other lakes and tourism is not as developed as on Garda and Como. This is one of its attractions, as is the ever-changing landscape and its location. Straddling

the provinces of Bergamo and Brescia, it's well-placed for a number of excursions. South, you find the wine-producing area of Franciacorta. East of the lake there's the impressively named Pyramids of Zone, bizarre rock formations with Ice Age origins. The Val Camonica lies to the north of the lake – the longest valley in Italy (55 miles long) and home to the National Rock Engravings Park, with hundreds of prehistoric rock carvings that date from the Neolithic period to the Iron Age. Farther east there's the beautiful town of Bergamo.

Location/Geography

The lake is 15½ miles long and up to three miles wide. It was formed by the Valcamonica glacier and lies at the foot of the southern Alps. It is fed by the Oglio River, a tributary of the Po, which enters the lake in the north near Lovere.

The biggest towns on the lake – and they are not particularly big – are Iseo, Sarnico, Lovere and Pisogno. Monte Isola is the largest lake island in Italy, and one of the largest in Europe.

Economy

Tourism, industry, wine and fruit production, mining, fishing and, a related industry, net production (both for fishing and for soccer goals)!

The Climate

 Lake Iseo has a mild climate but its size means it does not have the pseudo-Mediterranean climate of Garda, Como and Maggiore. You won't find lemon trees in abundance here or masses of palm trees. Instead there are olive trees (the olive oil produced here is prized for its delicacy) and chestnut trees. In April and October the temperature averages around 18°C/45°F, while summer temperatures can reach 29°C/84°F in August – a good few degrees less than on Lake Como or Lake Garda. June and Sept are lovely months to visit – temperatures average around 25°C/77°F. If you want to tale a dip, the water temperature on the surface is around 20-22°C/70°F in July and August.

Getting Here

There are a number of airports within easy reach of Lake Iseo: Bergamo, Brescia, Verona, Milan Linate and Milan Malpensa. Brescia and Bergamo (Orio Serio) are the nearest and are used by low-cost carriers such as Ryanair, which may well be of interest if you are flying from another European destination. Long-haul flights generally land at Milan Malpensa.

By Car

 Avis, Hertz, National Car Rental and Europcar all have a presence at the airports above. If you are driving from Milan, take the Milan-Venice freeway (A4) and exit at Sarnico. Journey time is around an hour and 40 minutes. If approaching from Brescia you take the SS11 after Brescia city, and then the SS510. It will take around 40 minutes.

From Bergamo, take the A4 freeway, toward Venice. Exit at Rovato, then take the SPXI to Iseo. Time is around 35 minutes.

By Train

 From Brescia, along the east coast of the lake to Pisogne. The service is half-hourly and takes around 35 minutes.

Traveling from Bergamo or Milan involves a change in Brescia. Check www.sbb.it for timetables.

Tourist Offices

 Lovere, Piazza X111 Martiri, ☎ 39 0359 62178, turismo.lovere@apt.bergamo.it. Iseo, Lungalago Marconi 2, ☎ 39 0309 80209, iat.iseo@tiscali.it.

Getting Around

 The best method of transport for the lake itself is of course a boat. The road that runs around the lake is not an easy drive on the west, and if you lose your concentration on the east you could find yourself on the bypass – a tunnel effectively.

There are seven boats on the lake, some with bar and restaurant facilites. Information on times can be found at www.navigazionelagoiseo.it.

For exploring the valleys and villages around the lake, and the Franciacorta region, a car is recommended.

Tours

Navigazione Lago d'Iseo organizes a variety of cruises on the lake, from brief two-hour jaunts and full-day excursions including guided tours of the most important towns on the lake, to evening candlelit dinner cruises. ☎ 39 035 971483, info@navigazionelagoiseo.it.

Alessandra Piccinelli is an authorized guide available for tours (in English or Italian) to the Franciacorta region and Lake Iseo, the Val Camonica and the city of Brescia. Contact her at a.piccinelli@iseolake.it.

What to See & Do

★★Iseo

 Iseo town is one of the prettiest spots on the lake. The views over the lake and Monte Isola – which from here doesn't look like an island at all – are lovely.

Lake Iseo

The historic center allows virtually no cars and the atmosphere is tranquil, even at the height of the season. The main square is **Piazza Garibaldi**, with a statue of Garibaldi himself standing on a large, mossy mound.

The small church of **Santa Maria del Mercato** has frescoes from the 14th and 18th centuries. It's here too that regular markets are held: a small market on Tuesday, the main market on Friday, and an antique market on the third Sunday of every month.

Iseo town dock (Catherine Richards)

Other things to see here before you take a leisurely lunch by the lake include the parish church of **Sant'Andrea**, in its present from dating from the 12th century, which has an important Romanesque bell tower. To the right of the unfinished façade is the mausoleum of Giacomo Oldofredi. The **Oldofredi Castle**, dating from the 11th century, was recently restored and now functions as a cultural center and library – it was originally in private ownership.

South of Iseo town is the **Nature Reserve of Torbiere del Sebino**, an area of marshland and former peat bogs, which were heavily exploted in the 19th century. The wholesale excavation of peat has resulted in much of the area returning to its post-glacial state of thousands of years ago and it's now home to a great variety of fish, flora and fauna. If you want to know a little more about this, have a look at www.torbiere.it.

Moving west, you reach the village of **Clusane**, small town with a pretty historic center. Most interesting is the **Castello di Castagnola**, a gift to Giacomo Oldofredi in 1429 from the famous Venetian, Count Castagnola. The fishing fleet here is important, and the boats are peculiar to the area – they're called "naecc" in the local dialect. The castle is privately-owned and not open to the public.

Il Castello di Castagnola

★ Sárnico

Sárnico is an attractive town, though the main road on which it sits can be get busy in the summer. Situated at the end of the lake where it becomes the River Oglio, it has some nice little streets and piazzas, and is a good place for a wander. The center of Sarnico dates from the Middle Ages, with **Via Lantieri** the most important street in the historic center.

The impressive parish church of **San Martino** sits above the medieval center: it was built in the early 18th century, though the belltower dates from the 15th century.

Worth seeing too is the tiny church of **San Nazario and Rocco di Castione**, near the Guerra waterfall. Though little remains of its medieval origins, there are some very old frescoes both within and on the exterior of the church. Another is the church of **San Paolo**, on Via San Paulo, which leads off from the main street in the medieval quarter, Via Lantieri. It was originally built in 1429 on the remains of Sarnico castle, though restoration in the 17th and 18th century left little of the original structure untouched. There are no museums here but there is the **Bellini Art Gallery** – 150 works from the 1500s to the 1700s, housed in Palazzo Gervasoni, dating from the 15th century and once a convent. There are also a handle of Art Nouveau villas here, the finest being the **Villa Faccanoni** and its mausoleum, built by Milanese architect Giuseppe Sommaruga in 1907-8.

Lake Iseo

Riva, one of the oldest and most respected names in the shipbuilding world was set up in 1842 in Sarnico by a local, Pietro Riva. Their boats are synonymous with elegance, quality and craftsmanship. Celebrities who have owned a Riva boat include Brigitte Bardot, Sean Connery,

A Riva boat

Prince Rainier of Monaco, King Hussein of Jordan and Richard Burton

 Something else to buy: If you're looking to taste a few local wines, pop into the **Enoteca Lantieri** on Via Lantieri. A wine store, and next door a simple restaurant and bar with a very friendly, helpful owner.

Predore

Predore

A good jumping-off point for walks and treks in the surrounding hills, and for watersports, Predore has a couple of interesting churches. Driving on from Predore, the road enters a tunnel, and turns north for Tavèrnola Bergamasca, with its view across to Monte Isola. Tavèrnola's protected location makes for a mild climate, and was a favorite spot a century ago for well-heeled visitors who built their summer villas here, long before the cement and stone quarries cut into Monte Saresano.

The drive along the lake continues to Riva di Scolto, about five miles. It has to be said that this is not an easy drive as the road is narrow and in the summer busy with holiday traffic. The rugged beauty of the rocks, the ravines and the coves at Riva di Scolto is best appreciated from a boat.

The village has a pretty center and a popular campsite right on the lake.

Did You Know? The background to Leonardo's *Mona Lisa* is said to have been inspired by the rocks and ravines of Riva di Scolto, with the Adamello mountains on the horizon.

Lake Iseo

★★Lovere

Lovere is the biggest town on the lake, with a medieval center, some impressive architecture including a number of medieval towers (torre) and a fine art gallery, the **Galleria dell'Accademia Tadini** (Via Tadini, ☎ 39 035 960132, acc.tadini@tiscali.net. Open mid-April through mid-Oct, 3-7 pm, Tues-Sat; 10 am-noon and 3-7 pm on Suns and holidays). The gallery is housed in the Palazzo Tadini, and contains a huge collection, including sculpture, prints, bronzes, armor, furniture and lighting, with works by Tiepolo, Bellini,Tintoretto, Lorenzo Veneziano, Strozzi, Hayez and Canova. The gal-

Madonna con Bambino, Accademia Tadini

lery was established by Count Luigi Tadini as a memorial to his only son, who died in Lovere in 1799.

Lovere has some lovely churches. The large **Church of Santa Maria in Valvendra** dates to the late 15th century and contains some interesting 16th-century frescoes. In contrast, the **Cappella di San Martino** is tiny – and the oldest in Lovere. It dates from the 12th century though it was built on the ruins of a much earlier structure.

Lovere was an important center for textile production from the 15th century, when it was under the rule of the Venetian republic – the "Serenissima Repubblica di Venezia." It produced a woollen cloth known as "panno grezzo," which was exported to countries such as Germany and Austria. In the 19th century, Lovere was the first town in the area to initiate steel production, which, though economically important for the inhabitants, has not left the landscape intact.

Lovere

★★Valle Camonica

North of Lovere, on the way to the village of Pisogne, is the beginning of the Camonica Valley – at 55 miles it's the longest in Italy, and contains some 40 villages.

The highlight of the valley is the ★★**National Rock Engravings Park**, at Capo di Ponte, a UNESCO Heritage Site, and the location of more than 150,000 prehistoric rock engravings, spread from the bottom of the valley up to a height of about 3,300 feet.

Prehistoric engravings

The earliest engravings date back to the Palaeolithic era, between 8000 and 4000 BC, before the practice of farming and agriculture. The engravings from the Neolithic period (4000-2800 BC) represent symbols, objects, and figures involved in hunting and farming. The engravings from the Enolithic period (2800-2000 BC) are the first examples of narrative scenes. Historically, this was a period when farming was developed, techniques such as irrigation were introduced, and tools were increasingly made of metal. The engravings continued through the Bronze Age, and the Iron Age, then the Celts

Il Pizzo Badile

and the Romans continued the practice, which incredibly only died out in the Middle Ages.

Just why the area around Capo di Ponte was considered sacred, particularly the peak of **Pizzo Badile**, may well be explained by an optical phenomenon called a "glory." Caused by the relection of light towards its source by a cloud of uniformly-sized water droplets, a glory often produces giant shadows surrounded by colored rings – similar to but smaller than a rainbow. In China this phenomenon was referred to as Buddha's light.

Pisogne

In the Middle Ages, Pisogne was a fortified town, with three entrance gates – evidence of its economic and strategic importance. By the 16th century, Pisogne's trade was primarily in arms and iron, sourced from the Valle Camonica. A weekly arms market was held in the **Piazza del Mercato**. Here too is **Torre del Vescovo** – Bishop's Tower, built in 1250 – where public humiliations often took place. Rebels were punished here, confessions extracted, and in 1518, a number of local women were imprisoned here and later burned as witches. In Contrada della Longa, north of the center, is the church of **Santa Maria delle Neve**, which dates from the first half of the 15th century. Very well preserved, it contains frescoes by the artist Romanino, painted between 1532 and 1543 (open 3-5 pm Tues-Sun, Sat and Sun; also open in the morning from 9:45-11:15 am).

The oldest church in town is **Santa Maria in Silvis**, built in the early 15th century on the site of an earlier eighth-century church. The frescoes are by a local painter, Giovanni di Marone. Recently restored, they were rediscovered in 1933, having been painted out on order of St Calro Borromeo at the end of the 16th century. There are other examples of Marone's work in neighboring churches, most notably in Cislano, in and on the church of San Giorgio. You'll pass the church if you're heading from Marone to see the Pyramides of Zone.

Marone & the Pyramids of Zone

After Pisogne you head south for Marone, with three or four tunnels en-route. After the second tunnel you pass through the little hamlet of **Vello**, with its pretty harbor. The tiny cemetery church here, 15th century, has work by the local artist Giovanni di Marone.

On entering **Marone** you'll see the remains of the Roman villa of **Co del Hela**, dating from the first century AD. Marone is a favorite spot for cyclists, walkers and swimmers, with a history of wool production and dolomite quarrying. Today tourism is the principal industry, along with felt production.

Marone sits on the crossroads of the Roman road, **Val Valeriana**, which runs through the stunning landscape east of the village. Built in the first century AD to connect Brescia to the Valle Camonica via Zone, it's a wonderful place to walk.

★★★**The Pyramids of Zone**, sounding very much like a high-school rock band, and looking like something out of 1960s sci-fi movie, are technically erosion pyramids, formed by a glacier thousands of years ago. Many of these pyramids –

Amid the Pyramids of Zone

known as the fairies of the forest or stone witches locally – have granite boulders sitting on top, protecting them from erosion. You can't drive farther than the village of Cislano. Leave the car here and enjoy a leisurely walk through the woods. The village of **Zone** itself is pretty and has a couple of interesting churches: the 18th-century **Beata Vergine di Lourdes** and the 17th-century parish church of **St. Giovani Ballista**. For those looking to walk, it's the starting point for a number of treks up to the Corna Trentapassi and Monte Guglielmo (1,946 m/6,384 ft).

★★**Sale Marasino** is one of the prettiest villages on the lake – a long-time favorite vacation destination. There are some lovely 16th-century buildings

Sale Marasino

here – **Palazzo Dossi**, **Palazzo Sbardolini**, **Casa Mazzucchelli** and **Villa Martinengo**, and a number of churches. Of these, the 18th century cathedral of **San Zenone Vescovo** is particulary fine.

★★★Montisola

You can reach the island of Monte Isola – or Montisola – from Sulzano, a village a little farther south and a favorite spot for sailing. Once the hunting reserve of the local aristocrats, Monte Isola has a resident population of around 1,700, which is swelled considerably in the summer season by day-trippers

Montisola

and those with second homes here. Most of the local population is employed in the fishing industry, boatbuilding or net building.

Monte Isola is carless, though not traffic-free, since motorbikes are allowed. You can take a bus around the island, walk or rent a bicycle. For bus information ask at Iseo Tourist Office or have a look at the website: www.lagodiseo.org/turismo/guida/montisola. It's a very tranquil place, though less so in the height of the summer and on Sundays, with chestnut groves, olive groves and a scattering of pretty villages that seem untouched by time. The island rises to an altitude of 600 m/1,968 ft and covers about 7½ square miles.

There are a number of villages to visit, each with its own character. **Peschiere Maraglio** is where the boats arrive from Sulzano. It's a fishing village and you will see the tables of drying fish (shad) and the local fishing boats called naecc or nae't in the local dialect. Net-making is big business here too, both for sport and for fishing.

Other villages to see are **Siviano**, on the north of the island, with fabulous views over to the west coast of the lake and the 14th-century Martinego tower. Or visit **Sensole**, walkable from Peschiere Maraglio, well-known for its olive groves and its view of the impressive fortress, the Rocco

Sanctuary of the Madonna of Ceriola

degli Oldofredi. **Cure** is the highest village on the island, with a path that takes you to the **Sanctuary of the Madonna of Ceriola**. The village of **Masse**, near Siviano, is the oldest on the island, with beautiful houses and courtyards. Then there are the ancient villages of **Novale** and **Olzano**, sitting one above the other, with characteristic stone and wood houses.

Excursions

★★★ Franciacorta

Franciacorta is the wine-growing area between Lake Iseo and the city of Brescia, as well as the name given to its wines: Terre di Franciacorta DOC is the still wine (both white and red) while Franciacorta DOCG is the region's sparkling wine – Italy's champagne.

DOCG WINES

DOCG stands for Denomination of Controlled and Guaranteed Origin and is the highest wine appellation awarded to any wine. Franciacorta sparkling wine was awarded its DOCG status in 1995. If you have little time to spend in the region but would like to buy a few bottles of Franciacorta, stop at the store **Le Cantine di Franciacorta** in Erbusco. With more than 1,000 local labels, you're bound to find something you like. And it's not only wine – the store sells a huge range of local products: cheeses, olive oil, honey, preserves, salami, cookies and cakes. Their website, www.cantinedifranciacorta.com, also has listings of local producers with and without websites.

Wine has been grown here for centuries. There is documented evidence of the existence of vines here as far back as second century AD, though the industry was badly hit by the devastating vine louse that hit Europe in the 19th century. It was not until the 1960s that the region started to recover, thanks to the introduction of new grape varieties, the boom in the global wine trade, a new generation of innovative wine producers (driven by passion rather than economics) and, in the 1980s, a nationwide and local tightening of regulations and standards.

Unlike the Champagne region in France, the majority of wine producers are small to medium-sized in Franciacorta, and number fewer than 200 in the entire region. The region covers around 50,000 acres, though the area given over to vineyards is only 4,200 acres. The annual production of Franciacorta DOCG is about four million bottles, while production of Terre di Franciacorta is three million.

Though there are many excellent Franciacorta producers, some of the best include Contadi Castaldi, Bellavista, and Ca del Bosco.

Probably the best way to enjoy the region is to stay a few days – preferably at an **agriturismo**.

Have a look at the site for **Vacanze Verdi** for a list of proper-ties in the area, www.vacanzeverdi.com . The site is only in Italian, though you can click on the map of Italy to select any region. Most of the agriturismos offer apartments as well as rooms, restaurants, and the opportunity to taste or buy their wines (if they are wine producers). The website of **Strada del Franciacorta**, www.stradadelfranciacorta.it, has listings of carefully chosen accommodation, restaurants, wines and local products. In English.

★★★Bergamo

A must-see sight if time allows – one of the most beautiful Medieval and Renaissance towns in Lombardy. It's a place with two halves: Bergamo Alta (the upper, historic part) and Bergamo Bassa (the lower, modern part) and it attracts the urban Milanese on weekends either to their second homes or for day-trips.

 To get an idea of its beauty have a look at Virtual Bergamo on www.bergamotour.it/uk. If you would like a guided tour in English organized by the Bergamo Tourist Office, e-mail them at orio@ turismo.bergamo.it or call ☎ 39 035 320 402. Their website is www.turismo.bergamo.it.

Bergamo had Etruscan and Celtic populations, and was an important Roman municipality. The Commune of Bergamo came into being in 1100, then came under the rule of Milan, followed by

Piazza Vecchia, Bergamo (FototecaENIT)

Venice in 1427. In common with much of Northern Italy, it was conquered by the French and then the Austrians in the 18th century. The lower half of Bergamo has wide streets, shops and a smattering of hotels, though it's the upper town that is the place to see. If you have a car, don't attempt to drive up. Park in the lower town and take the funicolare (7 am-12:30 am).

The **Piazza Vecchia** is a delight. This small piazza was begun in the 15th century, though a number of the buildings here have much earlier origins. The **Palazzo della Ragione** (the town hall) is medieval, the bell tower – the **Campanone** – is Gothic-Renaissance in style, and the town's library, the **Angelo Mai**, is Neo-Classical. Just behind the piazza is the **Cathedral**, dating from the latter half of the 15th century (though the façade is a 19th-century addition). The Cathedral contains an altar piece by Tiepolo.

Check out the **meridian line** in the collonade opposite the main door. If it's a sunny day and you're here in late morning, watch the ray of light move through a hole high up on one of the arches and across the meridian line. When it's on the line it's solar noon precisely.

Alongside the Cathedral is Bergamo's finest building, the 12th-century **Basilica of Santa Maria Maggiore**. Also in the piazza is the 14th-century **Baptistry** built by Giovanni

Santa Maria Maggiore

da Campione and the 15th-century **Colleoni Chapel**, the mausoleum of Bartolomeo Colleoni, who secured his fortune fighting as a mercenary for Milan against Venice, and Venice against Milan. Leaving Santa Maria Maggiore by the south door, you reach **Piazza Rosate**, with the temple of **Santa Croce** (10th-11th century) and a bakery with medieval origins.

Piazza Cittadella lies at the end of the main street, to the west of the Basilica and the Duomo. The **Aldaberto Tower** was begun in the 10th century. There's an archaeological museum here and a museum of natural science. Carry on through the piazza for some great views over the Brescian landscape.

Donizetti

The great composer **Gaetano Donizetti** was born and is buried in Bergamo. His tomb can be seen in Santa Maria Maggiore. He composed over 70 works, including *Lucia di Lammemoor*. The house where he was born can be found at Borgo Canale, just outside Bergamo Alta's walls.

On the road up from the lower town to the upper is an excellent art gallery – the **Accademia Carrara**, with works by Rafaelo, Tiepolo, Botticelli, Mantegna, Lotto, Bellini and Canaletto. (Piazza dell'Accademia 82d, Tues-Sun 9:30 am-1 pm, 2:30-6:45pm, ☎ 39 035 399643.)

Tip: There is a surprising lack of decent accommodation in Bergamo, so it may be better to come here for the day only, or even for half a day.

Adventures

On Foot

 There are lots of walks around Lake Iseo, in the Franciacorta and Valcalepio areas (the region west of the lake in Bergamo province). The Tourist Office in Bergamo publishes a leaflet on various itineraries by foot, bicycle or car. Check **iat.iseo@tiscali.it** and **iat.brescia@ tiscali.it**. **Inntravel**, an award-winning British company, offers a couple of walking vacations (with good accommodation and a gastronomic angle to boot!) on Lake Iseo and in the Franciacorta area. Find out more at **www.inntravel.co.uk**.

On Wheels

 Bike rental is often available at hotels and agrriturismos. The **Bergamo Tourist Board** has cycle itineraries in English or check out their website at www.apt.bergamo.it.

Le Baccanti has scooters available in the Franciacorta region – and vintage Vespas if you think of yourself as an extra in a Fellini epic! Contact them for more details through www.lebaccanti.com.

In the Kitchen

 The **International Kitchen** offers a three-night stay in the Franciacorta region at the luxury L'Albereta Hotel, owned by the famous wine-producing Moretti family. Included in the price is a gourmet meal at the Ristorante Gualtieri Marchesi, a cooking lesson in a local restaurant, a half-day visit to Bergamo, a guided vineyard tour and wine tasting. www.theinternationalkitchen.com.

Le Baccanti has an interesting three-day tour, which includes a day in the Franciacorta, wine tasting, a day exploring Lake Iseo, Monte Isola and Bergamo and the third day in Brescia, where you will have a cooking class with a renowned chef and restaurant owner. www.lebaccanti.com.

On the Golf Course

 Golf di Franciacorta, near Rovato, has an 18-hole and nine-hole course, with all the usual club facilities. Proof of handicap required, and advance booking recommended. There's no website but you can e-mail or phone for information. Località Castagnola, 25040 Nigoline di Cortafranca. Open only from June to Sept, the club is closed Tues. franciacortagolfclub@libero.it, ☎ 39 30 984167.

The **Golf Club of Bergamo** is an 18-hole course designed by the English team of Cotton/Sutton. All the usual facilities. Around eight miles northwest of Bergamo. Via Longoni 12, 24030 Almenno San Bartolomeo. Their website is currently in Italian. E-mail or call for information: segretaria@golfbergamo.it, ☎ 39 (0) 35 640 028.

On the Court

 There's a huge leisure complex called **Sassabanek**, near the Sebino nature reserve and right on the lake. Tennis courts, swimming pools, beach volleyball as well as watersports on the lake. A great place if you're traveling with kids. www.sassabanek.it.

On Water

 The **Sassabanek** leisure complex (see above) is right on the lake – rent windsurf boards, canoes and pedalos here. www.sassabanek.it.

The **Acquasplash Franciacorta** at Corte Franca is a water park that is bound to be a big hit with the kids. A huge park with many different water chutes and slides. Open every day from 9:30 am until 7 pm. www.acquasplash.it.

Liberavventura is an Italian organization based in Brescia. They organize a wide variety of outdoor programs and activities for singles and groups – canyoning, rafting, sailing and kayaking included. E-mail them at guido@liberavventura.it. They also offer paragliding, parachuting, ballooning, hiking, free climbing and ballooning.

At Sulzano the **Associazione Nautica Sebina** offers sailing lessons. ans.sulzano@libero.it.

At the tourist port of Lovere at the northern end of the lake, the **Associazione Velico Alto Sebino** has sailing courses and lessons to suit all levels of ability. Also windsurfing. No guarantee that courses will be in English, though, so check if you don't speak Italian. scuolavela@avas.it, ☎ 39 035 983509.

In the Air

If you'd like to do some paragliding, contact the **Associazione Sportiva Volere Volare** at Via Roma 80, Timoline di Corte Franca, ☎ 39 030 984184. In Brescia there's an organization called **Brixia Flying**, which offers tandem paraglide flights. You do nothing but enjoy the experience, while the experienced instructor does the rest. Flights in various locations throughout the Brescia region. E-mail for information: info@brixiaflying.it.

On Horseback

There are a number of stables in the area, as well as agriturismi with horses available for lessons or treks. Ask at the local Tourist Offices if Italian isn't your strong point as none of the stables listed below have websites.

Il Casale, Provaglio d'Iseo, ☎ 39 030 9883113.

Le Foppe, Paratico, on Via Malighetti, ☎ 39 035 911924.

Le Meridiane, Cellatica, on Via XXV Aprile 88, ☎ 39 030 318627.

With Wine

As you might imagine, there's no end to the wine tastings and tours to be had in the Franciacorta region. If you're staying at an agriturismo that happens to be a vineyard you're in luck; otherwise contact the addresses below or ask at the Tourist Office.

The **Associazione della Strada del Franciacorta** conducts tailor-made wine tours to the vineyards of the region, either day-trips and longer. Contact them at ☎ 39 0307 760870 or associazione@stradadelfranciacorta.

Cellar Tours runs a number of gourmet tours, a day or longer, in the Franciacorta region. You can customize the tour to suit your requirements. www.cellartours.com.

La Montina is a well-known winery surrounding the 17th-century Villa Baiana. It's seven km/4.2 miles east of Lake Iseo in a place called Monticelli Brusati. Have a look at their website and book your visit using their online form. You can call them too at ☎ 39 030 653278.

Where to Stay

Clusane

 Hotel Ristorante Rosmunda. Lovely location, simple family-run place with restaurant. Some rooms with lake view. info@rosmunda.it, www.rosmunda.it. €€

Erbusco

L'Albereta. Sheer luxury this – a 19th-century mansion, superb restaurant headed by Italy's most famous chef, Gualtiero Marchesi, and a spa are just some of its attractions.

L'Albereta

☎ 39 030 776 0550, info@albereta.it, www.albereta.it. €€€€€

Iseo Town

Iseo Lago Hotel. A 15-minute walk from Iseo town, and close to the Sassabanek leisure complex. Modern hotel with attractive décor. Also has a variety of apartments. ☎ 39 030 98891, info@iseolagohotel.it, www.iseolagohotel.it. €€€

I Due Roccoli. Very elegant hotel in its own park. Views over the lake, and a good restaurant, with a pretty courtyard for summer eating. 16 rooms and suites, some with lake views. There's a tennis court, swimming pool and gardens too. Colline di Iseo, Via Silvio Bonomelli, Iseo, ☎ 39 030 982 2977, relais@idueroccoli.com, www.idueroccoli.com. €€€

Hotel Milano. The location is the draw here and the prices – right on the lake at less than €80 a night! A clean, simple, family-run place. There's a restaurant with a terrace and you can rent motorboats and bicycles too. Always specify a lake view to avoid disappointment

HOTEL PRICE CHART	
Double room with tax & breakfast	
€	Under €80
€€	€80-€130
€€€	€131-€180
€€€€	€181-€250
€€€€€	Over €250

and book well in advance. Via Lungolago Marconi 4, ☎ 39 030 980449, info@hotelmilano.info, www.hotelmilano.info. €

Sarnico

Hotel Ulvi. Modern, with a great view over the lake. Secure car parking, a swimming pool and garden with palm trees and olive trees. Rooms are air-conditioned and have satellite TV. A good one if you're traveling with kids. Viale Madruzzo 11, Paratico, ☎ 39 035 912932, www.ulivihotel.it. €€

Corte Francia

Relais Franciacorta. Very comfortable and very popular, so book ahead. Located in the countryside less than a mile from Lake Iseo. The building dates from the 17th century. There's a restaurant here and a vineyard. Access to a car is highly recommended. Via Manzoni 29, Colombaro. ☎ 39 030 9884234,

Relais Franciacorta

info@relaisfranciacorta.it, www.relaisfranciacorta.it. €€€

Riva di Solto

B&B Il Palazzo. In the area known as the Solto Collina between Rovere and Bergamo. Around two km from Riva di Solto. A restored 18th-century palazzo with just a few rooms. There's a suite here that sleeps up to four which could suit a

B&B Il Palazzo

family. Great views over the lake, lovely terrace and garden. Only suitable if you have a car, and there is no restaurant – but a great choice if you want charm and views at a good price. Via dei Fantoni, 16, Solto Collina, Bergamo. ☎ 39 33 9770 0078, info@palazzoincollina.it, www. palazzoincollina.it. €

Monte Isola

In Siviano, try the **Bellavista**, which has exactly what the name suggests. Simple rooms, great prices, wonderful views (remember to clarify that you want a room with a view) and a restaurant. Book ahead – at these prices it gets booked up fast. There's a complimentary taxi shuttle service. Remember, no private cars on the island! Via Siviano 88, Siviano. ☎ 39 030 988 6106, bellavista@monteisola.com or info@ albergo-bellavista.it. €

Apartments & Villas

Castello di Zorzino, in Riva di Solto, has beautiful apartments to rent – open year-round – with fabulous views over the lake. You'll need a car to get here though, or a scooter. Very reasonable rates too. Around €400 a week for an apartment that sleeps three. ☎ 39 035 98243, www.castel-zorzino.com, or www.castelli.net (look under Lombardy).

On www.lake-iseo.com you will find a small selection of apartments, mostly around Lovere, and the very charming, rustic **Casa Teresa** in the village of Artogne. In the heart of Iseo town there's **La Mansarda** – an attic apartment, brightly furnished and with two bedrooms. The owner speaks English. graziap@lombardicom.it, www.lamansardaiseo.it.

Bed & Breakfast

Il Mondo in Casa (The World at Home, www. bebilmondoincasa.com) is a local organization set up by a group of women from Bergamo, with the aim of developing the B&B and self-catering market in the Brescia and Bergamo region. A sizeable number of their properties are in the

Bergamo area (which is good news, as Bergamo lacks accomodation) though they also have a selection of properties near Lake Iseo.

Check out **www.bed-and-breakfast-in-italy.com**. They have a good range of places in the Iseo, Bergamo, Franciacorta and Brescia regions. The site is also in English. Search under Lombardy first then select the province of Brescia.

Agriturismi

If you want to stay in the Franciacorta region, an agriturismo might be a good idea. There are a huge number of farms and/ or vineyards offering anything from a couple of simple rooms to very comfortable accommodation, with restaurant and leisure facilities. Renting a car is almost essential for these properties. The Tourist Offices in Lovere, Iseo, Bergamo and Brescia should have a list of properties in their regions – though they will not be recommendations.

Agriturismo Forest. This is close to Iseo town and to the Torbiere Nature Reserve. Nine rooms including a couple of triples, a restaurant and wonderful views – every room has a view. Red wine is produced here, along with olive oil, honey and jam. There are small farm animals too. It's a good place if you're traveling with young children. Contact them for rates. ☎ 39 030 981640, agriturismoforest@inwind.it, www. agriturismoforest.com.

Ricci Curbastro. An agriturismo at Capriolo, a few miles from Lake Iseo. It's a converted farmhouse on a big estate offering a number of apartments, named after birds, flowers or fruit. Unlike some apartment rentals, all extras are included in the price, so there are no surprises at the end of your stay! Ricci Curbastro is a vineyard too. ☎ 39 030 736094, info@riccicurbastro.it, www.riccicurbastro.it.

Al Rocol. In the heart of the Franciacorta region in a place called Ome, between Lake Iseo and Brescia. Rooms and a couple of apartments in a lovely restored building – this was one of the first vineyards/farms to open up to tourists in the region. Olive oil, honey, grappa and wine are produced here, along with cooking classes (English language lessons too), wine tasting and olive oil tasting courses. Mountain bike rental available. Via Provinciale 79, 25050 Ome (BS). info@alrocol.com, www.alrocol.com.

Camping

 There are a huge number of campsites around the lake – if you know where you want to stay, contact the local Tourist Office for information. Many of the campsites are no frills, just the basics. In high season (August particularly) they get full, so remember to book ahead.

The two campsites below are high-quality, big, and right on the lake.

The leisure complex **Sassabanek** is also a four-star campsite, packed with facilities for those who want them. sassabanek@sassabanek.it, www.sassabanek.it.

The four-star **Camping del Sole** lies a little farther west, between Iseo town and Parzanica. Rent a tent for a week, a mobile home, chalet or even an apartment if you're fond of your creature comforts. Swimming pool, tennis courts, activities for younger kids, bike rental, etc. Via per Rovato, 26. info@campingdelsole.it, www.campingdelsole.it.

Hostels

Lovere has a nice hostel, **Ostello del Porto**, at the harbor, with all rooms overlooking the lake. Each room has four beds with en-suite bathrooms. There's Internet access, swimming pool, free car parking, restaurant and it's wheelchair-friendly. Per-person the cost is around €25 – a group of four would pay about €100 for the room. Via Paglia 70, Lovere. You can book at www.hostels.com. In Bergamo there's the **Nuovo Ostello di Bergamo**. A member of the International Youth Hostels Association, it's clean, big and bright, with wheelchair access, 24-hour reception and bike rental offered. Per-person the cost is around €26 in a shared four-person room, a little less in an eight-bed dorm. Via G. Ferraris 1. You can book online at www.hostels.com or www.ostellodibergamo.it, ☎ 39 035 361724, hostelbg@libero.it .

Where to Eat

REGIONAL DISHES

The provinces of Bergamo and Brescia – Lake Iseo lies in both – feature a ravioli-style pasta dish called **casônsei** (casoncelli in Bergamo) and a another called **polenta e osei** – the osei being little birds cooked until crispy! Polenta is very common, particularly in Bergamo province and around the lake.

Taleggio, the famous cheese, comes from the Taleggio Valley north of Bergamo, while lake restaurants serve lake fish, including **tinca** (tench), **luccio** (pike) and **anguilla** (eel).

Brione

La Madia. Nestled in the green hills east of Iseo town, La Madia is a simple trattoria with a great menu, combining the tastes of the lake, the countryside and the mountains. Great prices too. Via Acquilini 5, ☎ 39 030 894 0937. Closed Tues. €

DINING PRICE CHART	
For three courses, excluding wine	
€	Under €20
€€	€20-€40
€€€	€41-€70
€€€€	Over €70

Clusane

Al Porto. Between Iseo town and Paratico, Al Porto is a lovely trattoria, in a villa that's been in the same family for more than a century. It's a fish restaurant with local specialties. Porto dei Pescatori 12, ☎ 39 030 982 9090, info@ alportoclusane.it, www.alportoclusane.it. Closed Wed outside of the high season. €

Erbusco

Mongolfiera dei Sodi. Tuscan-Lombard cuisine. A good place if you're hankering after a steak. Lovely interior with a terrace for summer eating. Via Olina 18, ☎ 39 030 726 8303. Closed Tues. €€€

Gualtiero Marchesi. Just past his 70th birthday, Gualtiero Marchesi is considered Italy's most famous chef and one of the top chefs in the world. Blow your budget for a sublime experience in a beautiful setting. Via Vittorio Emanuele 11, ☎ 39 030 776 0562. €€€€

Gualtiero Marchesi

Iseo

Osteria Il Volto. Tucked into the corner of a tiny square, this is not so much an osteria (though it once was) but a restaurant with an imaginative menu. If you really want to go to town, there's the menu degustazione at €70. Seven dishes and a meal to remember. It is not expensive, though some guides refer to it as a cheap place to eat. It is not – but it does offer great value for money. Closed Wed and Thurs lunchtime. Via Mirolte 33, ☎ 39 030 981 462. €€€

La Santissima. A nice, inexpensive place with good service. Popular with the locals. At lunchtime, choose the fixed price menu – probably a pasta dish followed by meat. At around €20, you can't go wrong. Via Bonomelli 14, ☎ 39 030 981 083. Closed Mon evening and Tues. €

Marone

Trattoria Glisenti is in the village of Vello on the old coast road between Marone and Pisogne. A simple place serving only fish. Very cheap and a good place for an after-dinner stroll – turn right as you leave the trattoria and walk the now-abandoned road along the lake. Closed Mon. ☎ 39 030 987222. €

Monte Isola

Trattoria del Sole. Lovely setting in Sensole on the lake's island, in a pretty garden complete with olive trees and a view of Val Camonica. Predominately fish, local dishes, though with some options for meat eaters or vegetarians. Via Sensole 17, ☎ 39 030 988 6101. Closed Wed. €€

Rovato

South of the lake in the village of Rovato, the **Ristorante Due Colombe** is a treat. A superb menu of local and regional dishes and a good choice of wine by the glass. Via Roma 1, ☎ 39 030 772 1534, prenotazione@duecolombe.it, www. duecolombe.com. Closed Sun evening and all day Mon.

Sarnico

Al Desco. Great fish in Sarnico's central piazza – Piazza XX Settembre. Appears in a lot of guidebooks, so it's popular. ☎ 39 035 910740. Closed Mon and Tues lunchtime. €€€

Ristorante Pizzeria Amphora. Fish and pizzas in the same square as Al Desco. Piazza XX Settembre 2, ☎ 39 035 910 828. Closed Mon. €€

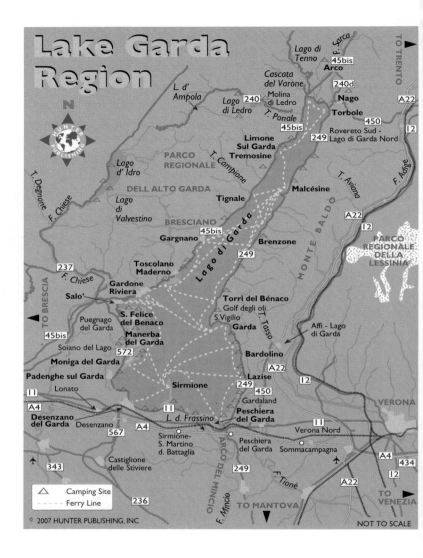

Lake Garda

This is Italy's largest lake, perenially popular, and a great place for watersports and family holidays. This is the one lake that seems both Alpine and Mediterranean. The northern reaches of the lake are quite mountainous, with rugged cliffs. The south, where the lake fans out into the Lombardian plain, is

altogether softer, with more Mediterranean flora. Lake Garda was originally called Lake Benacus, a name of Celtic origin. In 268 AD, the Emperor Claudius confronted the Alamanni at the Battle of Lake Benacus. The Alamanni were routed, forced back into Germany, and did not threaten Roman territory for many years afterwards.

There are a number of beautiful lakeside towns, and lots of strolling or sitting in lakeside cafés to be done. The beautiful city of Verona is a short drive away. If you're traveling with kids, (or even without) Gardaland, Italy's largest theme park makes for a fun day out.

Lake Garda is well-known for its lemon cultivation, but did you know that it is the northernmost lemon-growing area in the world?

Location/Geography

Garda was formed more than 10,000 years ago by a glacier, which, having thrust its way south into the Lombardy plain, receded, leaving the lake. More than 30 miles long, its maximum width is 10 miles, its circumference 100 miles. The maximum depth is 1,135 ft, though 488 ft of that is a moraine deposit (moraine is the name given to the rocks and soil deposited by a glacier). The lake extends over three provinces: Verona, to the southeast, Brescia to the southwest and Trento in the north.

Economy

 Tourism is the primary activity on Garda, along with agriculture, wine production and some industry.

The Climate

 Lake Garda has a temperate climate, and doesn't suffer the cooler evening winds that the other lakes do (so you can leave your cardigan in the hotel). Of all the Northern Italian lakes, Garda has a Mediterranean climate, and has been described as a giant solar battery, resulting in very mild winters.

Average temperature in April and October is 13°C/55°F; in July and August the average is around 25°C/77°F, though August can see highs of 32°C/90°F. May, June and Sept are lovely months to visit – temperatures average 22°C/72°F, and the water is at its warmest in Aug and Sept – 27°C/81°F and 22°C/72°F degrees respectively. Though many restaurants and hotels close during the winter, if you can find some that are open, Garda, of all the lakes, is a great place to visit off-season.

There are, particularly in the north of the lake, local winds that make for great windsurfing and sailing. The wind called the "sover" blows from the north in the morning, while the "ova," from the south, takes over in the afternoon and evening.

Getting Here

By Air

 Verona (Villafranca) and **Venice** are the nearest airport cities, though **Bergamo** (Orio al Serio) and **Milan's** Linate and Malpensa airports are do-able too. The freeways that cut across Northern Italy make the drive from Milan to Garda less than two hours. Verona and Bergamo (Orio al Serio) primarily serve European airlines.

By Car

 Avis, Hertz, National Car Rental and Europcar all have a presence at the airports above. If you're driving from Milan on the A4 freeway (Milan-Venice) you exit at Peschiera del Garda.

By Train

 There's a regular half-hour service from Milan's Central Station to Peschiera del Garda. It takes 80-100 minutes. Check www.trenitalia.com for timetables and to book online. If you are coming from Verona, take the connecting bus service into Verona city; the trains leave from Verona Porta Nuova station and take 15 minutes. See www.trenitalia.com for timetables and to book online.

By Bus

 The **SIA** bus service has some routes between Milan (Autostazione Garibaldi) and a number of towns on Garda's west coast, such as Manerba and Gardone Riviera. You change at Brescia. You can book online at www.sia-autoservizi.it (the site is in Italian only).

Tourist Offices

 There are three main Tourist Offices representing each of the three provinces. Each town on the lake has a smaller tourist information office as well.

Lombardy: Sirmione, Desenzano sul Garda, Salò, Gardone Riviera, Toscolano Moderno, Gargnano, Campione and Limone sul Garda. APT Brescia, Corso Zanardelli 38, 25121 Brescia, ☎ 39 030 45052, www.bresciaholiday.com.

Trentino: Riva del Garda. APT Garda Trentino, Giardini di Porta Orientale 8, 38066 Riva del Garda, ☎ 39 0464 554444, www.gardatrentino.it.

Veneto: Torbole, Malcesine, Torre del Benaco, Garda, Bardolino, Peschiera del Garda. APT Garda, Lungolago Regina Adelaide 3, 37016, Garda, ☎ 39 045 6270384, www.aptgardaveneto.com.

Lake Garda

Getting Around

 The best method of transport for the lake itself is, of course, a boat. For timetables on the ferries and other boats, check www.navigazionelaghi.it.

The local bus company has an extensive service around the lake and the provinces. Check their website, www.apt.vr.it, then look under "Orari e linee." Every town or village that is served appears in a listing with bus route numbers. The same company runs tourist specials to Verona and Venice. As an example, Bardolino to Venice takes 2½ hours. Again, check their website or ask at the Tourist Office.

Tours

Sirmione Boats has a variety of motorboat tours of the lake, from 30-minute tours to the entire day. Generally, they are for groups but contact them for a price if there are fewer than 10 of you. ☎ 39 030 990 5235, info@sirmioneboats.it, www.sirmioneboats.it.

Viaggi Molinari is a local firm that organizes bus tours around the lake (short boat trip included) as well as a host of other trips in area and beyond. Multilingual tour guides on board. Reasonable rates too. A tour of Lake Garda costs around €35. Book online or in their local offices (addresses on website, www.gardalake.it/viaggi-molinari).

Limontours, a local company, offers a range of day bus/boat tours around the lake and farther afield. On Wednesday and Saturday, they operate a lake tour, Friday, Verona and a wine and nature tour to Trentino. Thursday destinations include Milan, Venice, the Dolomites and even Florence. If you're visiting between June 24 and August 27, the company conducts a trip each night to the opera at Verona's Arena. All details are in the company's brochure, which you can download at www.lagodigardamagazine.com/pdf/escursioni_limtours.pdf. Their e-mail is excursions@limtours.it.

Markets

Bardolino . . . . Monday & Thursday
Desenzano . . . . Tuesday & Sunday

Garda . . . . Friday
Gargnano . . . . Alternate Wednesdays
Limone . . . . Tuesday (not the 4th in the month)
Malcesine. . . . . Saturday
Manerba del Garda . . . . Friday
Moniga del Garda . . . . Monday
Padenghe. . . . . Saturday
Peschiera . . . . Monday & Friday evening
Polpenazze. . . . . Saturday
Riva . . . . Wednesday (not the 1st in the month)
Solferino. . . . . Saturday
Sirmione. . . . . Monday & Friday
Salò . . . . Saturday
Tignale . . . . Tuesday
Tremesino . . . . Tuesday
Toscolano Moderna. . . . . Thursday

What to See & Do - Western Shore

★★★Sirmione

The "pearl of all islands and all peninsulas," said the Roman poet Catullus, and indeed Sirmione is a delight, with great views, ancient cypress groves, olive and lemon trees and palms.

One of the best-known resorts on Lake Garda, Sirmione sits at the end of a narrow peninsula that juts northward into the southern end of the lake. On weekends particularly, the town is bursting with weekenders and day-trippers, who throng the elegant streets and make finding a spot to enjoy a coffee a little tough, though mid-week and out of high season it can be remarkably peaceful. Sirmione's sulphur springs have been attracting visitors seeking a cure for over 2,000 years.

The **Rocca Scaligera** (the Scaligera Castle) sits at the entrance to the old town, and was built by the wealthy Della Scalla family from Verona in the mid-13th century. Completely surrounded by water and beautifully preserved, the castle's defensive walls cut the town off from the mainland.

The Rocca Scaligera

Open Oct-Mar 9 am-1 pm, April-Sept, 9 am-6 pm, except Thurs, when it closes at 12:30.

The **Grotto di Cattulo** is one of the most impressive Roman remains in Northern Italy. The villa, dating from the first century BC, may or may not have belonged to the Roman poet Catullus, though it is known that he had a family villa in Sirmione. The entire complex of Grotto di Cattulo was huge, including thermal baths (you can smell the sulphur), pools, shops and gardens, and hosted the likes of Julius Caesar in its day. Many of the objects unearthed during the excavations in the 1950s are on display. The Grotto is at the tip of the peninsula. Walk there by footpath or take the little train, the "Treno del Grotto." The Grotto is open daily.

The Grotto di Cattulo

 Historians believe that the Grotto di Cattulo may have been more than a spa and getaway. It may well have been where Roman emperors, traveling through the northern reaches of the Empire, met important political and military leaders.

Near Sirmione is the lovely church of **San Pietro in Mavino**, with stunning views over the lake. It's the oldest church in

Sirmione, with eighth-century origins. Remodeled in the 11th and 14th centuries, the church contains some beautiful 13th- and 16th-century frescoes.

★★★Desenzano

Desenzano

One of the most popular resorts on Lake Garda, and the largest, with a population of 25,000. Desenzano is very attractive, with bustling restaurants and harbor cafés, and it makes a good base for exploring the lake, particularly if you're looking for nightlife.

Named after the wealthy Roman, Decentius, who established a country estate here, by the Middle Ages it had become a prosperous, though much fought-over city, and it was in this period that the town's impressive castle was built. In 1426 Desenzano passed to the Venetian Republic and began to enjoy a period of prosperous tranquility.

A must-see relic is **Villa Romana** (second-fourth century AD) with its superb mosaic floors – over 2,150 square feet have survived – depicting scenes of hunting and local life. Discovered in 1921, the villa lies on the ancient road between Brescia and Verona. It is at Via Crocefisso 22. (Open

Villa Romana

Mar to mid-Oct, Tues-Sun 8:30 am-7:30 pm; between Oct 15 and the end of Feb it closes at 4:30 pm.)

The **Antiquario** (Via Anelli 22, open Tues and Fri-Sun, 3-7 pm) has a collection of archaelogical finds excavated from the villa. Desenzano's **Archaeological Museum Rambotti**

Lake Garda

Villa Romana mosaic

has some impressive Bronze Age exhibits, recently unearthed from the peat bogs southwest of town. One of the most impressive objects is an oak plough, more than two m/ 6½ ft long, that dates from 2000 BC. The Museum is in the 15th-century former convent of Santa Maria de Senioribus, Via Anelli 7. (Open Tues, Fri-Sun and holidays, 3-7 pm.)

See too the town's cathedral – **Santa Maria Maddalena** – remodeled by the local architect Todeschini between 1586 and 1611. The façade dates from 1702. Inside there are 27 enormous paintings by 17th-century Venetian artist, Andrea Celesti, and an unusual *Last Supper* by Tiepolo.

The town's main square is **Piazza Malvezzi**, the site of weekly markets since the 15th century (these days they're on Tues). The port, Porto Vecchio, also dates from the 15th century. It was from here that corn was traded for olive oil, citrus fruits, wine and cloth from the northern part of Lake Garda.

THE FOUNDING OF THE RED CROSS

The hills south of Desenzano have huge military and historical significance, for it was here, amid the carnage of war in 1859, that the International Red Cross was born. Napolean III and Victor Emmanuele II fought as allies and won a number of decisive but bloody battles against the Austro-Hungarian empire. Their victory gave life to the quest for Italian union, but at huge cost. Thousands of troops died in just a few days, and Desenzano and the hill towns became huge hospitals full of thousands of wounded.

Henry Dunant, from Geneva, on his way to seek concessions for Algeria from Napolean, was so horrified by what he saw in the town of Castiglione, and deeply moved by the dedication of those who tried to care for the wounded of both sides, that he was prompted to set up a permanent organization that would provide professional care for those hurt in battle. That organization was established in 1863 by Dunant, and became known as the International Committee of the Red Cross.

There is a museum – the only one in the world – dedicated to the history of the Red Cross in Castiglione delle Stiviere. (Open Oct-Mar 9 am-12 pm and 2-5:30 pm, April to Sept 9 am-12 pm and 3-7 pm.) In the town of Solferino, there is a simple monument erected in 1959 to commemorate the centenary of the campaign's bloodiest battle, and the founding of the Red Cross. The town also has a very moving site, the Cappello Ossuaria behind the church of S.Pietro. This chapel contains the remains of 7,000 mostly French and Austrian troops.

Moniga (Ernst Stavro Blofeld)

The **Valtenesi** is the area north of Desenzano, on the west coast of the lake, made up of seven districts, including the villages of Padenghe sul Garda, Moniga and Manerba. It's an area of olive plantations and vineyards – producing some of

Brescia's best-known wine and great olive oil. The region has many example of early medieval architecture, with Moniga being particularly impressive.

Historians believe the village **Moniga** was named after the goddess Diana Munichia, the Greek goddess of the full moon. The old town is surrounded by castle walls that date from the 10th century, built against the threat of invasion by Hungarians. The castle itself is rectangular, and well-preserved, given its age. Down by the harbor, with its view across to Sirmione, there are a number of bars, restaurants and trattorias.

 Chiaretto is the name given to the wine produced around Moniga. First made at the end of the 19th century, the wine has a fruity and floral bouquet, with a dry, full-bodied flavor.

Manerba

A short drive from Moniga is Manerba, a district made up of five villages, and often known as Rocca di Manerba for its eighth-century fortress – of which nothing remains. The district spreads itself along the promontory, and below

Manerba

the rocky outcrop there are a number of lovely coves and pebbly beaches. There's a causeway here to the tiny island of **San Biagio**, also known as the Rabbits Isle. The parish church of **Santa Maria**, near the lake, dates from the seventh-eighth centuries and was built on the site of an earlier church. Nearby there are Roman ruins. Its interior, with superb frescoes from the 12th and 13th centuries, is well worth a look.

 Kid-Friendly: If you're traveling with small children, the local **beaches Il Torcolo** and **La Romantica** are considered safe and child-friendly.

The peninsula of San Felice has a lovely view across to the lake's largest island, the private **Isola di Garda**.

Just outside the village is the **Carmine Sanctuary**, consecrated in 1482. It was suppressed in 1770 and lay empty nearly 200 years. In 1952 the Carmelites returned, and the sancuary has been restored. It contains some fine 15th- and 16th-century frescoes. If you want to swim here, head for **Baia del Vento**.

★ ★ ★ Salò

The capital of the Upper Garda in the Brescian province, Salò is an elegant town with a population of around 10,000. In spite of an earthquake at the turn of the 20th century, a number of fine houses from the 15th and 16th centuries survived, as did the cathedral. In the 14th century, Salò became the seat of the Consiglio della Magnifica Patria, essentially the regional council. Some 600 years later, it was the seat of another council – Mussolini's puppet republic. The headquarters of the republic was at the village of

Santa Maria Annunziata

Barbarano, in the 16th century Palazzo Terzi Martinengo.

See the late Gothic cathedral in Salò, dedicated to **Santa Maria Annunziata**. With some Renaissance additions to its façade, the church contains work by Romanino and Moretto. The **Museo del Nastro Azzurro** is a military museum, housed in **Palazzo Fantoni** (16th century), with items from the 18th century through to 1945. Via Fantoni 49, ☎ 39 0365 208 04.

Gasparo da Salò is the name used by one Gasparo Bertoletti (d. 1609) who was born in Salò. He was a founder of the Brescian school of violin makers. Though the claim is now disproved, he was credited with developing the violin in the shape we know today.

★★★ Gardone Riviera

Gardone Riviera (sfonditalia.it)

With the highest winter temperature in Northern Italy, Gardone Riviera has been a popular resort for well over a century. Towards the end of the 19th century, German doctors began to promote the therapeutic effects of its mild, dry climate – particulary if visitors were prepared to stay quite a while. The development of the town as the place to be was due to one Luigi Wimmer, who was so impressed by his own rest cure that he decided to build the first grand hotel here in 1881. It wasn't long before European royalty and the wealthy began flocking here in search of a little R&R. For his trouble, Wimmer became Mayor of Gardone Riviera.

Known internationally as a garden city (though it's hardly a city) for the richness of its planting, Gardone also has a famous botanical garden, the **Giardino Botanico Hruska**, with more than 500 species of plants. Via Motta 2. Open Mar 15-Oct 15, 9 am-6 pm daily.

Gardone has more than its fair share of villas, two of the most famous being **Villa Alba**, an early-20th-century imitation of the Acropolis now owned by the town, and **Villa Fiordaliso**, a beautiful lakefront villa that played host to Mussolini and his mistress, Claretta Petacci, in the autumn of 1943. The villa is now a hotel and restaurant (see *Where to Stay* and *Where to Eat*).

The most famous resident of Gardone Riviera was Gabriel D'Annunzio (1863-1938), whose house and adjacent museum, **Il Vittoriale degli Italiani**, named for Italy's victory over Austria in 1918, is a must-see sight for its beauty and its incredible collection of objects. There are 33,000 books, an aircraft, the 1913 Fiat that he drove to capture Fiume in 1919 (see below), a coffin that served as a day-bed, and a bronze embalmed tortoise -- D'Annunzio's former pet. It's fascinating and fun, though extremely popular, so get here just as it opens to avoid the crowds. (The museum is open April-Sept, 8:30 am-8 pm daily; Oct to end Mar, Mon-Fri 9 am-5 pm, Sat and Sun 9 am-5:30. The villa itself is open April-Sept, 9:30 am-7 pm, closed Mon. From Oct-Mar it's open 9 am-1 pm and 2-5 pm. Closed Mon.

GABRIEL D'ANNUNZIO

Gabriel D'Annunzio was a journalist, poet, novelist, dramatist, war hero and a political agitator. He fought with the Italian army and air force during the First World War, and in 1918 he flew a dare-devil 700-mile round-trip to drop propaganda leaflets – penned himself – onto Vienna. Immediately after the war he was responsible for the capture of the port of Fiume (now Rijeka, Croatia) in 1919, leading a band of like-minded agitators and nationalists. Though his nationalism found sympathy with the general population, the Italian government was less keen and he was forcibly removed from Fiume (which he held on to for two years!) by the Italian navy in December1920.

After this, D'Annunzio retired to Garda, wrote, campaigned and generally led a hedonistic existence until his death from a stroke in 1938.

His literary influence on generations of Italian writers is uncontested, and the impact his work had across Europe was considerable. His reputation became tainted because of his relationship with Mussolini and Fascism, though D'Annunzio never became directly involved in the Fascist politics of the day.

Reading Material. *If D'Annunzio interests you, or you would like to read more about Europe immediately before the "war that was to end all wars" (and changed Europe irrevocably), or if you have an interest in the history of flight, pick up a copy of the excellent* **The Air Show at Brescia 1909** *by Peter Demetz. Published by Farrar, Straus & Giroux (2002).*

Toscolano-Maderno

The next village you meet is Toscolano-Maderno. Aside from the two towns that make up its name, it includes another seven villages and one of the best beaches on the entire lake. Toscolano was the site of the ancient "Benacum," the Roman name for Lake Garda, which, according to legend, was swept away by a freak storm in the third century BC. Maderno was the administrative center for the western part of the lake for 500 years from the ninth century. It was also the summer home of the powerful Gonzaga dynasty, the princes of Mantua. The **Palazzina del Serraglio** (17th century) was built by the Mantovan princes primarily for amorous get-togethers.

The parish church of **Sant'Ercolano**, right near the lake in Maderno, dates to the 18th century and contains paintings by Veronese and Celesti. The Romanesque church of **Sant'Andrea** dates back to the 10th century, though it was remodeled in the 12th century. In Toscolano, the tiny **Sanctuary of the Madonna of Benaco** (not to be confused with the church of the same name that sits on a hill above the town) was built in the 10th century on the site of a much earlier temple dedicated to Jupiter. This is one of the oldest centers of Christian worship in the Garda area. Also in Toscolano is the parish church of **Santi Pietri e Paolo** (1584). It contains several interesting pieces of wooden sculpture and many paintings by Andrea Celesti.

Also worth a visit is the **Ghiradi Botanical Garden**, with plants from five continents. ☎ 39 0365 71449.

Toscolano has a long history of **paper making** – it was a flourishing industry as far back as the 14th century – and became synonymous throughout Italy with quality. The first print shops in the area were set up in the villages of Messaga and Cecina. A Bible was printed here in 1487 that Martin Luther used for his translation into German. There are still many paper businesses in the Toscolano valley – it's the area's largest industry.

Gargnano

Gargnano

Known primarily for the famous yachting regatta – the **Centomiglia** – Gargnano has Roman origins. In the 13th century the Franciscans arrived and the lovely church of San Francesco was founded. As the story goes, on his return from Syria, Saint Francis received a gift of some land and a small house on the shores of Lake Garda, which some believe was at Gargnano. Take a walk along the lake heading north to Calino, to the church of **San Giacomo**. It's just over a mile. Sitting amid citrus groves, this is the oldest building in Gargnano and one of the oldest Christian churches on the lake. The church dates from the 10-11th centuries and has several 13th-century frescoes on its façade, one of which, on the lakefront, is of the patron saint of travelers, San Cristoforo.

Villla Feltrinelli, designed by architect Solmi, was used by Mussolini as his summer residence during the puppet republic in the years 1943-45. For the last few years it's been a luxury hotel (see *Where to Stay*).

Lake Garda

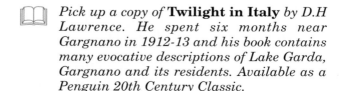

Pick up a copy of **Twilight in Italy** *by D.H Lawrence. He spent six months near Gargnano in 1912-13 and his book contains many evocative descriptions of Lake Garda, Gargnano and its residents. Available as a Penguin 20th Century Classic.*

The lake is already narrowing at Gargnano, but as you drive north, through Tignale, Campione and onwards to Limone sul Garda, the lake narrows further still, and the landscape changes considerably. Tunnel after tunnel has been cut into cliffs that plunge into the lake. This part of the lake is wind-surfing heaven, known throughout the world for the quality of its surfing, The World Championship has been held here since 1979 and the place is invariably packed with windsurfers – particularly on the weekend. If you're a windsurfer yourself, or have always wanted to learn, have a look at the listings in *Adventures*, below.

Tignale

At Tignale, if you're driving, head up to the **Santuario di Montecastello** – the views are amazing. Down by the lake itself, the harbor, called "Pra de la Fam" in local dialect, has an impressive limonaia – a lemon house. Restored, the limonaia is open to the public. For information, contact Tignale Tourist Office at info@tignale.org.

Tignale is the collective name given to six hamlets sitting below Mount Denervo (1,500 m/4,921 ft) with a total population of around 1,300. It's a good place for a gentle stroll or a more serious hike. There are endless olive grooves, ancient stone walls and paths along old mule tracks. The **walk** to the village of **Aer** from Tignale proper is easy, and passes through the **Valle dei Canài**, a pretty place with small waterfalls and inviting mountain water pools. Or walk to the village of **Prabione**, a little farther, a little steeper, and have lunch in this tiny stone-built village. There's a free shuttle bus that connects the villages with the beach at Pra de la Fam.

Limone

Oddly enough, the name Limone is a happy coincidence for a town that was at the center of the historic lemon production in the area. Historians believe the town's name has nothing to do with citrus fruit but may derive from the Latin word for boundary – limen – referring to the historic boundary that ran north toward Riva.

There is evidence that the Franciscans grew lemons as far back as the 13th century, though it wasn't until the 17th century that lemon-growing took off. By the 18th century, lemon production was a full-scale industry. Special glass houses were built to protect the lemons between November and March. These were called limonaias. In the 18th century, lemons were grown on an almost industrial scale, and at that time countless greenhouses were built to protect the plants during the winter. Recently the historic value of these limonaias has been appreciated.

★★★Riva del Garda

At the northern tip of the lake, Riva del Garda lies in the province of Trentino, below the impressive Monte Brione. It's the second-largest town on the lake, with a population of 13,000. An important town commercially as early as the 11th century, Riva fell under the control of Verona, Milan, and Venice in the years prior to the 16th century. It suffered a lot of damage in the 18th century as the French and the Spanish fought it out, though its fortunes revived, and for most of the 19th century – when under Austrian rule – it was an extremely popular resort. In the early years of the 20th century Riva welcomed as many as 38,000 tourists annually (mostly German and Austrian), including the likes of Thomas Mann, Nietzsche, Kafka, Stendhal and D.H. Lawrence. Lawrence stayed here for a fortnight in 1912, before finding cheaper lodgings farther down the lake at Villa.

There are two defensive structures worth seeing in Riva: the **Rocca** (12th century), which today houses the city's Museo Civico, and in Piazza III Novembre, which faces the lake, the **Torre Apponale** (1220 – shown at right in the picture on the following page). The tower (35 m/115 ft) was extended in 1515, and functioned at various times in its history as a corn and

Riva del Garda (Fototeca ENIT)

salt warehouse, a bank, a prison, and during the First World War, as an observation post. The tower's bell dates to 1532. On top of the tower is an angel, Riva's symbol. Also in the piazza is the **Palazzo Pretorio**, built around 1370. High up on the east façade are the arms of the Prince Bishop Giorgio di Neideck (around 1510) which were carved over the Lion of San Marco, symbol of Venice.

The castle, the Rocca, contains the **civic museum**, with archaeological exhibits and a collection of 14th- to 20th-century art. Open Tues-Sun, 9:30 am-6:30 pm.

Churches worth seeing include the **Inviolata** (1603), built by the Governor of Riva, Gaudenzio Madruzzo, who employed an unknown Portuguese architect. Its exterior is plain, its interior anything but. Considered the finest Baroque church in Trentino, Inviolata's interior is sumptious in the best Baroque tradition, with gilt, stucco, marble and wood carving. The church contains work by Palma il Giovane, Guido Reni, Paolo Ricchi and Teofilo Turri.

Just outside Riva, around two miles to the north, is the splendid ★★★**Cascate del Varone** (Varone Waterfall), 80 m/ 262 ft high. The water crashes down through a narrow gorge formed by erosion over 20,000 years. The rate of erosion is just under an inch per year. There's ample car-parking here, a picnic area and visitors get close to the waterwall via walkways. (May-Aug, open daily, 9 am-7 pm; Mar, April and Oct, daily, 10 am-12:30 pm and 2-5 pm; Nov-Feb, Sun and holidays only, 10 am-12:30 pm and 2-5 pm.)

★★Lake Ledro

West of Riva in the mountains is Lake Ledro, set in stunning scenery, and for those who want to, walkable from Riva. The shortest route is four miles – drive from Riva along the SP37 and then leave your car at the beginning of the SS240. You could continue driving to the lake, passing Molina di Ledro and then walk around the lake (eight km/five miles) or you can head up to Cima d'Oro, for superb views of seven lakes, the Dolomites and the Appenines. But, at 20 km/12 miles and 5,900 ft elevation, this is for serious hikers only.

The area around Lake Ledro is archaelogically fascinating. In 1929 a Bronze Age settlement of pile dwellings (lake dwellings raised on stilts) was discovered, and one has been reconstructed around ★★**Molina di Ledro**. Excavations unearthed some superb examples of bronza ax heads and triangular-bladed daggers, along with earlier Stone Age tools. The quantity of amber discovered – used primarily for jewelery – points to the existence of a barter-trade between Central European pile dwellers. The museum, **Museo delle Palafitte**, houses the objects discovered during the excavations. (Open July-Aug, daily, 10 am-6 pm, Mar-June and Sept-Nov, 9 am-1 pm and 2-5 pm. Closed Mon.)

Arco

Sitting behind Riva is the ★★**Castello di Arco**, built to defend the Sarca Valley against armies from the north. Sited high up on a rock overlooking the lake, the oldest part of the castle dates from the sixth century. In the 12th century the castle, essentially a bell-tower, was appropriated by the Arco family, who built a palace tower here among the cypresses and olive trees. Little of it remains today.

The town of Arco, below the castle, was a fashionable resort in the 19th century and, thanks to its mild climate, has been dubbed "the Nice of Trentino."

Lake Garda

There are a number of interesting 19th-century structures – built as the health resort developed – but also earlier Renaissance and Baroque churches and palazzi. The church of **Santa Maria Assunta** was built on the site of a much earlier church, that was, without ceremony, demolished. In its place, in 1613, the new church was built, inspired by architect Palladio, and is one of Trentino's most important churches. In the square in front of the church is the Fountain of Moses, with the Arco family crest, the Baroque town hall and the **Palazzo Marchetti**, built in 1550 by Felice Arco.

Castello di Arco

FESTIVAL FUN

If you're around Arco in late February/ early March, check out the carnival. It harks back to the days when Arco was part of the Hapsburg empire, and was a favorite resort for the court. In addition to the traditional street parade, there are costumed balls, events for the kids, concerts and plays – and free gnocchi!

Torbole

At the mouth of the River Sarca is the resort of Torbole, sitting beneath the impressive 2,000-m/6,000-ft Mount Baldo. Tobole today is known as windsurfers' heaven, thanks to the fact that

motoboats are pro-
hibited on this
stretch of the lake,
and to the the
ever-present
winds, the morn-
ing Pelér and the
afternoon Ora,
which blows from
the south. There
are international
surf competitions

Torbole

from May through to Sept, including an early June surf festival that attracts more than 20,000 people. A short distance
inland from Torbole is **Nago**, which is well worth a wander.
See the 13th-century church of **San Vigilio**, the Baroque
Trinità church, and the house of the 19th-century Italian
poet Gazzoletti.

AN AMAZING FEAT

The Santa Lucia Valley lies between the Adige Valley and Lake Garda. In the 15th century, only an ancient Roman road ran through it. In 1439, the
Venetians were at war with the Viscontis of Milan,
who controlled the southern half of the lake. At the
suggestion of a Greek sailor, the Venetians sailed to
Razzone at the the end of the River Adige, and then,
incredibly, dragged 25 boats and six galleys over
Monte Baldo to Lake Garda. At Ponale, the Venetians defeated the Milanese and then took Riva on
May 5, 1440. A very impressive feat.

What to See & Do - Eastern Shore

★★Malcésine

Lying in the province of Verona, Malcésine is one of the most
attractive towns along the eastern shore of Lake Garda, with
a well-developed tourist infrastructure. The swimming
around the town is known to be good, there are lots of opportu-

Malcésine

nities to windurf, cycle or hike, though, if you wish to do nothing, the town has plenty of cafés and restuarants.

The town has Roman origins, followed by years of occupation, before being granted independent-city status in the 12th century, with the right to mint its own currency and pass its own laws. The impressive castle, the **Rocco Scaligero**, was built by the Bishops of Verona in the 12th century, on the site of a sixth-century castle. It was made a national monument at the beginning of the 20th century, and today houses a small natural history museum dedicated to the geology, flora and fauna of Monte Baldo. This is also the place to come if you want to know just how the Venetians got those boats over Monte Baldo! Also on show are the sketches made by Goethe when he was here in 1786. (Open Apr-Oct, 9:30 am-6:30 pm daily, Dec-Mar, 10 am-4 pm on Sat and Sun).

The historic center of Malcesine is very attractive and the parish church of **Santo Stefano** is worth a visit. It contains some 17th-century altars, a 16th-century altar piece by Girolamo dai Libri and a 15th-century ciborium (a communion vessel).

Hiking Tip: On the slopes of Monte Beldo in the San Zeno valley is the **San Benigno and Carlo Hermitage**. Benigno and Carlo were hermits, who lived between the eighth and ninth centuries. The Hermitage sits 800 ft above sea level, so it's a tough climb. You'll need about three hours if you're fit.

Monte Baldo

Looming above Malcésine is the impressive Monte Baldo. This limestone ridge rises to around 2,218 m/ 7,000 ft and stretches for more than 50 miles between the lake and the Adige Valley. Known as the

Rifugio Monte Baldo

Botanic Garden of Europe for its incredible variety of flora, there is a superb view to be had at the top: the Venetian and Lombard Pre-Alps, the Po Valley, and the Dolomites. Nor do you need to hike up to appreciate the view. The new cable car takes you up nearly 1,760 m/5,800 ft to Tratto Spino in around 15 minutes. Not only that, but the cable car has rotating cabins, guaranteeing panoramic views. You can take bicycles with you for a small fee. Operates April 1 to Nov 1. Around €16 round-trip, ☎ 39 045 740 0206.

Torri del Benàco

Torri del Benàco

Driving south from Malcesine, through the Riviera degli Olive, you pass a number of small villages: Assenza, Brenzona and Pai, with several attractive beaches, until you reach Torri del Benàco. Called Castum Turriam by the Romans, it was an important stop between the towns of Garda and Riva in the north and was, from the 10th century, considered the controlling center of the lake. The remains of **Scaliger Castle** are here, built in 1383 by the ruling Della Scala family to defend the important harbor and fortified town. The castle today contains a small museum, with displays on the local industries – olive oil, fishing and citrus fruit production. There are also some rock engravings dating from 2,000 BC. Open Apr-May and Oct, 9:30 am-12:30 pm daily, Jun-Sept, 9 am-1 pm, 2:30-7:30 pm, Dec, 2:30-5:30 pm on Sun. The church of **Santa Trinità** has frescoes from the 14th century and is well worth a look. Alongside the church is the 10th-century **Torre (Tower) Di Berengario**.

★★★Punta San Vigilio

Torri del Benàco and the beautiful Punta San Vigilio immediately to the south are known to be among the most exclusive of all the resorts on Lake Garda. Fans over the years have included writer André Gidé, poet Stephen Spender, Sir Laurence Olivier and Vivien Leigh, the great Maria Callas, and a touch of royalty provided by Prince Charles and King Juan Carlos of Spain. There's a locanda here (**La Locanda L'Albergo San Vigilio**). One of the oldest hotels in Italy, it comes highly recommended, if your budget allows. If your

Punta San Vigilio

budget doesn't allow, you can stop for a drink at the nearby taverna and appreciate the tranquility and the sublime view. For details of the locanda see *Where to Stay*, below.

The beautiful 16th-century **Villa Guarienti** is the work of the Venetian military architect Michele Sammichele (1484-1559), who was commissioned by a wealthy lawyer from Verona, one Agostino Brenzone. More of Sammichele's work can be seen in Garda, just a couple of miles south, and in Verona. The villa itself is not open to the public.

KID-FRIENDLY

The **Parco Baia delle Sirene** is a private beach area in Punta San Vigilio with reclining chairs and loungers, a children's playground with organized activities, ping pong tables, a picnic area, plus a snack bar and ice-cream parlor. It's a perfect place to spend the day if you or the kids are tired of sightseeing. You pay a fee to enter.

★★Garda

The town that gives its name to the lake (and not the other way around), Garda is an attractive place, with over a mile of lakeside promenade, most of it traffic-free, lined with bars and restuarants. This is a small but lively place without the noise or too many of the day-trippers that some of the southern lake towns see. Narrow alleys, cobbled streets and tiny piazzas characterize the old town.

The name Garda comes from the Lombard word "guardia," meaning lookout or watchtower and in the 12th century the name, which had already been applied to the area around the town, was used for the lake itself, previously known as Benàco. The historic center of Garda is surrounded by its ancient walls, which surround a small piazza – once the port. In the piazza there are some fine historic buildings: the **Palazzo dei Capitani** (15th century) in Gothic-Venetian style, the **Palazzo dei Fregoso**, built for a wealthy family from Genoa, and the **Palazzo Parlotti**, with its loggia, designed by Sammichele in the early 1500s. The 16th-century church of **Santa Maria Maggiore** in Piazzale Roma has a 15th-century cloister and work by Palma il Giovane. The bell tower was built in 1571.

QUEEN ADELAIDE

Otto I at the defeat of Berengario

Sitting high above the lake at Garda there was once a castle, scene of dark goings-on in the 10th century. Queen Adelaide, successor to and widow of the murdered Lothair of Arles, was abducted by one Count Berengario of Ivrea, who named himself King of Italy and attempted to legitimize the title by forcing Adelaide to marry his son. When Adelaide refused she was locked up in the castle. A monk discovered her, and spent some time plotting her escape, which happened a year later. In 951, Otto I of Germany invaded Italy, Berengario was killed and Adelaide and Otto were married. Otto later became Holy Roman Emperor, and died in 973. He was buried next to his first wife – Edith of Wessex, who happened to be Alfred the Great's grand-daughter.

Bardolino

Synonymous with the wine that takes its name, the village of Bardolino sits on a natural harbor created by the headlands of Cornicello and Mirabello. There is evidence of prehistoric civilizations – pile dwellers – prior to it becoming an important Roman camp. Once a city-state, it was sold to Verona in 1193. The wine industry in the

Bardolino

area took off once Bardolino passed into the hands of the Venetian Republic.

San Zeno

There are three interesting early churches in or around Bardolino. **San Zeno**, eighth-century, belonged to the monastery of Verona, who built it for collection of local taxes or "tithes." The layout is the original Latin Cross, with six red marble columns. **San Severo** is considered the most important church in town. Built in the ninth century, it was remodelled 300 years later. It contains 12th- and 13th-century frescoes depicting the

The Creation of Eve, San Zeno

Apocalypse and the Recovery of the Cross. In the hamlet of Cisano, the parish church of **Santa Maria** dates to the 12th century, with some 16th-century frescoes.

The wine museum at the **Cantine Zeni** is interesting (Via Costabello 9, Mar-Oct, Mon-Fri, 9 am-1 pm and 2-6 pm, Sat 9 am-1 pm), as is the **Museo dell'Olio**, in Cisano, dedicated to the story of olive oil production. Displays include a 19th-century water-powered press and a host of other tools and implements. (Open 8:30 am-12:30 pm and 3-7 pm, Mon-Sat.) If you're a wine-lover, or simply a landscape-lover, you may be interested in following the **Bardolino Wine Route** organized by the Bardolino Wine Consortium. The Wine Route includes 71 wine producers and stretches from Garda down to Pachengo. The consortium's website is currently only available in Italian, though the map is fairly clear. www.winebardolino.it/ita/strada.php. The Bardolino Tourist Office can give you more details. (Piazza Matteotti 53, ☎ 39 045 721 0078.)

San Severo

The **Wine Festival** takes place in Bardolino in October – again, ask for the dates from the Tourist Office.

Lazise

In the days when the area was in the hands of the Venetian Republic, Lazise was the main port and it retains a number of buildings from that era, including the Customs House, which had previously been built as an arsenal by the powerful Della

Lazise

Scala family. It was the Della Scala family who built the town's walls – which still survive – in the 14th century. The name Lazise comes from "laceses," which means "place on the lake." It's a charming village, with a pretty harbor and has a well-developed tourist infrastructure.

Under the Venetians, Lazise became a central hub on the lake: all tranported products, be they grains, olive oil, paper, or cloth, had to pass through the Customs House. Its history is quite interesting. From being the place where dynamite was produced, it later became a textile factory, and then the headquarters of the local Fascist Party.

The **Castle** in Lazise, which sits in the Villa Bernini park, was first built in the ninth century, to protect the town from the Hungarians. Much of what remains dates from the 11th century. This is one of the best surviving castles in the Lake Garda area, still retaining its five towers and keep. The arms of Bartolomeo and Antonio Della Scala can still be seen on the entrances, in spite of Emperor Maximilian's attempts to get rid of them. Speak to the Tourist Office about visits.

 Lazise locals had an uneasy relationship with the Della Scala family, whose coat of arms included a dragon. They used to say: "La giustizia del mondragòn la ghe dà torto a chi g'ha rasòn" (The justice of the dragon punishes he who is right).

The church of **San Zeno** (13th century) and the church of **San Nicolò** (12th century) are worth a visit. San Nicolò sits by the harbor, and was consecrated again in 1953 after being used for years as a store room, theater, a barracks, home and a movie theater! On the north wall is a fresco depicting *Madonna Enthroned with Child* from the 14th century.

KID-FRIENDLY

Italy's biggest theme park, **Gardaland** will be a sure-fire hit if you are traveling with kids. Or even if you're not! Among 38 attractions, the Magic Mountain rollercoaster and the Blue Tornado are probably the scariest, while smaller kids will love Fantasy Kingdom, with its talking trees and singing animals. Be warned: Gardaland is very, very popular. You can avoid waiting in line to enter by booking your tickets online; they're good for any date. Adult entrance is around €26. From mid-June until the first week of Sept, Gardaland is open continuously from 9:30 am-midnight. www.gardaland.it.

Peschiera del Garda

One of the biggest ports on the lake, Peschiera del Garda is an important center for tourism. Named Piscaria by the Lombards for the vast quantity of fish here, it is the one town on the lake that has retained its military aspect. The town is surrounded by a **star-shaped wall**, rebuilt and extended by the architect Sammichele for the Venetian Republic in 1556. The Austrians added two forts a couple of hundred years later. The church of **San Martino** was rebuilt in 1822 on the site of one of the oldest churches in the province of Verona. The interior is surpisingly modern, however. The work of Pino Saoncella, it was decorated in 1937.

Santuario della Madonna del Frassino

A couple of miles outside Peschiera, near Lake Frassino, is the **Sanctuary of Madonna del Frassino**. Built in the 16th century and renovated in the early 1900s, the sanctuary contains a beautiful frescoed cloister, works by Paolo Farinati and Andrea Bertanza and 17th-century frescoes by Bernardone Muttone il Giovane. The sanctuary is a place of great religious importance, thanks to a vision of the Madonna that appeared to a local farmer here, Bartolomeo Brogglia, in 1510.

 Tip: If you're looking for a quiet, simple and economical place to stay, complete with a sense of authenticity, you can stay at **Casa Francescana**, a hostel attached to the Sanctuary. There are a number of rooms available, singles, doubles, triples and quads, and a restaurant with simple, local cuisine for around €15. A double room in high season costs around €55. www.casafrancescana.org.

The ★★**Sigurtà Garden Park** lies five miles from Peschiera on the edge of the Mincio National Park. There are 125 acres of woods, lawns, trees and planting, which began life in the mid-17th century as a walled-garden. Internationally renowned, the park is a must for garden lovers, and for those who want a cultivated stroll. If you don't like walking or have kids with you, there's a small train that does a round-trip of some five miles through the park. You can also rent golf carts or bicycles. Snack bars and picnic areas are available

Sigurtà Garden Park

as well. (Valeggia Sul Mincio, ☎ 39 045 637 1033, www.sigurta.it. Open Mar-Nov, 9 am-7 pm. Last entrance at 6 pm.)

Excursions

★★★Verona

The Roman Arena

Only 20 miles south of the lake, this is a must-see destination for those traveling to Lake Garda. The setting for Shakespeare's *Romeo and Juliet* (the Capulets and the Montagues did exist, the rest is primarily fiction), Verona is best-known for the superb **Roman Arena**, which dates from the first century AD. With an interesting history – it served as a red-light district in the Middle Ages and was the setting for public executions in the Renaissance – the Arena today is a marvelous open-air venue for

Castelvecchio

opera, with seating for 20,000 spectators! The season runs through June, July and August, and a night at the opera is highly recommended. Book well ahead though – this event is world-famous. You can book online at www.arena.it.

Sacra Famiglia (Mantegna), Museo di Castelvecchio

Castelvecchio, the castle, was built in the 14th century by Cangrande II della Scale, and was used thereafter by all of Verona's rulers. Today it houses the city's **museum and art gallery**, with works by Tintoretto, Pisanello and Veronese (Corso Castelvecchio, open Tues-Sun, 9 am-6:30 pm, ☎ 39 045 806 2611). The bridge that runs through the castle and across the Adige River is called the **Ponte Scaglieri**. Part of the original design of the castle, this bridge, along with the Roman **Ponte Pietra**, was restored after retreating Germans destroyed it in 1945.

Corso Porta Borsari leads to **Piazza delle Erbe**, once a Roman forum and herb market, and now considered the heart of the city. There's a regular market here, some lovely buildings and lots of bars and cafés where you can unwind. Adja-

Ponte Scaglieri and Castelvecchio

cent is the **Piazza dei Signori**, former political and financial center of the city, with its central statue of Dante, and some wonderful palazzi, including the 15th-century **Loggia del Consiglio** (not open to the public).

The **Mercato Vecchio** is here as well, and for some great views over the city take the lift to the top of the 12th-century **Torre Lamberti** (closed Mon morning).

Verona's **Duomo** was begun in the 12th century, completed in 1423, and tweaked in the 17th century. It's a mixture of Romanesque and Gothic, and contains interesting art, including a painting by Titian. More charming perhaps is the church of **San**

San Zeno Maggiore Cloister

Triptych detail (Mantegna), San Zeno Maggiore

Zeno Maggiore in Piazza San Zeno, built between the ninth and the 12th centuries to house the remains of Verona's first bishop and patron saint, the African San Zeno. The church contains a triptych by Andrea Mantegna.

For a bit of greenery, cross the river and visit the **Giardini Giusti**, a small 14th-century garden designed by Agostino Giusti. You can climb the stone turrets here, and the monster balcony for some great views of the city. (Via Giardino Giusti 2; small charge to enter.)

LA CASA GIULIETTA

La Casa Giulietta (Via Capello 23) was never the home of the Capulets, nor was Juliet serenaded as she stood on the balcony – it was added to the house in 1923. Romeo's house, in Via Arche Scaligere, probably did belong to the Montague family, though it's not open to the public.

To stay in Verona, book ahead, particularly in the high season. Try **Hotel Gabbia d'Oro** (www.hotelgabbiadoro.it) if budget is no option, for luxurious and intimate rooms in the heart of the city. For cheaper stays, try **Hotel Aurora**, with a terrace that overlooks Piazza Erbe. Basic accommodation, clean and comfortable, in a great location. Around €120 for a double room. www.hotelaurora.biz.

For dining try **Al Pompiere** (Vicolo Regina d'Ungheria, near Piazza delle Erbe, ☎ 39 045 803 0537) or **Osteria al Duomo** (Via Duomo 7a, ☎ 39 045 800 4505). For a relaxed drink try **Al Mascaron** on Piazza San Zeno.

Adventures

On Foot

Strolling, walking, hiking, trekking or climbing – they're all possible in the Garda region.

Liberavventura is an organization that offers all manner of activities, including hikes and free climbing. Qualified guides and instructors available. Contact them for details of what they offer. guido@liberavventura.it, www.liberavventura.it.

Friends of Arco offers a huge variety of activities: Nordic walking, trekking and climbing, to name but a few. They also offer river trekking and rock climbing courses for kids. Arco is in the north of Lake Garda, near Riva. info@friendsofarco.it, ☎ 39 333 166 1401, www.friendsofarco.it.

Alpin Guide is near Arco. They have a range of treks or hikes, from a fairly relaxing four- to five-hour hike from the

Val di Ledro to Limone (€35 per person) to a three-day trek across the Brenta Dolomites (about €245 per person). guide@alpinguide.com, ☎ 39 0464 422273, www.alpinguide.it.

The Internet site, **www.lagodigardamagazine.com**, has a number of hikes and treks around the lake that you can print out. Look under "Sports and Nature."

   Pick up a copy of **Via Ferrata of the Italian Dolomites Vol 2** *by Graham Fletcher and John Smith. It covers the southern Dolomites, Brenta and northern Lake Garda. Cicerone Books. ISBN 1 85284 380 2.*

On Wheels

 Renting a bike is easy on Garda – the local Tourist Office will have information (or even the bikes themselves), while many hotels and campsites also have them to rent. Ask at the local Tourist Offices for biking itineraries too – they are too numerous to list here – or check out **www.lagodigardamagazine.com**, and look under "Sports and Nature."

Sky Climber is an organization based at Tremosine, not too far from Limone. They rent mountain bikes and offer a huge variety of tours on bikes, complete with a guide and a shuttle service. They also have Nordic walking and climbing – both with guides and itineraries. Their website is in German, though they can usually speak English and Italian as well. Via Dalco 3, Tremosine, ☎ 39 0365 917 041, mail@skyclimber.it, www.skyclimber.it.

Adventure Sprint in Sirmione, Via Brescia 15, rents cars, scooters and motorbikes. ☎ 39 030 91 9000, http://web.tiscali.it/adventuresprint.

In Salò, **Ciclimata** rents bikes and scooters, ☎ 39 0365 541 1492.

In Torbole, **Torbole Tour** offers a bike shuttle service to/from selected destinations. info@torboletour.com, ☎ 39 0464 551 925.

Coast to Coast has something similar. info@coasttocoast.it, ☎ 39 0464 506 115.

In Desenzano, **Girelli**, Via Annunciata 10, rents out bikes, ☎ 39 030 912 7222.

In Riva, the **Santorum Autonolegio** rents scooters. Viale Rovereto 76, ☎ 39 0464 552282.

If you'd like to try driving around an Italian lake in a classic car, check out **Sprintage**. They have a number of suggested excursions in their vintage cars: a Triumph, Alfa Romeo, MG or, for all you romantics, the tiny Fiat 500. Custom or pre-planned itineraries (available on all the lakes too!). info@sprintage.it, www.sprintage.it.

In the Kitchen

A company named **I Will Haute Cuisine** offers a range of cooking classes – from one to seven days in various beautiful locations near Verona and midway between Lake Garda and Verona. English spoken. info@iwillcuisine.it, ☎ 39 045 810 9031, www.iwillcuisine.it.

Arte Culinaria is some distance east of Lake Garda, 30 miles north of Venice. English-speaking host Antonella Tagliapietra offers three-day or one-week courses in her beautiful home, complete with a small indoor swimming pool. arteculinaria@tiscali.it, ☎ 39 0438 975 510, www.arteculinaria.it.

On the Golf Course

In Peschiera del Garda, **Golf Club Paradiso del Garda**, Loc. Paradiso. Via Campaldo, ☎ 39 045 6405802, info-golf@parchotels.it, www.golfclubparadiso.it. A little inland, this is a modern hotel and golf course development.

Ca degli Ulivi is on the eastern side of Lake Garda – a couple of miles from Garda town and with great lake views. Hotel and golf course, with nice club house. Nine- and 18-hole courses. info@chincerini.com, ☎ 39 045 621 2277.

Bogliaco is on the western shore of Lake Garda, near Toscolano Maderno, one of the oldest courses in Italy (1912) and recently extended to 18 holes. info@golfbogliaco.com, ☎ 39 0365 643 3006, www.golfbogliaco.com.

Garda Golf, 27 holes, designed by Cotton, Pennick and Steel in 1986. Very popular and respected course that extends over 300 acres in a stunning location between the Rocca di Manerba, Soiano Castle and the Valtenesi hills. ☎ 39 0365 674788, www.gardagolf.it.

Palazzo Arzaga is a luxury hotel, spa and golf complex, with an 18-hole course designed by Jack Nicklaus II and a nine-hole course by Gary Player. Known for its bunkers and water hazards. Five miles from Desenzano. info@palazzoarzaga. com, ☎ 39 030 680 600, www.palazzoarzaga.it.

On the Court

 If you want to play tennis or improve your game, **Tennis Clinic** at the **Club Hotel Olivi** is run by trainer Klaus Moik – junior courses available, as well as private lessons. www.tennisclinic.it.

The **Tennis Center** near Tremosine has 13 courts in a superb location. Take lessons or just play. Via Dalco 3, Tremosine. info@tenniscenterlagodigarda.com, ☎ 39 0365 917 041, www. tenniscenterlagodigarda.com.

On Water

 You've come to the right place if you're looking for adventures on water. There is no end of windsurfing schools and sailing schools – either to learn or to rent equipment. If you're a beginner, you'll be surfing in the morning – the afternoon Ora wind is more for people who know what they're doing!

There will be no difficulty in renting boards once you arrive, but if you'd like to take some lessons, the following companies will be useful. In Riva, **Pier Windsurf** is well-known, run by Dutch windsurfing champion Miki Bouwmeester. Lessons, courses, rental and stuff for kids too. info@pierwindsurf.it, ☎ 39 0464 550 928, www. pierwindsurf.it.

Surf Segnana has a number of centers between Riva and Torbole. They offer a huge range of courses for all ages and all levels of ability. Many of the centers also have kayak, catamaran and bike rental. info@surfsegnana.it, ☎ 39 0464 505 963, www.surfsegnana.it.

Vasco Renna is based in Torbole, and offers windsurfing rental and courses for all levels and ages. info@vascorenna. com, ☎ 39 0464 505 993, www.vascorenna.com.

In the south of the lake, at Sirmione, there's **Centro Surf Martini Sport** at Galeazzi, ☎ 39 030 916208, and **Centro Surf Sirmione**, at Brema Beach, ☎ 39 338 624 3650.

For boat rental, in Salò, check out **Arcangeli**, ☎ 39 0365 43443. For lessons, contact the **Centro Nautico Velico**, ☎ 39 0365 43245.

For sailing lessons in Desenzano, at Porto Maratona, contact **Fraglia Vela**. Courses for all ages. info@fragliavelia.it, ☎ 39 030 914 343, www.fragliavelia.it (only in Italian). In Padenghe there's the **West Garda Yacht Club**. They offer courses for all ages and levels (Via Marconi), ☎ 39 030 990 7295. And in Manerba, **Circolo Nautico**, ☎ 39 030 990 7217.

The **Garda Yachting Charter** in Toscolano Maderno rents motorboats and offers courses. gyc@gyc.it, ☎ 39 0365 548 347. In Sirmione contact the **Yachting Club**, ☎ 39 030 9904078. If diving is your thing, contact the **Peschiera Garda Diving Center**, at Camping San Benedetto, Via Bergamini, ☎ 39 045 755 0544. Also in Peschiera is the **Sub Club Peschiera**, ☎ 39 045 755 2702. In Malcesine, contact the **Malcesine Dream Sub**, ☎ 39 045 740 0216. In Desenzano there's **My Dive**, on Viale Andreis 74, ☎ 39 030 999 1541, and **Diansub**, on Via Valtenesi 21, ☎ 39 030 914 4821.

Near Salò, in Barbarano, there's the **Diving Center Garda Beach**, ☎ 39 0365 20225.

 Warning! If you meet boats on Lake Garda with bicolored sails, brown at the top and white at the bottom, be aware they are piloted by blind people, part of the Homerus project, which aims to give blind people an independent life. Pay attention and give way to them. (homerus@tin.it, ☎ 39 0365 599656, www. homerus.it.)

In the Air

There are a number of paragliding clubs in the area that offer tandem flights and courses – though lessons for beginners tend to take place on weekends over four months. If you're looking for an intensive course it's worth asking.

Arcobaleno Fly is located in a place called Passo Bordala, west of Rovereto. They offer tandem paragliding flights from

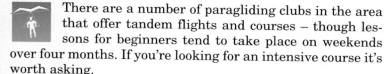

a couple of points in the area – the full tandem is from Monte Baldo above Malcesine and lasts 30-40 minutes. Cost is about €90. freepara@tin.it, ☎ 39 348 709 989, www.arcobalenofly.com. In Malcesine, the **Paragliding Club Malcesine** organizes flights from Mount Baldo. info@paraglidingmalcesine.it, ☎ 39 0355 676 4675. In Bardolino, contact Herbert Planatscher at **Camping Serenella Bardolino**, ☎ 39 045 721 1333. Also water-skiing and other activities.

At Gardone there's **Volere Volare**, located at the Hotel Colomber, in the San Michele district, ☎ 39 0365 21108.

On Horseback

 Riding is increasingly common in the Garda area and you shouldn't have too much difficulty finding stables that offer trails or lessons.

Arco

Club Ippico S.Giorgio, L. San Giorgio. Stables and a riding school, ☎ 39 348 443 8307.

Lonato

Centro Ippico La Pampa, Via Cappuccini 4. Stables, riding trails and riding school. ☎ 39 030 913 0335.

Cascina Spia d'Italia, Via Cerutti 61. Stables, riding trails and riding school. ☎ 39 030 913 0233

Riva del Garda

Cavalli & Carrozze, L. Cèole. Riding school and riding trails. ☎ 39 347 790 4556 (cell).

San Felice del Benaco

Pony Club la Fontanella, Via Mazzini 14. Riding school for children and riding trails. ☎ 39 0365 62200.

Solferino

Cascina le Volpi, L. Solgive. Stables, riding school, trails and treks, ☎ 39 0376 854 028.

Toscolano-Maderno

Scuderia Castello, Via Castello 10. Stables, riding school, trails and treks. ☎ 39 0365 644 101.

Valle di Ledro

Haflinger Cadrè, Molina di Ledro, L.Pur. Riding school for kids, riding trails. ☎ 39 0464 508 292.

With the Language

Global Language School has modern premises in Arco. Small groups start any Monday. Via Santa Caterina 60/a, Arco. italiano@globalschool.it, ☎ 39 0464 514 200, www.globalschool.it.

With Art

Il Chiostro, based in New York, offers three creative workshops in the Lake Garda area. Choose from photography, drawing or fiction writing. Workshops take place in early October, accommodation in a former Franciscan monastery. Il Chiostro, 241 W. 97th St, 13N New York, info@ilchiostro.com, ☎ 800 990 3506, www.ilchiostro.com/Garda.htm.

Where to Stay

Cassone

Hotel Cassone. Between Malcasine and Benaco, Hotel/Ristorante Cassone is a budget option, with clean, simple rooms, and near the lake. Rooms have air-conditioning. Be aware that any hotel which is also a popular restaurant is not for people who taurant is not for people who

HOTEL PRICE CHART	
Double room with tax & breakfast	
€	Under €80
€€	€80-€130
€€€	€131-€180
€€€€	€181-€250
€€€€€	Over €250

like to be in bed by 9:30. Bike rental. Minimum two night stay. Via Gardesana, info@hotelcassone.com, ☎ 39 045 658 4197, www.hotelcassone.com. €

Hotel Bellavista. Another budget option, though this time with a lake view. Seven rooms, very simply furnished, though with a/c, en-suite facilities and a balcony with lake view. Parking available. Also a restaurant/pizzeria with terrace. Breakfast is optional here so if you prefer to save €6 you can! Loc. Vendemme 5, info@bellavista-malcesine.com, ☎ 39 045 659 0219, www.bellavista-malcesine.com. €

Castelnuovo del Garda

Hotel Campanello

Hotel Campanello. A good place if you want to be near Gardaland or Peschiera, but away from the noise. Clean and simple, just a few feet from the lake and with a small garden, bar and car lot. Half the rooms have lake views, some with a terrace. Good value. Via Campanello 7/9, hotelcampanello@gardalake.it, ☎ 39 045 755 0253, www.gardalake.it/hotelcampanello. €

Desenzano

Vittorio. Nice location, right alongside a tiny harbor and next to the lake. Bar but no restaurant. Recently restored and, given its location, it offers good value. 43 rooms. Via Porto Vecchio 4, Desenzano, hotelvittorio@gardalake.it, ☎ 39 030 991 2245, www.gardalake.it/hotelvittorio. €€

Fasono

Grand Hotel Fasano. Elegant 19th-century building – a former hunting lodge of the Austrian royal family. Lake-side and with a tremendous amount of parkland. Corso Zanadrelli 190, info@grand-hotel-fasano.it, ☎ 39 0365 290 220, www.grand-hotel-fasano.it. €€€€

Grand Hotel Fasano

Villa del Sogno. Beautiful views here, lakeside, in a turn-of-the-century villa. Swimming pool, restaurant, tennis, etc. Via Zanardelli 107, villadelsogno@gardalake.it, www.gardalake.it/villadelsogno. €€€€

Gardone

Dimora Bolsone. In the hills overlooking the lake, four suites in a converted 15th-century manor. Surrounded by an enormous garden well-known by garden enthusiasts. dimorabolsone@

Dimora Bolsone

gardalake.it, ☎ 39 0365 21022, www.gardalake.it/dimora-bolsone. €€€€

Villa Fiordaliso

Villa Fiordaliso. Former home of Gabriele D'Annunzio. Lots of charm, a beautiful interior. Includes some rooms that even the hotel describes as small. Gourmet restaurant. Via Zanardelli 150, info@villafiordaliso.it, ☎ 39 0365 201 58, www.villafiordaliso.it. €€€€€

Villa Capri. Lovely position, right on the lake and set in a mature garden. Swimming pool and swimming jetty for those who prefer to swim in the lake. Car lot, bar, but no restaurant. All rooms have lake view and balcony or terrace. Via Zanardelli 172, villacapri@gardalake.it, ☎ 39 0365 21537, www.gardalake.it/villacapri. €€€

Villa Capri

Lake Garda

Gargnano

Hotel du Lac. Right on the lake, small family-run hotel (12 rooms, half with lakeview) close to Villa Igea, where D.H. Lawrence stayed. Restaurant and bar, private lakeside garden. Via Colletta 21, info@hotel-dulac.it, ☎ 39 0365 711 07, www.hotel-dulac.it. €€€

Hotel du Lac

Hotel Gardenia al Lago

Hotel Gardenia al Lago. Right on the lake, owned by the same family as the Hotel du Lac. Beautiful, fresh décor, garden lakeside, restaurant. Via Coletta 53, info@hotel-gardenia.it, ☎ 39 0365 711 95, www.hotel-dulac.it (homepage of hotel above). €€€

Villa Giulia. Neo-Gothic villa, lakeside, with 22 rooms and three suites. Lovely park complete with an historic "limonaia" or greenhouse for lemon trees. Rooms overlook the park or the lake. Restaurant, bar, piano bar, swimming pool.

Villa Giulia garden

Very close to the Golf Club Bogliaco. villagiulia@gardalake.it,
☎ 39 0365 71022, www.gardalake.it/hotel-villagiulia. €€€

Limone

Hotel du Lac. Family-run, modern hotel in its own gardens right on the lake. Modern rooms, most with air-conditioning. Swimming pool, kids' pool, lots of sports and activities offered or organized, including windsurfing, trekking, horseback riding and tennis. Apartments available too. Via Fasse

Hotel du Lac, Limone

1, dulac@limone.com, ☎ 39 0365 954 481, www.limone.com/dulac. €€

Malcesine

Hotel Meridiana. Modern, almost mininalist, interior, lots of wooden floors, carefully chosen furniture and soft lighting. A few extras too – Finnish sauna, outdoor hot tub, gym, shiatsu treatments available. In the heart of Malcesine, close to, but not on, the lake. info@hotelmeridiana.it, ☎ 39 045 740 0342, www.hotelmeridiana.it. €€

Club Hotel Olivi

Club Hotel Olivi. Set in several acres of park, very close to the lake, Club Hotel Olivi is a hotel and tennis resort. Nine courts. Perfect your game with qualified instructors or simply take the opportunity to play a lot of tennis. Swimming pool, basket ball, beach volley ball, gym, sauna. A few minutes walk away there's the **Sportcamp**, run by Heiz Stickl, a world champion in windsurfing and sailing. www.stickl.com. Club Hotel Olivi has attractive rooms – no chintz in sight – and also suites and some accommodation suitable for families. Via Gardesana 160, info@clubhotelolivi.it, ☎ 39 045 7400444, www.clubhotelolivi.it. €€€

Manerba

Villa Schindler

Villa Schindler. Set amidst olive grooves, this is a 19th-century villa with a lovely interior. Swimming pool, tennis, garden, car lot and bar. Anna Brotto, the owner, also arranges various courses for guests, including sculpture, painting, furniture restoration, yoga and massage. Very good value for money and an ideal spot if you want to get away from the crowds. Via Bresciani 68, villa-schindler@gardalake.it, ☎ 39 0365 651 046, www.gardalake.it/villa-schindler. €€

Peschiera del Garda

Hotel San Marco. Modern hotel right on the lakefront, with restaurant, terrace, and car lot. The location is the thing here. Some triple and quad rooms; good for families or those on a budget. Lungolago Mazzini 15, sanmarco@gardalake.it, ☎ 39 045 7550077, www.gardalake.it/sanmarco. €€

Riva del Garda

Du Lac et Du Parc. Large hotel and resort set in a beautiful park right on the lake. What the rooms lack in charm or individuality the hotel makes up for in facilities and location, with indoor and outdoor pool, tennis courts, fitness and beauty center. More than 400 rooms. Viale Rovereto 44, Riva Del Garda, ☎ 39 0464 566600, hoteldulac@anthese.com, info@dulacetduparc, ☎ 39 0464 551510, www.dulacetduparc.com. €€€€

Hotel du Lac et du Parc

Albergo Ancora. Lots of character and good value in this small (11 rooms) albergo in Riva's historic center. Bar and restaurant/pizzeria. Some triple and quad rooms plus a junior suite. Open year-round. Via Montanara 2, ☎ 39 0464 522131, hotelancora@gardalake.it, www.gardalake.it/hotelancora. €€

Punta San Vigilio

Locanda San Vigilio. Seven double rooms and seven suites in a 16th-century villa. Stunning location – very possibly the best spot on the entire

Locanda San Vigilio

lake. Elegant, without being stuffy or formal, a favorite with royalty and celebrities, the villa is right on the lake, surrounded by cypress, olive and lemon trees. Some of the suites are in an adjoining building. ☎ 39 045 725668, sanvigilio@gardalake.it or info@punta-sanvigilio.it, www.gardalake.it/sanvigilio or www.punta-sanvigilio.it. €€€€€

Salò

Hotel Duomo. Right on the lakeside. Some rooms have lake views, others have views of Salò's Duomo. Sun terrace, small fitness area, restaurant, bar and car parking. The rooms have attractive décor. Lungolago Zanardelli 63, hotelduomo@

gardalake.it, ☎ 39 0365 210 26, www.gardalake.it/
hotelduomo. €€€

Hotel Lepanto. Restaurant with six rooms, all overlooking
the lake. Great value, so book early! Lungolargo Zanardelli
67, hotel.lepanto@libero.it, ☎ 39 0365 20428. €

Sirmione

Grand Hotel Terme bedroom

Grand Hotel Terme.
Luxury hotel with spa
facilities. Private
beach, pool and gym,
and lakeside restau-
rant. One of the best
known hotels in
Sirmione – and very
expensive. Viale
Marconi 7, info@
termedisirmione.com,
☎ 39 030 916 261, www.termedisirmione.com. €€€€

Hotel Eden. In the center
of Sirmione, right on the
lake and close to the castle. Ezra Pound stayed
here in 1920. Terrace and
sun area right on the lake.
The interior is modern, the
rooms have air-
conditioning, though no
restaurant. Piazza
Carducci 18, hotel.eden@
gardalake.it, ☎ 39 030 916
481, www.gardalake.it/hotel-eden. €€€

Hotel Eden

Hotel Corte Regina. In the city center, simple but bright
and well-priced rooms, with some family rooms available.
Restaurant. All rooms have air-conditioning and some have
disabled facilities. Via Antiche Mura 11, lorenzoronchi@
libero.it, ☎ 39 030 916 147, www.corteregina.it. €€

Hotel Grifone. You'll have to book ahead to get in here – it
appears in all the guidebooks, and rightly so. You pay for the
location, though you don't pay much. Inexpensive and simple

rooms, fabulous views over the lake and the Rocca Scaligera. Via Bocchio 4, ☎ 39 030 916 014, ☎/fax 39 030 916 548. €

Hotel Speranza. In the heart of Sirmione's historic center, nice rooms, and great value. No lake view here but only a hundred yards from the Rocca and the lake. Via Casello 2, hotelsperanza@tiscali.it, ☎ 39 030 916 116, www. hotelsperanza@sitonline.it. €

Tignale

Hotel Elisa. At an elevation of 1,968 ft, and with a great view over the lake. Simple, basic rooms, but outdoor swimming pool, restaurant and good value. Via Don Bosco 7, hotelelisa@ gardalake.it, ☎ 39

Hotel Elisa

0365 760263, www.gardalake.it/hotelelisa. €

Torri del Benaco

Hotel Al Caminetto. A lovely family-owned place that seems more like a home than a hotel. At the foot of Monte Baldo, close to the lake and set in a pretty garden, with restaurant/ bar and car lot. Reasonable prices too. Via Gardesana 52, info@hotelcaminetto.it, ☎ 39 045 722 5524, www.alcaminetto. com. €€

Tremosine

Hotel Miralago. Great views and good prices. The Miralago sits on a cliff that juts out over the lake. At times the cliff even makes an appearance inside the hotel. Fabulous views, simple rooms and restaurant/pizzeria. The owners also have a leisure complex a few moments away, with swimming pool, seven tennis courts complete with instructor and sauna. Try to ignore the curtains. Pieve di Tremosine, miralago@gardalake.it, ☎ 39 0365 953 001, www.gardalake.it/miralago. €

Hotel Miralago

Villa Selene. 1,640 ft up in the Alta Garda Bresciano National Park. Great views, nice interior and perfect for those who want to get away from the roads and the crowds. Big terrace, garden, mountain bikes available at no charge and buffet breakfast served until 12 pm. Sauna, solarium and massage also available. Via Lò 1, villaselene@gardalake.it, ☎ 39 0365 953 036, www.gardalake.it/villaselene. €€

 Tip: Garda Pass is an organization representing the Hoteliers Association of the Riviera dei Olive – the east coast of the lake, in the Veneto, from Malcesine to Peschiera. They have an efficient, free booking service, though with a three-day minimum, so it could be useful if you've left your booking a bit late. Search online, book online at www.gardapass.com.

Bed & Breakfast & Apartments

Il Nido. A small B&B in a village called Raffa di Puegnago, close to Salò. Situated in olive grooves, around 10 minutes to the nearest beach on the lake. Run by an English/Italian couple who also have a small restaurant. Six double rooms, some with air-conditioning. nidoraffa@libero.it, ☎ 39 0365 651 864, www.ilnidobed-breakfast.it. €

Il Nido

Cervano. Set in the hills near Toscalano Moderna in the Alta Garda Bresciano National Park. 18th-century house and farmhouse with three suites/apartments, two with lake view. Right next to the Bogliaco golf course – guests receive 10% discount on greens fees. Three-night minimum stay. info@cervano.com, ☎ 39 036 554 8398, http://xoomer.virgilio.it/cervano. €€

Villa San Pietro

Villa San Pietro. Around nine miles from Desenzano, and 14 miles from Brescia, set in the medieval town of Montichiari. Run by an Italian/French couple, Anna and Jacques, who also speak English and Spanish. Four rooms, nicely furnished with antiques. The property also contains 16th-century frescoed ceilings. The hosts provide a five-course dinner on request, arrange wine tours and offer Italian- and French-language classes (Anna is a qualified translator). villasanpietro@hotmail.com, ☎ 39 030 961 232, www.abedandbreakfastinitaly.com. €€

The tourist website, **Lago di Garda Magazine**, has an extensive range of apartments to rent throughout the Garda Lake area. Select Hotel and Residence, then the town or village that you want, then click the Apartments tab. www.lagodigardamagazine.com.

Tip: Don't be alarmed if a hotel or residence is termed a "lagobiker" hotel. This does not refer to gangs of leathered motorbikers but lycra clad mountain bikers.

Lake Garda

Camping

 Lake Garda is well-equipped for campsites, with room for more than 6,000 pitches. Sites range from the very simple "green field and great view," to sites with restaurants, bars, sports facilities, bungalows and trailers to rent. Given that there are so many sites, the best approach is to decide where you want to be, then have a look at the following websites, which list campsites and their facilities. Bear in mind, the bigger the site, the busier it will be. Book ahead and, if you're desperate for simplicity and peace, try to find smaller sites with fewer facilities.

■ www.gardalake.com/campings.

■ www.campeggi.com (do a search for Lombardy and then select Brescia, or Veneto, then Verona).

■ www.camping.it (the home page has a link for Lake Garda under "Tourist Area").

Youth Hostels

Surpisingly, given the number of young people who flock to Garda for holidays, there are few youth hostels. If you're looking for budget accommodation, check out campsites, where trailers, cabins, bungalows or little apartments are often for rent.

In Riva del Garda there's the **Benacus** youth hostel, right on the lake. Some family rooms are available. Rates are about €17 per person in a family room. Credit cards accepted and you can book online. Piazza Cavour 10, info@ostelloriva.com, ☎ 39 0464 554911, www.ostellionline.org/ostello. php?idostello=600.

Agriturismi

Gardalake has a great list of agriturismi in the area. Some are working farms, some beautifully restored historic houses, while others are simpler operations. Some have restaurants, some don't. The majority are country properties, which means a car is a must, unless you intend to rent scooters or bikes. "Only 10 minutes to the lake" may well mean in the car, at high speed, downhill.

The great thing about agriturismi, "farm holidays," is the price, and the opportunity to experience Italian life, and food,

a little more closely. Check out www.gardalake.com/
agriturismo.

AGRITURISMI

Unlike hotels, almost all agriturismi are priced per
room or apartment, NOT per person. Also, don't pre-
sume that they all take credit cards or are able to act
as currency changers. Ask before it's time to pay,
and if you need to pay cash, make sure it's in the
right currency! Agriturismi are very popular, particularly with Italians, so if you have your heart set on
one, book ahead.

Agriturismo Cascina Cà Nov. In Puegnano del Garda, on
the Desenzano-Salò road, a 16th-century farmhouse, with
two rooms and five apartments, around 1½ miles to the lake.
Simply furnished. Weekly rates, except for weekends when
you can stay a minimum of two nights. Swimming pool, children's play area. Small restaurant and bread store a few minutes walk away. ☎ 39 0365 654319, canova@numerica.it,
www.primitaly.it/agriturismo/cascinacanova. €

La Murla del Gherlo is eight miles southeast of Peschiera,
in Gherla. A good choice if you want to combine a visit to the
lake with trips to Mantua and/or Verona. Very comfortable
rooms, pastel colors, stone walls and terracotta tiles. Eight
rooms and two studio apartments. All rooms have air-
conditioning, Internet connection, TV, phone and safe. ☎ 39
045 795 0773, info@lemuradelgherlo.it, www.lemuradel-
gherlo.it. €

Agriturismo Sangallo. In Bedizzole, a few miles from
Padenghe and the lake. Beautiful, vaulted brick ceilings,
terracotta tiled floors. Eight rooms, including a family room
for four. A deposit is required here and, strangely, breakfast is
not included in the room rate. You can eat here too – there's a
restaurant. ☎ 39 030 674 965, ☎/fax 39 030 675 604, info@
sangalloagriturismo.it, www.sangalloagriturismo.it. €

Il Bagnolo. Halfway between Salò and Gardone di Riviera,
in the hamlet of Bagnolo di Serniga. Nine pretty rooms. A

lovely spot, good for treks, walks and biking. You can rent bikes here. Restaurant (closed Tues), children's playground. ☎ 39 0365 21877, ilbagnolo@gardalake.it, www.gardalake. com/ilbagnolo. €

Where to Eat

Tip: No surprise that the a sizeable number of restaurants in the Lake Garda area feature fish, primarily lake fish, but sea fish too. As you move away from the lake, the restaurants are more likely to serve meat, local vegetables and staples such as polenta. All restaurants will have pasta on offer as a primo, though you are under no obligation to either have this course or to order a secondo – meat and fish dishes. Fish restaurants will often have a couple of meat or vegetarian dishes available.

Arco

Belvedere. One of the best trattorie in Arco, and great prices to boot. Local dishes, homegrown vegetables, fresh pasta, grilled meat. Closed Wed. Via Serafini 2, in Loc. Varignano, ☎ 39 0464 516 144. €

DINING PRICE CHART	
For three courses, excluding wine	
€	Under €20
€€	€20-€40
€€€	€41-€70
€€€€	Over €70

Da Gianni

Da Gianni. Some say the best food in the area, with an extensive wine list, and specialties that include gnocchi with two local cheeses, seasonal vegetables, and the wonderfully named priest chokers – strangolapreti – a kind of pasta. You can stay here too. There are eight lovely rooms (around €80 a night). The rates for half-board are particularly interesting. Closed Sun evening and Mon all day. Via S.Marcello 21, ☎ 39 0464 516 464, info@dagianni.it, www. dagianni.it. €€

Alla Lega. In an old palazzo in the heart of Arco. Vaulted and beamed ceilings. It serves Trentino cuisine. Not the place for an intimate evening as it's popular and often very busy. Closed Wed. Via Vergolano 8, ☎ 39 0464 516 205. €€€

Bardolino

Il Giardino delle Espiridi. In the center of Bardolino, a wine bar/restaurant with local cuisine and some non-local dishes. Meat and fish dishes. Via Mameli 1, ☎ 39 045 621 0477. €€

Brenzone

Belvedere. A pizzeria that also does simple local dishes. Cheap. Via Marnega 38, ☎ 39 045 742 0055.

Casteletto di Brenzone

Alla Fassa. One of the best fish restaurants on the lake, with some meat dishes too. Lakeside. Booking advised here as it's very well-known and gives great value. Closed Tues except in the summer. Via Monsignor Nascimbeni 13, ☎ 39 045 743 0319. €€

Al Pescatore. A small fish restaurant, family-run and with a good reputation. No menu here, since it changes according to the day's catch – if you like fresh fish and pasta, you won't be disappointed. Located right near

Al Pescatore

the little harbor in Casteletto. ☎ 39 045 743 0702, info@ osteriaalpescatore.it, www.osteriaalpescatore.it. €€

Castiglione delle Stiviere

Osteria da Pietro. South of Desenzano, in the hamlet of Castiglione delle Stiviere, Michelin-starred restaurant serving excellent regional cuisine. Via Chiassi 19, ☎ 39 0376 673 718. €€€

Desenzano

Esplanade. One of the best restaurants in the area, Michelin-starred and with a lovely view over the lake. Regional dishes, with an excellent choice for fish and meat eaters. There are two menu degustazione for those who like their food. Not a cheap option but a gastronomic experience guaranteed. Closed Wed. Via Lario 10, ☎ 39 030 091 433 61. €€€

Antica Hosteria Cavallino

Antica Hosteria Cavallino. A fish restaurant – from the sea and the lake – with classic and innovative dishes. Very pretty terrace for summer eating. Booking advisable. Closed Mon. Via Murachette 29, ☎ 39 030 912 0217, info@ristorantecavallino.it, www.ristorantecavallino.it. €€€

Al Portico. Predominately a fish restaurant with some meat items. Fresh interior with a terrace for summer eating. Conveniently located close to the center of Desenzano, near the lake and adjacent to the Rambotti Museum. Closed Tues. Via Anelli 44, ☎ 39 030 914 319. €€

La Taverna del Lago. Near the parish church in the district known as Rivoltella, this small restaurant is known for the quality of its food – primarily fish – and for the artwork covering its walls: reproductions of works by artists who became famous after their deaths! Good prices. Closed Tues. Via Parrocchiale, ☎ 39 030 911 0926. €€

Ortaglia. An agriturismo in the hills in the hills, halfway between Desenzano and Peschiera, near San Martino della Battaglia. A well-known restaurant with beautiful brick-vaulted ceilings. Local cuisine and everything produced on the farm or locally, including the wine. Booking advisable. Closed Mon and Tues. In Località Ortaglia, ☎ 39 030 991 0106. €€

Ristorante La Contrada. In the center of Desenzano, a very attractive restaurant that offers a menu of Lombard-Veneto cuisine at great prices. Closed Wed. Via Bagatta 12, ☎ 39 030 914 2514. €€

Caffè Italia. Wine bar and restaurant, close to the lake and the Duomo. Later hours than most: lunch served until 3 pm, dinner until 11 pm. Closed Mon. Piazza Malvezzi 19, ☎ 39 030 914 1243. €€

Gardone Riviera

Villa Fiordaliso. In the hotel of the same name, a renowned restaurant with both classic and innovative cuisine. The menu is primarily fish. The location is superb, the bill high. Closed Tues lunch and all day Mon. ☎ 39 0365 201 58, fiordaliso@relaischateux.com, www.villafiordaliso.it. €€€€

Belvedere da Marietta. A 19th-century villa with panoramic lake views from the terrace. Local and regional cuisine; good for fresh pasta and fish. Good prices too. Closed Thurs. Via Montecucco 78, ☎ 39 0365 209 60. €€

Agli Angeli

Agli Angeli. Close to the Vittoriale, in upper Gardone. Very attractive trattoria, family-run with tables that spill out into the tiny piazza in front. A short but mouth-watering menu. Agli Angeli has a number of rooms to let, with doubles around €120. Closed Mon. Piazza Garibaldi

Lake Garda

2, ☎ 39 0365 208 32, info@agliangelli.com, www.agliangeli.
com. €€

Gargnano

La Tortuga

La Tortuga. Justifi-
ably renowned and
popular, La Tortuga
serves regional dishes,
primarily fish, seasonal
vegetables, fresh pasta
and lovely desserts.
This place is tiny, only
seven tables, so book-
ing is highly recom-
mended. Closed Mon
evening and all day
Tues. Via XXIV Maggio 5, ☎ 39 0365 712 51, la.tortuga@
libero.it. €€€

Ristorante Allo Scoglio. In Bogliaco near Gargnano. Right
on the lake with a terrace and garden for summer dining.
Local and regional cuisine, largely fish. Closed Fri. Via
Barbacane 2, ☎ 39 0365 710 30. €€

Lazise

Trattoria Villa Pergole.
In the hills behind Lazise,
around two miles from the
lake, with nice views and,
for families, a small kids'
play area. Terrace for summer eating. Tables a little
close together for the
author's liking, but they
have a menu for meat eat-

Trattoria Villa Pergole

ers, with lots of steak and grilled meat. Via Bine Storte 1,
Contrada Pergole, ☎ 39 045 758 0248, info@ristorante-
trattoriavillapergole.com, www.ristorantetrattoria-
villapergole.com. €

Limone

Ristorante Gemma. In the heart of Limone, right on the lake, a family-run place with a varied menu. Very popular with tourists. Piazza Garibaldi 11, ☎ 39 0365 954 014, ristorantegemma@libero.it. €€

Ristorante Enoteca La Cantina del Gato Borracho. Over 1,000 wines in this attractive restaurant/enoteca, run by two brothers. In the center of Limone. Choose from the fixed menu of regional dishes or try the daily menu. Every course comes with a different wine. All wines available by the glass. Seasonal dishes, great pasta, including one for wine lovers. Via Caldogno 1/1, ☎ 39 0365 914 010, info@gattoborracho.com.

Lonate

Da Oscar. A family-owned trattoria, set in the Barcuzzi hills just outside Lonate. Set amongst olive trees, with a garden and a panoramic view of the lake. Local cuisine. Closed Mon and Tues lunchtime. Via Barcuzzi 16, info@myoscar.it, ☎ 39 030 913 0409. €€

Maderno

Osteria del Boccondivino. Tucked out of sight in Toscolano Maderno, this simple osteria serves simple regional cuisine accompanied by a great selection of wine. Terrace. Late closing (3 am). Closed Tues. Via Cavour 71, ☎ 39 0365 642 512. €€

Manerba

Capriccio. A family-run restaurant, with a Michelin star. Very attractive interior, terrace with lake view, and elegant, imaginative cuisine. Known also for its sublime desserts – if it's still on the menu, try the warm peach tart, flavored with lavander and lemon, with a sauce of wild strawberries. Closed Tues at lunchtime. Book ahead. In Loc. Montinelle. Piazza S.Bernardo 6, ☎ 39 0365 551 124, info@ristorantecapriccio.it, www.ristorantecapriccio.it. €€€

Capriccio

Il Gusto. Next door to Capriccio and run by the same team, this wine-bar has a great menu and a terrific selection of wines by the glass. If you're looking for something a little more informal than Capriccio but with the same attention to detail, give Il Gusto a try. The opening hours are a little different too: open from 5 pm until 1 am. Open at lunchtime only if you book ahead. ☎ 39 0365 550 297. €€

Moniga del Garda

Quintessenza. In Moniga del Garda's central piazza, an attractive restaurant with a good-sized terrace for summer eating. Local cuisine, fish – freshwater and from the sea – meat, pasta. Closed Tues, open every evening in July and Aug. Piazza S.Martino, ☎ 39 0365 502 116. €€

Padenghe

Seradel. Immersed in the countryside, a traditional trattoria/agriturismo serving local dishes, grilled meat and chicken, much of it their own produce. No fish. A good place for kids – set in its own park. An animal corner has goats, rabbits, and other animals. Via Meucci 75. Closed Wed. **No credit card**s, ☎ 39 030 990 7123. €€

Aquariva. A great spot – right on the lake – with terrific food (largely fish-based) and relaxed though professional service. Bright interior, and a terrace for summer eating. Always open from May through to Sept, otherwise closed for Tues lunch and all day Mon. Via Marconi, 57, ☎ 39 030 990 8899, info@ aquariva.it, www.aquariva.it. €€€

Peschiera

Al Combattente. A small trattoria near the tourist port of Bergamini. Simple dishes, predominately lake fish. Closed Mon. Strada Bergamini 60, ☎ 39 045 755 1566. €€

Pozzolengo

Antica Locanda del Contrabbandiere. In the countryside south of Peschiera in the hamlet of Martelosio di Sopra. A medieval farmhouse serving excellent local cuisine. Very attractive dining room and terrace/garden for summer eating. You can stay here too – there are three nice rooms, a good

Antica Locanda del Contrabbandiere

breakfast and a swimming pool for guests. ☎ 39 030 918 151, info@locandadelcontrabbandiere.com. €€

Prada

Sole e Neve. A good spot for lunch, after a morning's walk – 3,000 ft up on Monte Baldo behind the Prada cablecar station. An agriturismo, serving simple, regional dishes, with a terrace for great views. You can stay here too – there are seven rooms, priced at around €60 for a double room. Open April-Sept, 12-2 pm. ☎ 39 045 728 5693. €

Riva del Garda

Al Volt. In a 17th-century palazzo in the center of Riva, a couple of minutes from the lake. Nice interior – lots of white, red and antiques. Two degustazione menus (Trentino and Lake cuisine) at around €40. Closed Mon, except in Aug. Via Fiume 73, ☎ 39

Al Volt

0464 552 570, www.ristorantealvolt.com. €€€

Salò

Gallo Rosso. A small place in the center of Salò, with classic, regional dishes. Very good value here – the food and the prices mean it's popular, so book ahead. Closed Wed. Vicolo Tomacelli 4, ☎ 39 0365 552 0757.

La Campagnola. Set in a lovely garden, with a pretty terrace for summer eating. The food is imaginative, though always has its roots in the cuisine of Lake Garda. The pasta dishes are great, plus lake fish and meat. Extensive wine list. Via Brunati 11, ☎ 39 0365 22153. €€

Osteria dell'Orologio. Informal, relaxed and friendly place, closing only between 3 and 5 pm. Known for its traditional, regional dishes, with a good wine list that includes a number of very small local producers. A good spot for a couple of glasses of wine if you can't get a table – it's very popular so book ahead for lunch or dinner. Great value. Closed Wed. Via Butturini 26a, ☎ 39 0365 290 158. €€

Il Melograno. Fabulous views over the lake, with a terrace for summer eating, and good value. Lots of lake fish, and regional classics. South of Salò in the hamlet of Campoverde. Closed Mon evening and Tues. Via del Panorama 5, ☎ 39 0365 520421, info@ilmelogranoristorante.it. €€

Sirmione

Al Caciosalume. Informal place, adjacent to the store selling salami and cured meats, offers a selection of local dishes, cheeses and salami. The desserts are great too. At pretty much any time you can stop by for a glass or two of great wine and some salami. In Via Colombare 123, ☎ 39 030 919 331. €

Osteria Al Torcol. Closes very late – around 2 am. A good place for snacks and light meals accompanied by a glass of wine. Attractive garden. Via San Salvatore 30, ☎ 39 030 990 4605 €

Vecchia Lugana. One of the Garda's best restaurants, with a lovely menu in a quiet spot right on the lake. Garden for summer eating. The menu changes according to the season, and is mainly based on lake fish, though it always has some meat dishes. Book ahead here. Closed Mon and Tues. Piazzale le Vecchia Lugana 1, ☎ 39 030 919 012, info@vecchialugana. com. €€€

Al Progresso. Family-run, friendly and relaxed. In the center of town. Varied menu of local and regional dishes. Closed Thurs. Via V.Emanuele 18, ☎ 39 030 916 108. €€

Ristorante Signori is in the historic heart of Sirmione. Elegant, contemporary décor, with lakeside terrace. Traditional and local cuisine. Booking advisable – especially if you want a terrace table. Closed Mon. Via Romagnoli 17, ☎ 39 030 916 017, ristorantesignori@acena.it. €€€

La Rucola. In the historic heart of Sirmione near the castle, a very small, refined place for an intimate dinner. Very imaginative menu, as well as a degustazione menu. A gastronomic experience guaranteed – and not for those watching their budget. Closed Fri lunchtime and Thurs. Via Strentelle 3, ☎ 39 916 326. €€€€

Torbole

La Terazza. Lovely fish restaurant, well-known in the area, right near the lake and with lovely views. Via Benaco 14, ☎ 39 0464 506 083. €€

La Terrazza della Luna. In the hamlet of Coe, a 19th-century Austrian fort. Regional cuisine, lots of lake and sea fish. Closed Mon. ☎ 39 0464 505 301. €€

Al Forte Alto. Another restored Austrian fort, in Nago. Terrace for outside eating and with good views. Trentino cuisine. Closed Tues. ☎ 39 0464 505 566. €€

Index

Index